I0810400

IMAGES
of Modern America

MONESSEN

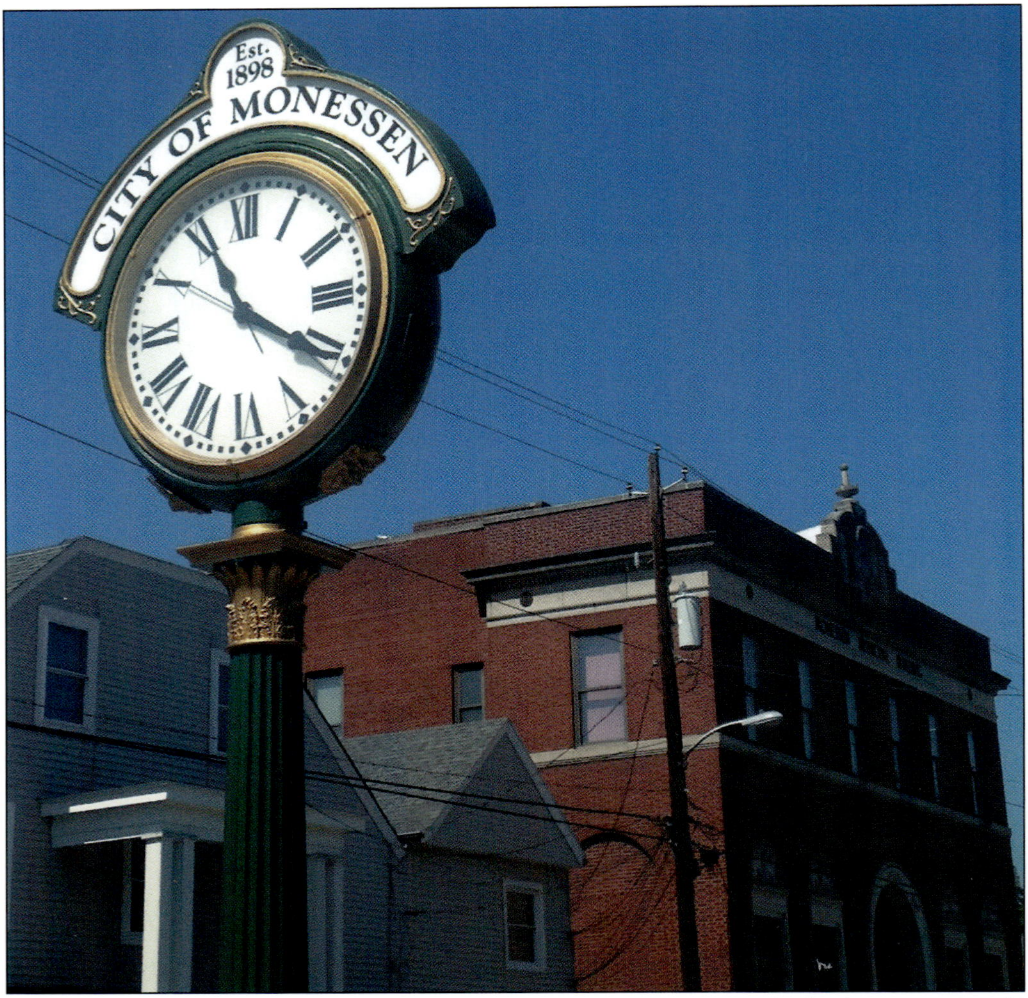

This is the newly installed Brown Street clock on Donner Avenue and Third Street. The old municipal building is visible in the background. Brown Street clocks were produced on Monessen's Donner Avenue throughout the early 20th century. The clocks were shipped around the country, but only a few remain in use today. (Author's collection.)

On the Front Cover: Clockwise from top left:
JFK gives a speech in downtown Monessen on October 13, 1962 (Courtesy of Greater Monessen Historical Society); Douglas Education Center emblem on one of its buildings in downtown Monessen (Author's collection); the clock on top of the old Monessen Municipal Building at Third Street and Donner Avenue (Courtesy of Karla Spangler); a flag ceremony on Donner Avenue (Courtesy of Linzi Troilo-Dalfonso); the Brown Street clock at Third Street and Donner Avenue (Author's collection)

On the Back Cover: From left to right:
ArcelorMittal coke works, the only portion remaining of Monessen's industrial past (Courtesy of Chad Jones); view of Third Street and Schoonmaker Avenue from the Reed Avenue Bridge (Courtesy of Greater Monessen Historical Society); a historical marker noting the achievement of Monessenite and Nobel Prize–laureate Christian Anfinsen (Courtesy of Karla Spangler)

IMAGES
of Modern America

MONESSEN

Matthew T. Shorraw
Foreword by Daniel Zyglowicz

ARCADIA
PUBLISHING

ISBN 978-1-4671-2296-2

Published by Arcadia Publishing
Charleston, South Carolina

Printed in the United States of America

Library of Congress Control Number: 2014947293

For all general information, please contact Arcadia Publishing:
Telephone 843-853-2070
Fax 843-853-0044
E-mail sales@arcadiapublishing.com

Visit us on the Internet at www.arcadiapublishing.com

To my grandparents, Irene (Sivak) and Earl Shorraw, for their love and support and their dedication to Monessen

Contents

Foreword		6
Acknowledgments		7
Introduction		8
1.	A Modern City	11
2.	Faith, Culture, and Ethnic Ties	19
3.	The Fall of Steel	37
4.	Hard Times	45
5.	A New Century, a New Era	55
6.	Pushing for a Renaissance	67
About the Greater Monessen Historical Society		95

FOREWORD

In January 1914, Monessen founder and Civil War hero Col. James Schoonmaker was the main speaker at the annual Monessen Board of Trade Banquet. He was quoted as saying, "I challenge the world to produce a town that in 15 years has made the progress and development Monessen has. To rise from a farm and wasteland, to a modern little city in this length of time is indeed a challenge to the world. I fill with pride and swell out my chest when I speak of Monessen."

If the colonel had been around in 1950, Monessen's growth and development would have given him extreme satisfaction and a sense of accomplishment. The industrial mills were booming, and the business district was filled with bustling stores and shops from one end of town to the other.

By the early 1970s, Monessen entered a period of decline. The aging mills began to cut back production, lay off workers, and close. The stores in the business district began to disappear as people moved away, and the old first- or second-generation shop owners died or retired. The close-knit ethnic neighborhoods vanished.

Since that time, Monessen has struggled to reinvent itself. Matt Shorraw, a voice in the new campaign to involve young people in making Monessen vital again, accepted the challenge to create this photographic history of Monessen from 1950 to the present. Many of the images used in this pictorial history came from the archival collections of the Greater Monessen Historical Society, which works to protect, preserve, and enhance the strong ethnic diversity and rich industrial heritage of Monessen and the Mon Valley. Shorraw's book defines over 60 years of triumphs, disappointments, and hope for a new future through carefully selected photographs that capture the determination of Monessen's people.

—Daniel Zyglowicz
President, Greater Monessen Historical Society

Acknowledgments

This book—Images of Modern America: *Monessen*—is not only dedicated to my grandparents, but also to my entire family: my parents, Tom and Karen Shorraw; my brothers, Nick, Matt, Donnie, and Seth; my sister, Nicole; my brother-in-law, Scott; my sister-in-law, Tracey; my niece, Grace; my nephews, Keith and Adam; and to all Monessenites who are striving to keep our city and its history alive. I would like to thank the Greater Monessen Historical Society board and volunteers for the opportunity to pursue this endeavor, as well as for their support and donation of many of the photographs throughout this book.

I would also like to thank Arcadia Publishing and my editor Abby Walker for her guidance and support; Linzi Troilo-Dalfonso and her mother, Kathy, for donating photographs from the collection of Mayor Dalfonso; the Monessen Public Library; the Monessen School District; the Monessen Amphitheater Committee; Monessen Communities That Care; the Monessen Community Development Corporation for guiding and motivating me to help and care for the city of Monessen; my parish family at St. Mary's Byzantine Catholic Church in Monessen and Fr. Stephen Wahal, Dea. John and Mrs. Hanchin, and Msgr. Andrew Parvensky for their love and support; my music department family at California University of Pennsylvania, especially Dr. Ikach, Rose Markovich, Dr. Kathy Sacco, Max Gonano, Prof. Greg Davis, Lisa Brovey-Kovach, and Greta Schottman; and all of my brothers in Alpha Chi Rho, Sigma Chi Phi Colony. Cassandra Vivian, author of *Monessen: A Typical Steel Country Town*, inspired me to pursue this endeavor.

Lastly, I would like to thank Teresa Seh, Katie Lucy, Chelsey Salay, Karla Spangler, Chad McCauley, Jackie Pierce, Nikki Lepresti, and Samantha Brown for their never-ending love, tolerance, and support.

Unless otherwise noted, all images appear courtesy of the Greater Monessen Historical Society.

INTRODUCTION

Like many cities in the Pittsburgh region, the city of Monessen, Pennsylvania, has its roots in industry that flourished along the Monongahela River throughout the 20th century. Monessen was officially founded as a borough in 1898, and its establishment was brought about mainly because of industrial interest in the area.

Before Monessen's founding, the land was made up of a series of farms that were purchased by the East Side Land Company. Interest in the area was primarily due to industrialist and philanthropist William Henry Donner's National Tin Plate Company, which was the first industry that opened in the city.

With the support and investments of Col. James M. Schoonmaker, who was part of the East Side Land Company and vice president of the Pittsburgh & Lake Erie Railroad, Donner and Schoonmaker set out to start a legacy that is still carried on today.

Monessen's story is one of triumphs and failures, much like the typical story of a city. Throughout its 116 years of existence since its official founding, Monessen has built itself up and torn itself down. It has not only faced its own disasters and difficulties, but also endured national crises as well. It has seen the late Victorian era, the Gilded Age, the space age, and beyond. Its existence has survived two world wars, the Great Depression, labor strikes, the women's suffrage movement, and the civil rights movement. Its own people were involved in the tragic sinking of *Titanic*; all of them survived and made it to Monessen. It has also seen 20 presidents in office and numerous other political figures and celebrities, both famous and infamous, pass through the national and international spotlights. The world has gotten faster, and Monessen has followed.

In its own history, Monessen is one filled with people who are determined and resilient. They are made up of many ancestral ethnicities: Italian, Greek, French, German, Slovak, Irish, and more. They and their ancestors have endured like so many others after first arriving upon these shores. They have known hard work and determination to be the driving force of this country and of Monessen.

In its early days, Monessen was booming, and buildings were constructed throughout the entire city. This boom continued until the Great Depression, when things slowed down for most of the country, including Monessen. Construction and progress picked back up again after World War II. Monessen embarked on many new projects throughout the city in order to modernize and attract new residents, especially younger families.

New projects included the New Town, Inc. Project, the Eastgate Project, the Westgate Project, the Mid-Town Revitalization Project, the Seneca Hollow Project, and the Park Plan Project.

After the booming years of the mid-20th century, Monessen took a hit. Like many other industrial cities throughout the country, it was losing its jobs to foreign companies. Throughout the 1970s and 1980s, businesses began to decline, and people began to move out of the city for better, more stable opportunities. The city assumed that it would bounce back and continued on with a business-as-usual attitude.

In 1986, Wheeling-Pittsburgh Steel, originally known as Pittsburgh Steel, which had been Monessen's major employer for the majority of the century, closed its doors for good. This caused Monessen to steadily decline for 20 years. Most businesses closed, more than half of the population moved away, and buildings sat vacant and went into disrepair.

Once the city recovered from the shock of the loss of its only major industry, its citizens attempted to push forward. Plans were made throughout the 1990s to demolish many of the abandoned buildings, including the empty Wheeling-Pittsburgh Steel facilities.

In 1998, the city celebrated its centennial with much pomp and fanfare. Ceremonies, festivals, and other celebrations occurred throughout the entire year, but Monessen was still hurting. The beginning of the 21st century would simply mean that more businesses would close and more people would leave. No matter what it did, the city could not manage to stabilize itself for long periods of time.

By the 2010s, Monessen had lost control of its vacant properties. The numbers rose to a large amount, but the resilient city continued to push onward. The administration built a new public safety building and the Monessen Public Library, among other improvements, marking the new decade.

The exit of the mill brought to Monessen a wave of crime that the city had never seen before. Throughout the 1990s to the present, the city has fought against gangs, violence, and drug problems. These are symptoms of a city that is hurting financially and morally. The lack of jobs have not only caused people to leave, it has caused the morale of the people that have stayed to fall to a low level. The citizens are still grieving the loss of Wheeling-Pittsburgh Steel, and it can be seen through the indifference and lack of motivation. Regardless of the situations that have been given to Monessen, most of its citizens are still resilient and motivated like their ancestors before them. Many are working hard to bring Monessen back.

As it stands in 2014, the city seems to be remaining still for the time being. Many groups have been trying to help get the city back on its feet, but it has become increasingly difficult due to lack of funds and political oppositions at multiple angles. The city's urgent goal is to stabilize its housing market and bring in jobs to attract younger families. Only then will crime be decreased and a sense of community be rekindled into the city.

One

A Modern City

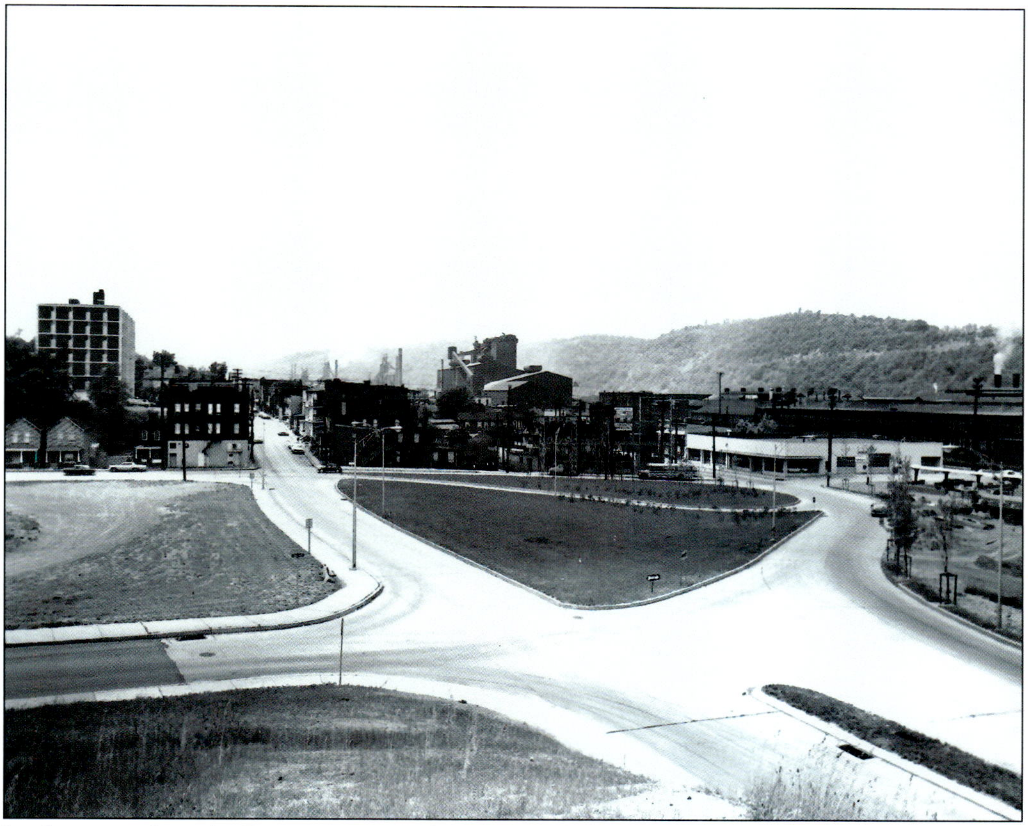

Looking west from the Eastgate section of Monessen, this 1960s photograph shows a neighborhood that was demolished and reorganized to modernize Monessen and ease its traffic problem. The Page Wire Mill can be seen to the right; the Eastgate sector is home to several offices as well as a shopping center.

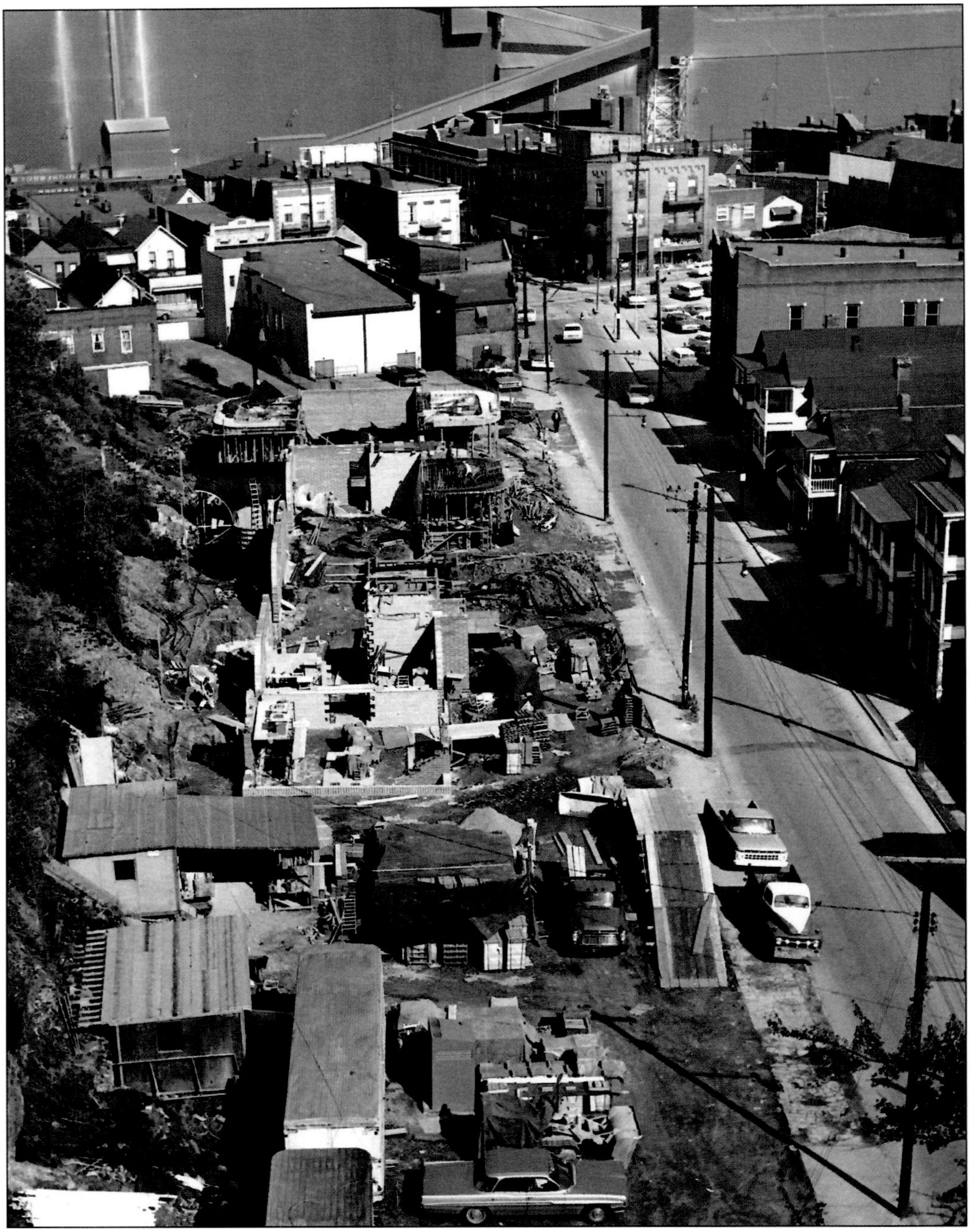

This view takes a look down Third Street towards the basic oxygen furnace of Pittsburgh Steel. Pictured here is the Valley Manor, one of Monessen's residential high rises that was built in the middle of the 20th century. The Valley Manor is still in operation today, although much of the street has changed due to the demolition of many buildings in that area.

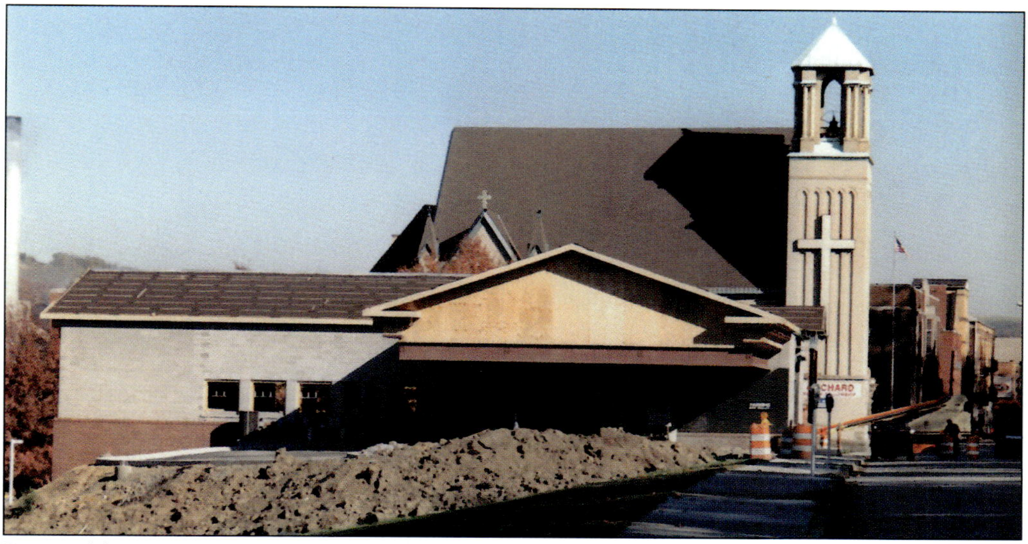

Pictured here is construction of the Valley First Federal Credit Union at Eighth Street and Schoonmaker Avenue in the 1990s. Valley First is a credit union that is locally operated in the Monongahela Valley.

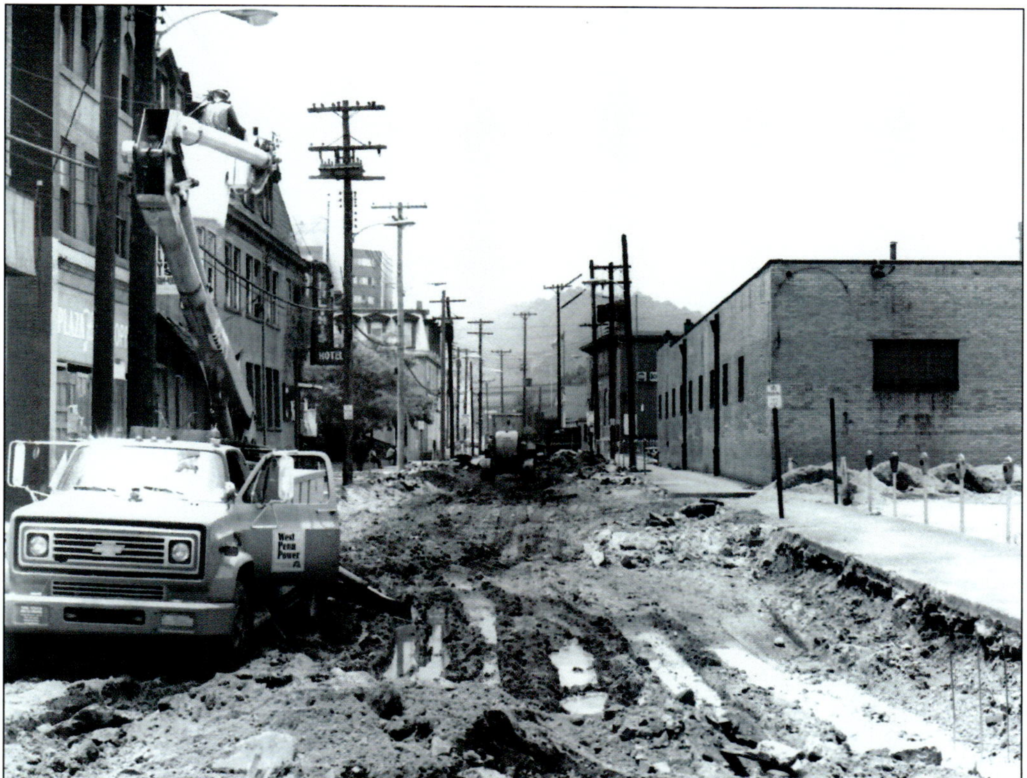

Looking west on Donner Avenue at Sixth Street, crews can be seen working to repave the road with concrete. Many Monessen roads were paved with concrete in the 1960s due to political influence and economic success. Monessen was in its height in the 1950s and 1960s, and many projects like these occurred in the city during this time.

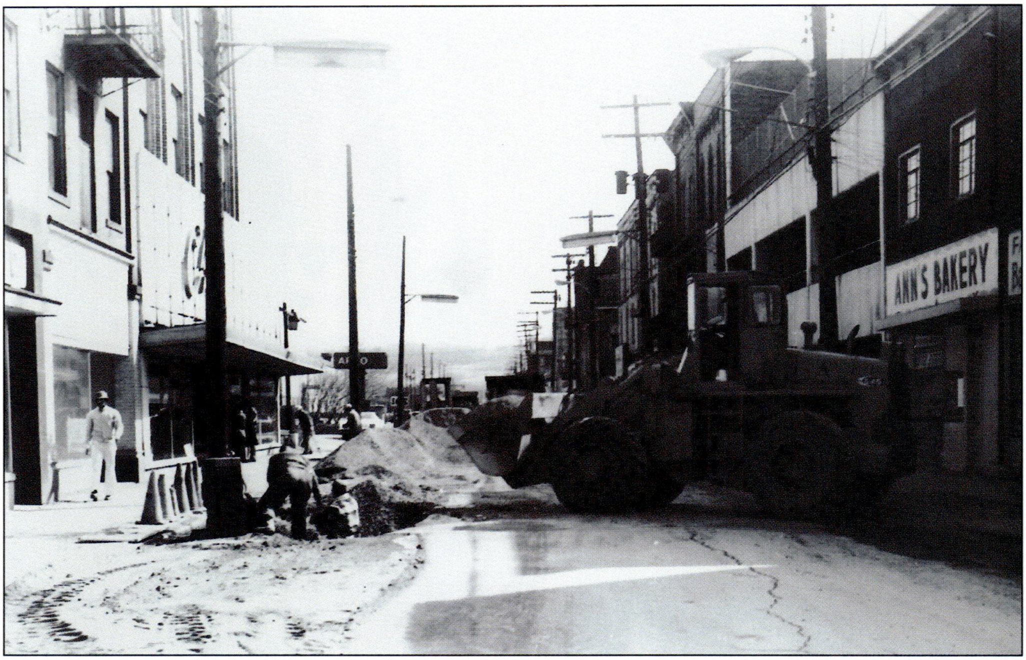

This photograph from March 1975 shows crews working on a road rehabilitation project on Donner Avenue, looking east toward Fourth Street. The project was part of the New Town, Inc. Project. New Town, Inc., brought together businessmen from various sectors to pledge physical and financial support to improving Monessen's business sector in the 1970s.

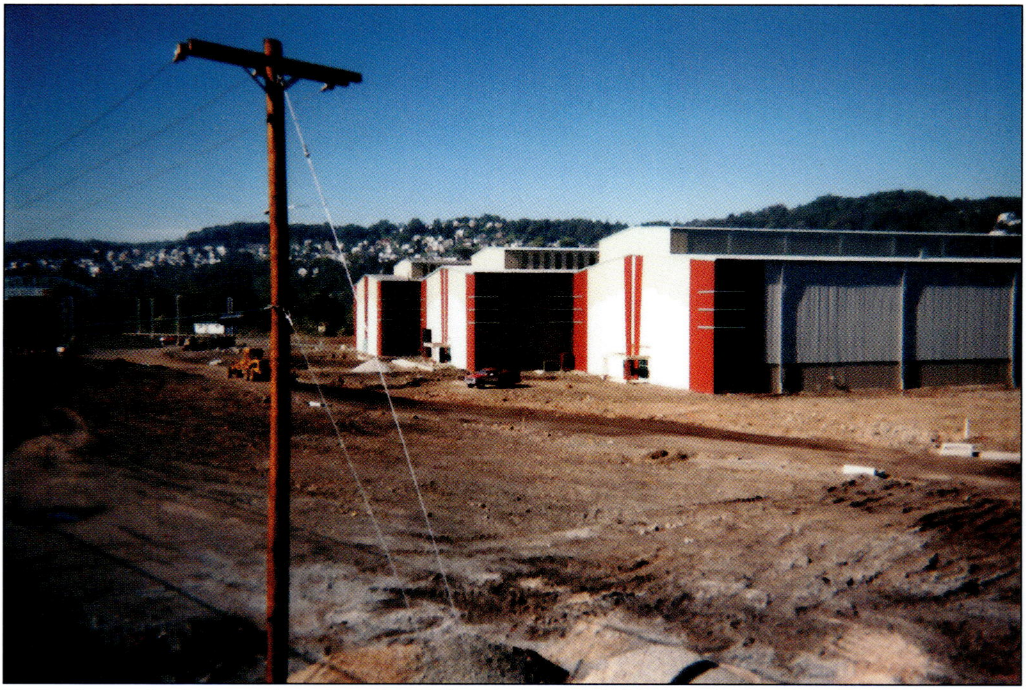

Some former buildings of Pittsburgh Steel were remodeled in the 1990s to house various small companies. Many of the companies that use the buildings today are clean industrial companies. The area was renamed Monessen Riverfront Industrial Park II.

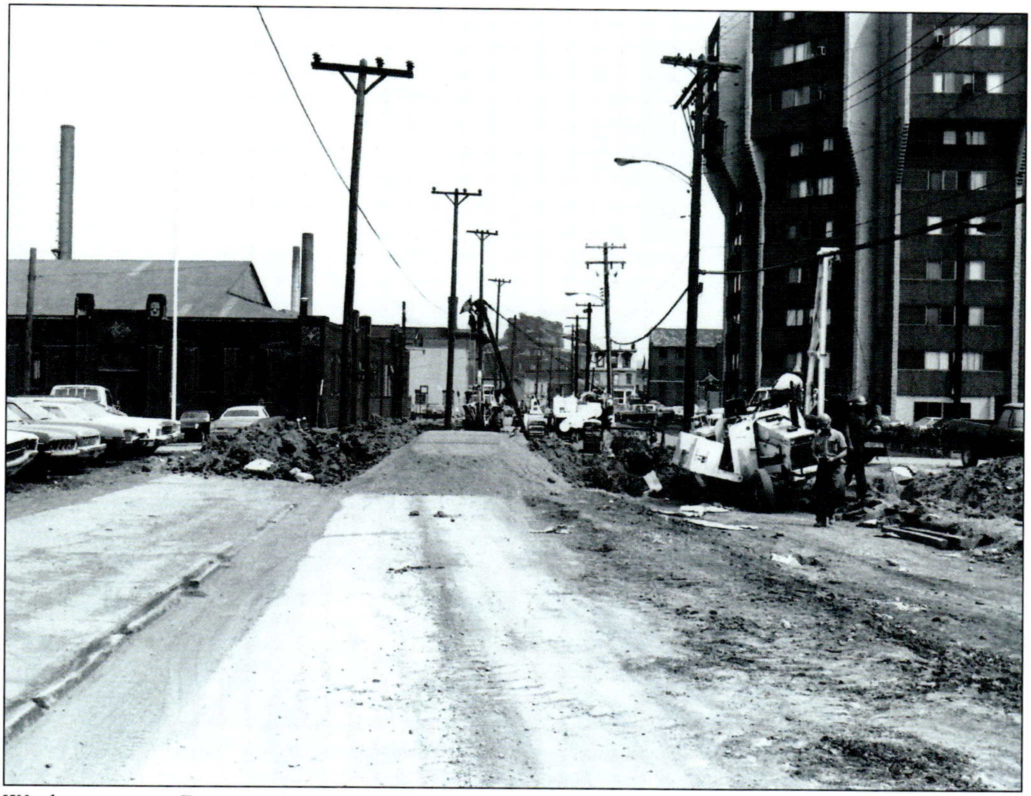

Workers repave Donner Avenue in the Westgate section of Monessen during the New Town Inc. Project in the 1970s. The former Monessen Armory building can be seen to the left, with the Westgate Manor to the right. The old armory building is now used as a civic center and the Monessen Recreation Authority headquarters.

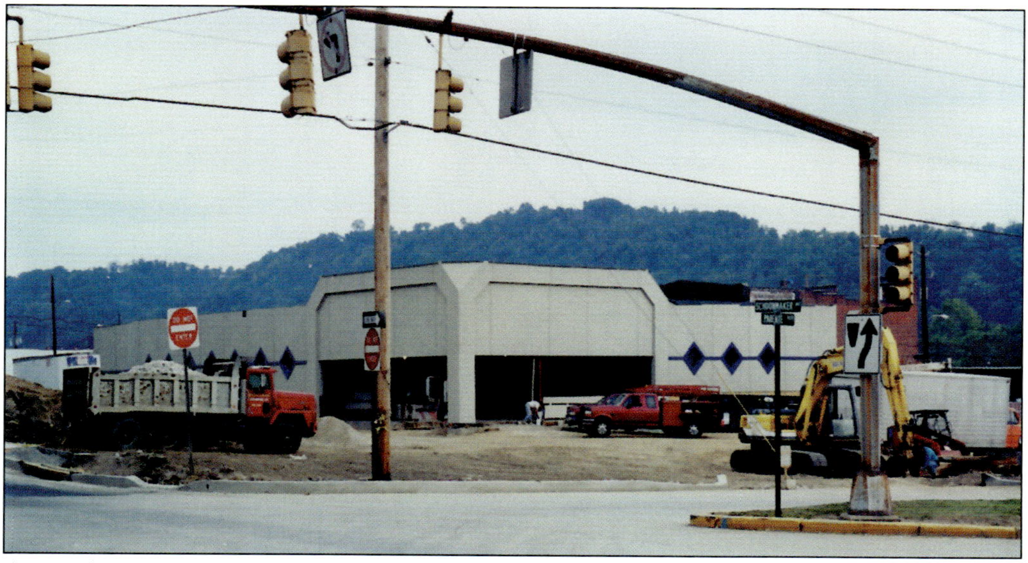

A new drugstore is being constructed at Parente and Schoonmaker Avenues in the 1990s. An entire block of residential and commercial buildings once stood in its place. The Rite Aid pharmacy was once located in the middle of the downtown area.

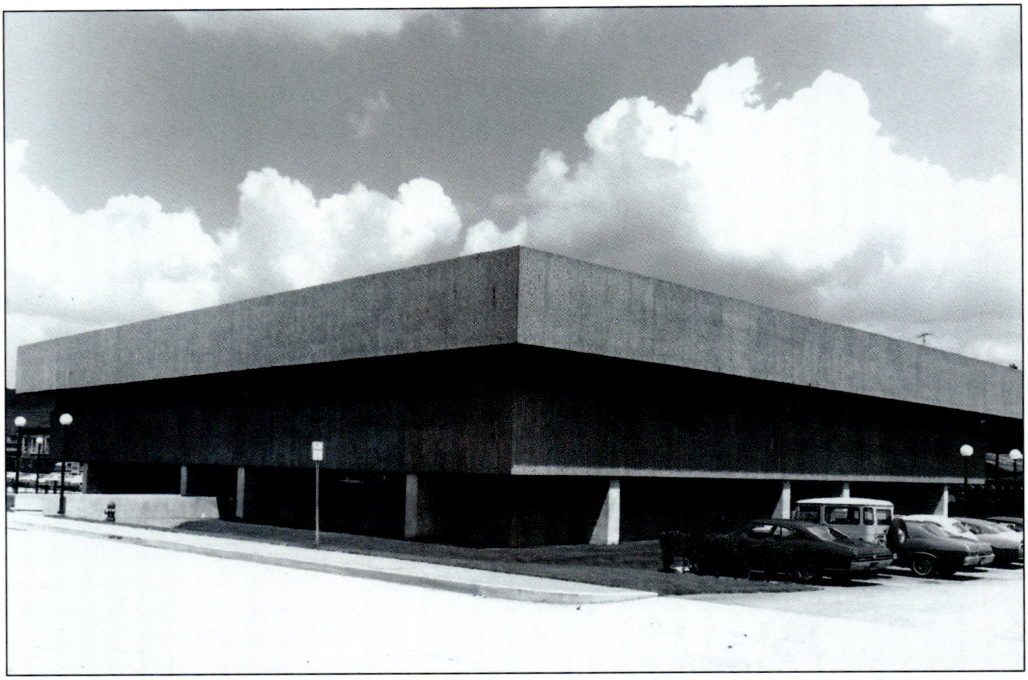

The Mon Valley Health Center Complex is pictured here before its third and fourth floor additions. The building served as the health center until the 2010s. The city administration moved from its building on Third Street and Donner Avenue, and the center is now the Monessen Municipal Complex.

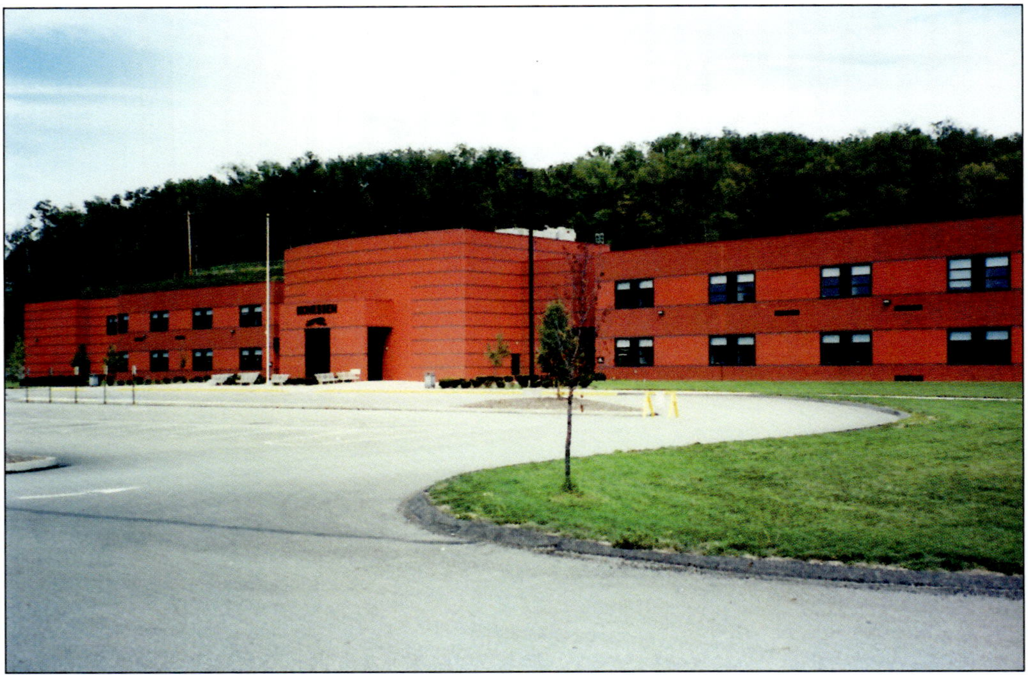

The new Monessen High School building on State Road was constructed in 1996 as part of the revitalizing Park Plan. On the grounds of the high school are a soccer field, track, softball field, tennis courts, and large parking lot.

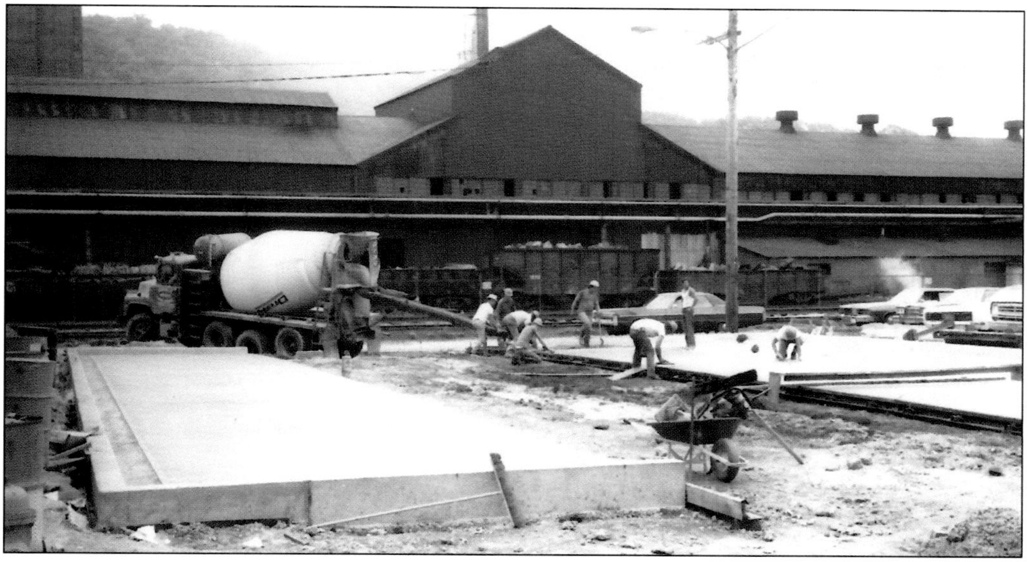

A new parking lot is being poured in downtown Monessen in the 1960s. This parking lot is located at Fifth Street and Donner Avenue. Part of the former Pittsburgh Steel plant is visible in the background.

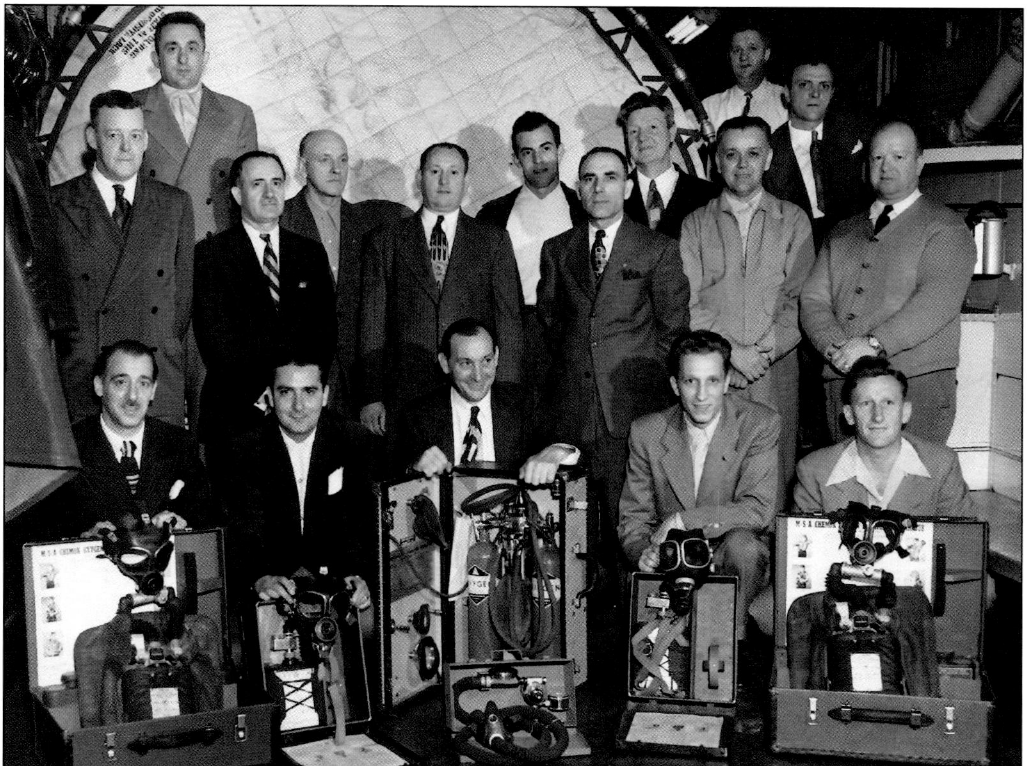

Members of the Monessen Fire Department pose with their new, modern equipment. Monessen boasts two fire companies: Department No. One, which is located in downtown Monessen, and Department No. Two (also known as Hilltop), which is located on Grand Boulevard. Both departments are active within the community.

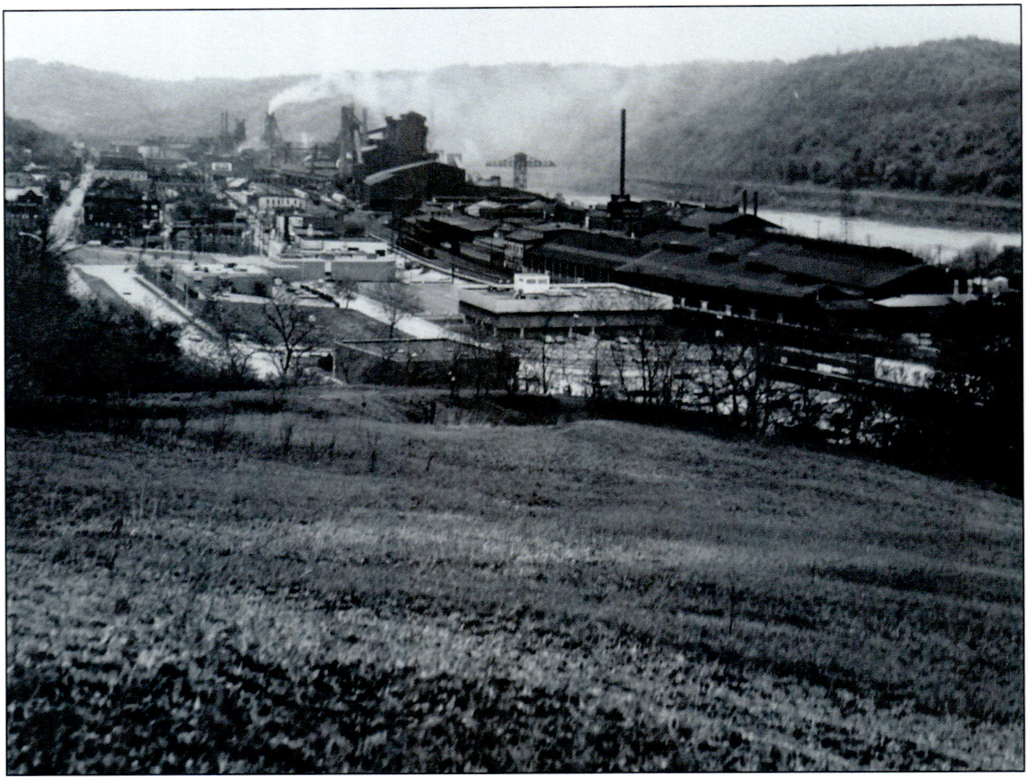

In this hilltop view of the Eastgate and Midtown sections of the city, the Page Wire Mill and Pittsburgh Steel can be seen in the distance. The wire mill operated in its same location until it caught fire in the 1970s.

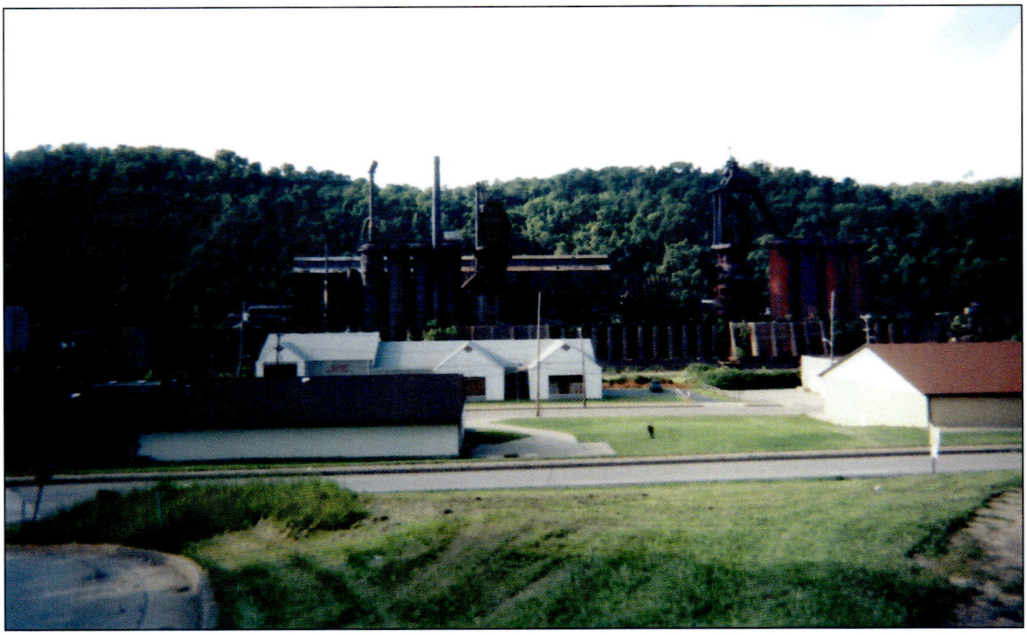

This is a unique view of the derelict blast furnaces of Pittsburgh Steel before their demolition in 1996. The demolished facilities spanned seven city blocks along the Monongahela River.

Two

Faith, Culture, and Ethnic Ties

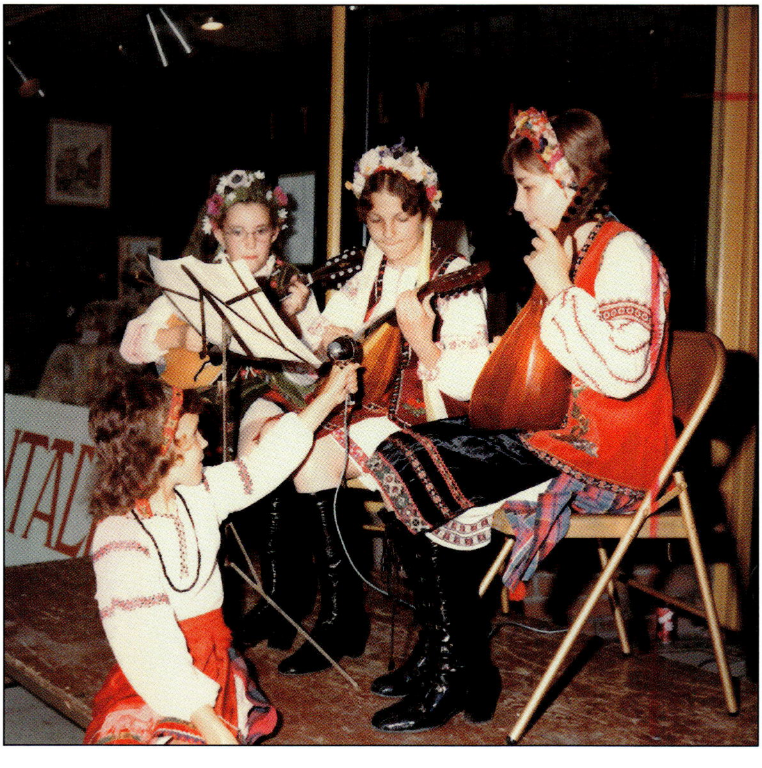

A group of young girls perform ethnic music at one of Monessen's annual cultural heritage festivals, which were held each year in the city. The festivals attracted thousands of people from the surrounding communities and the Greater Pittsburgh region each year. Participation and attendance decreased until the festival was abandoned in 2006.

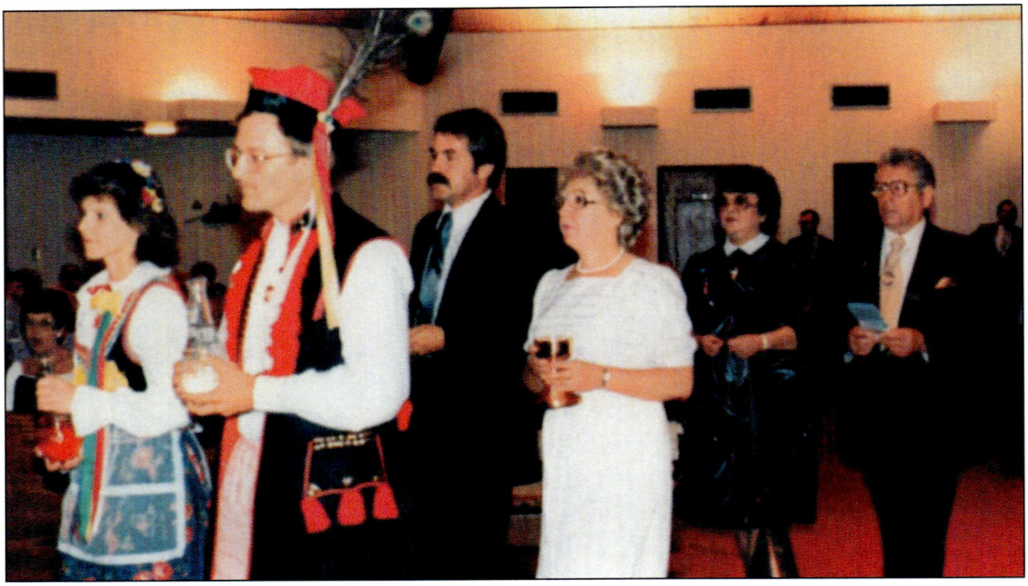

Members of St. Hyacinth Polish Catholic Church participate in a ceremony. St. Hyacinth was one of several Roman Catholic churches in the city. All of the ethnic Roman Catholic churches were merged into one unified church in 1991. The former St. Hyacinth building now serves a chapel site for the newly created Epiphany of Our Lord Catholic Church.

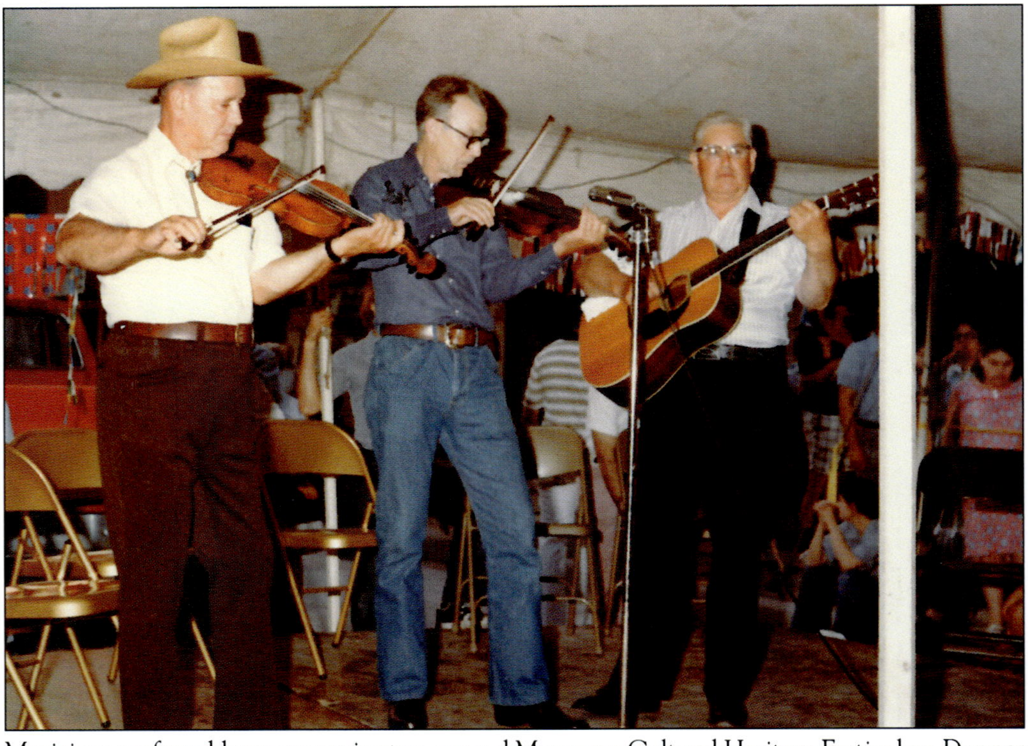

Musicians perform bluegrass music at an annual Monessen Cultural Heritage Festival on Donner Avenue. For most of the years that it ran, the festival was held on Donner Avenue in downtown Monessen, but the last few years of the festival were held at Monessen City Park. Participation waned, and the festival ceased to exist in the mid-2000s.

This building on Seventh Street in downtown Monessen houses one of the cities remaining ethnic-related organizations, the Italian Society of Mutual Aid. The building originally housed the Elks Lodge until it was moved to a newly constructed facility in the Park Plan area of the city. (Author's collection.)

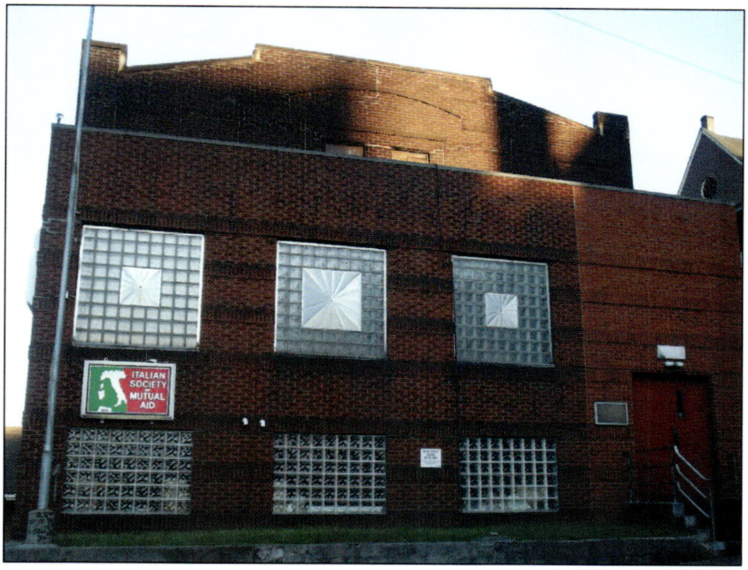

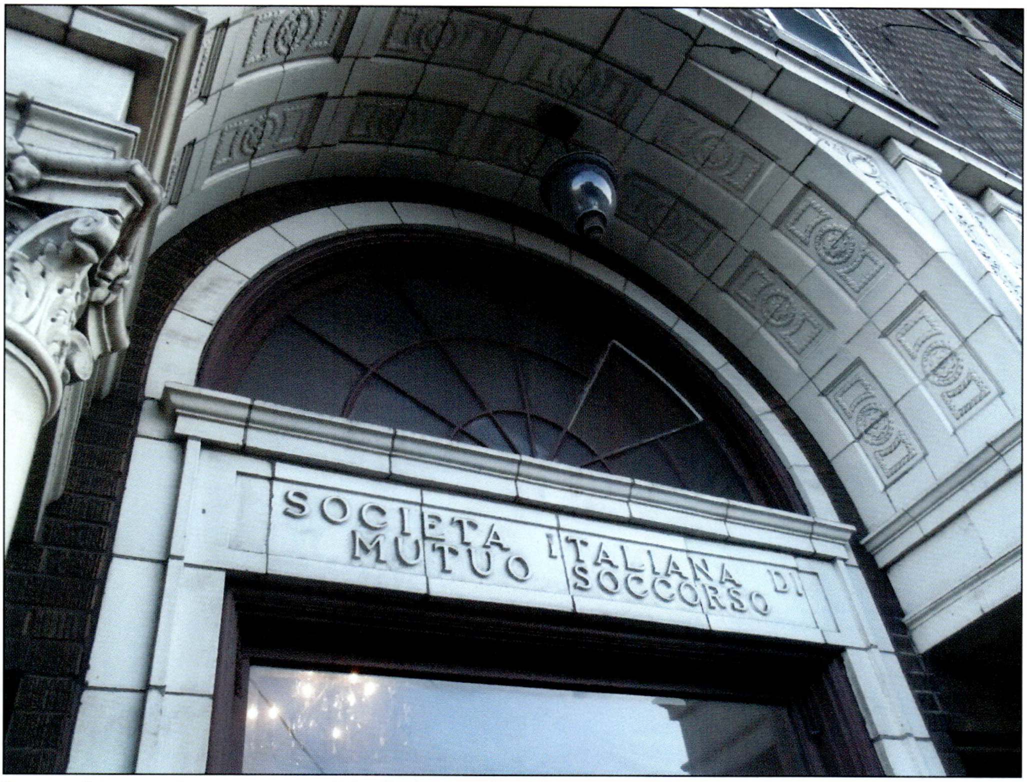

Pictured here is the entryway of the Italianate building that originally housed Monessen's Italian Society of Mutual Aid and the Italian Hall. The building now houses Felicia's Italian restaurant and lounge and is located on Schoonmaker Avenue near Fourth Street, in the heart of Midtown. (Author's collection.)

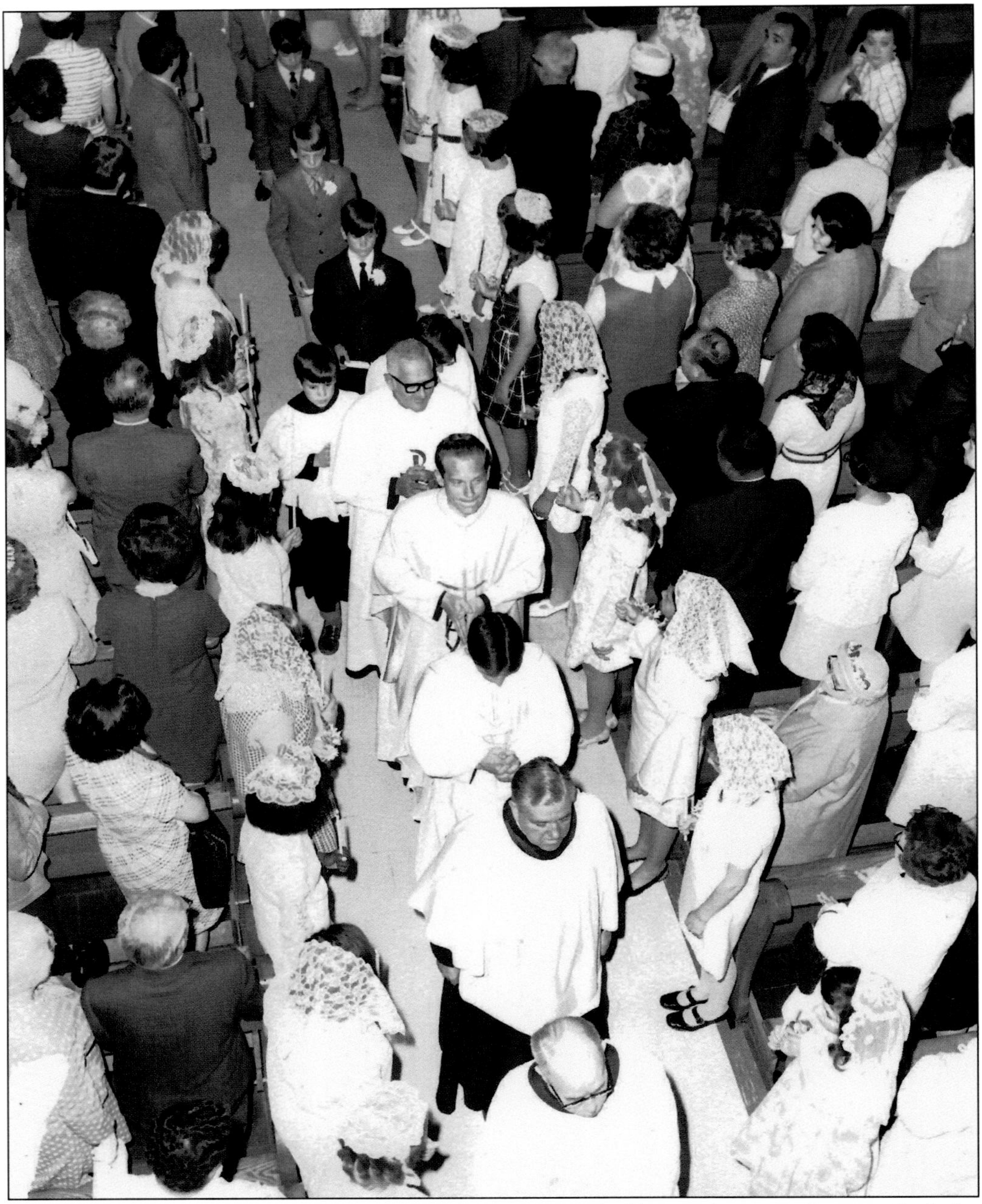

This 1969 photograph shows a procession during a mass held at Holy Name Roman Catholic Church on Reed Avenue. Holy Name served one the largest congregations in Monessen, but it closed with other churches in the early 1990s. Its congregation was made up of people with Slovak ancestry, and the property that surrounded the church also included a school and a nunnery. When the church was slated to close its doors, the parishioners appealed to the bishop and even to the papacy, demonstrating the determination of Monessenites. Sadly, their church was closed along with four others and merged into one parish in two buildings. The church building where the Holy Name parish worshipped now houses an alternative learning center. Most of the other buildings that were once on the church's grounds were torn down, and houses were built in their place.

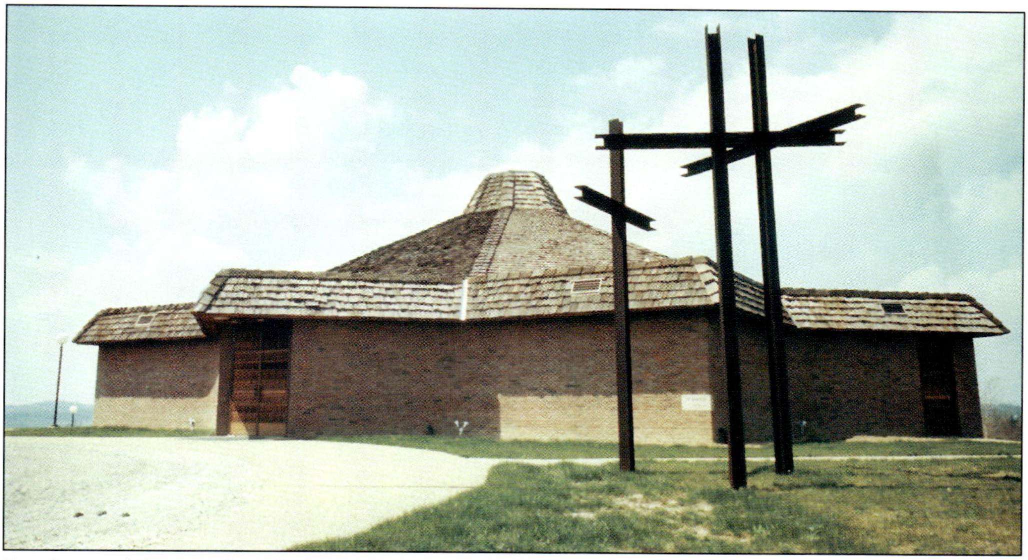

Epiphany of Our Lord Catholic Church sits on one of the highest points in Monessen. The chapel once served as the new site of the St. Hyacinth parish, which was a Roman Catholic parish with a mostly Polish congregation. St. Hyacinth was one of five Roman Catholic churches that were closed in Monessen in the early 1990s.

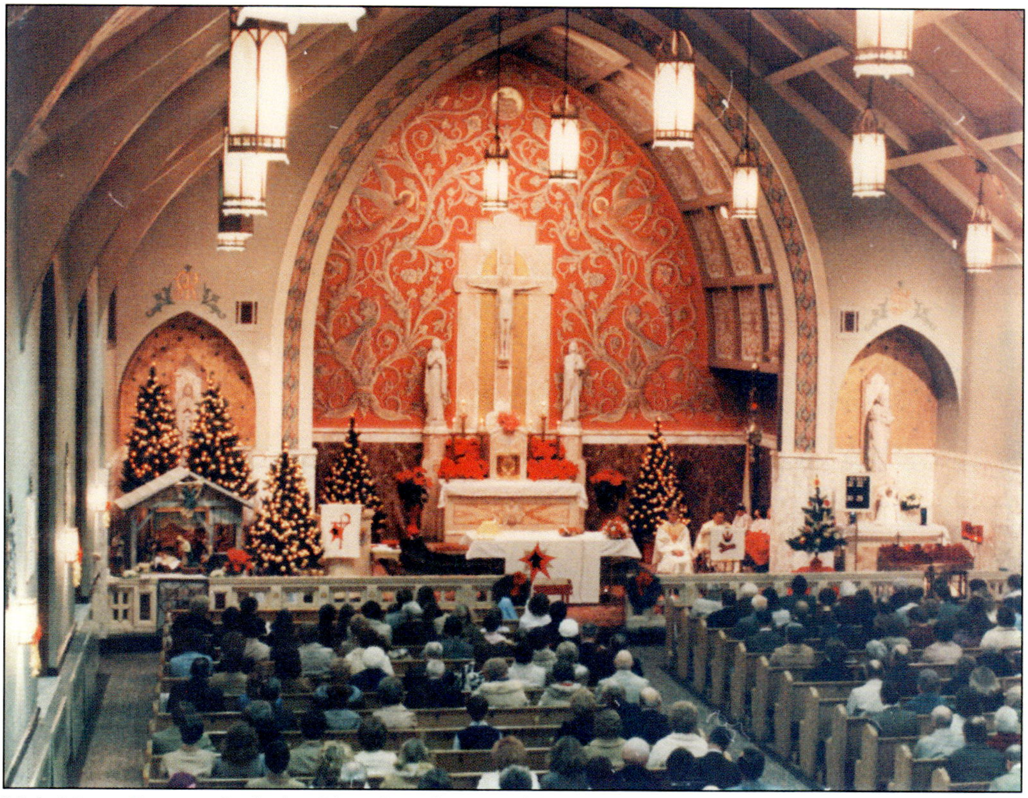

Holy Name Roman Catholic Church is decorated for Christmas Eve Mass. This photograph was taken before major interior renovations were started. Once one of the most successful parishes, the church was forced to permanently close its doors in 1991.

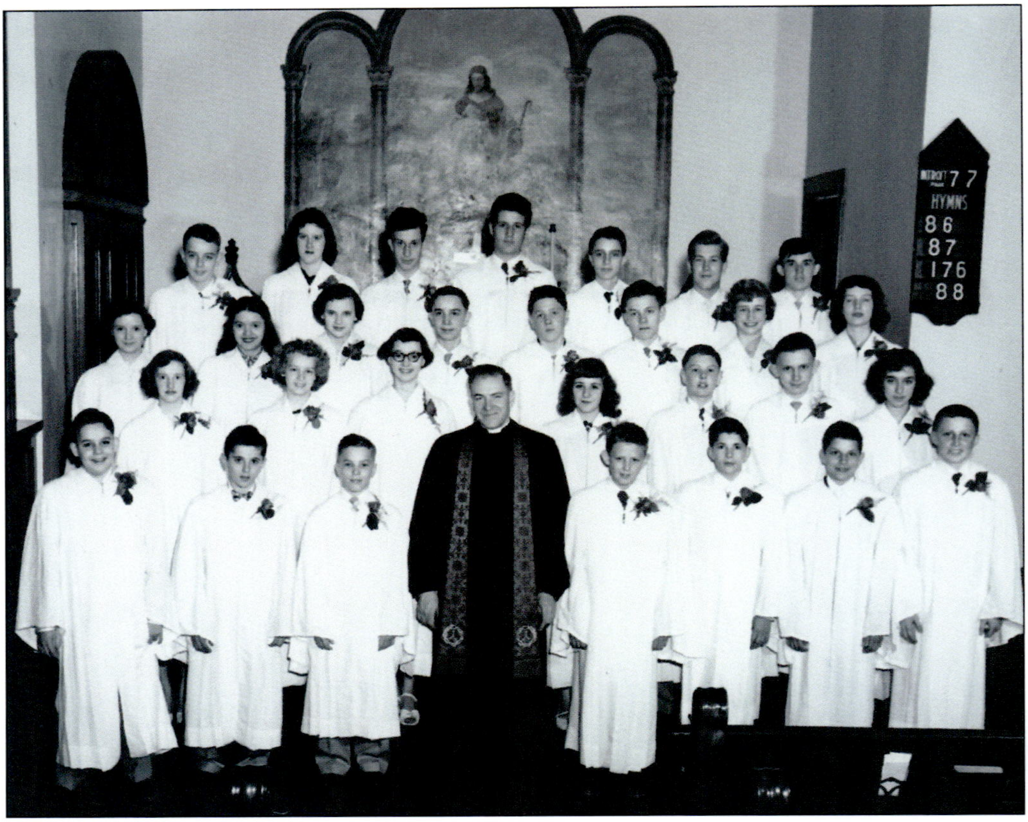

Pictured here is a confirmation class at St. Paul's Evangelical Lutheran Church. This photograph was taken when the congregation held services at its first location on Eighth Street in downtown Monessen. The church was demolished and relocated to Grand Boulevard and Watkins Street when the Westgate revitalization project was under way in the city.

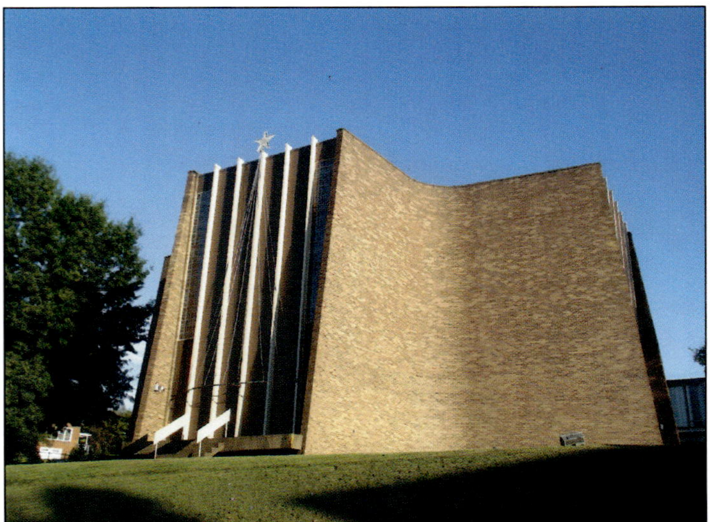

This is the new location of St. Paul's Evangelical Lutheran Church. Its congregation has continually practiced in this location at the corner of Grand Boulevard and Watkins Street since its move from Eighth Street in the 1960s. Like the majority of the city's churches, St. Paul's congregation has declined, but the church still remains active within the faith community. (Author's collection.)

St. Spyridon's Greek Orthodox Church is one of several Eastern Christian churches in the city and one of the most active. Every August, the church holds a food festival featuring traditional Greek food and dancing. The event is attended by hundreds of people throughout the region. (Courtesy of Karla Spangler.)

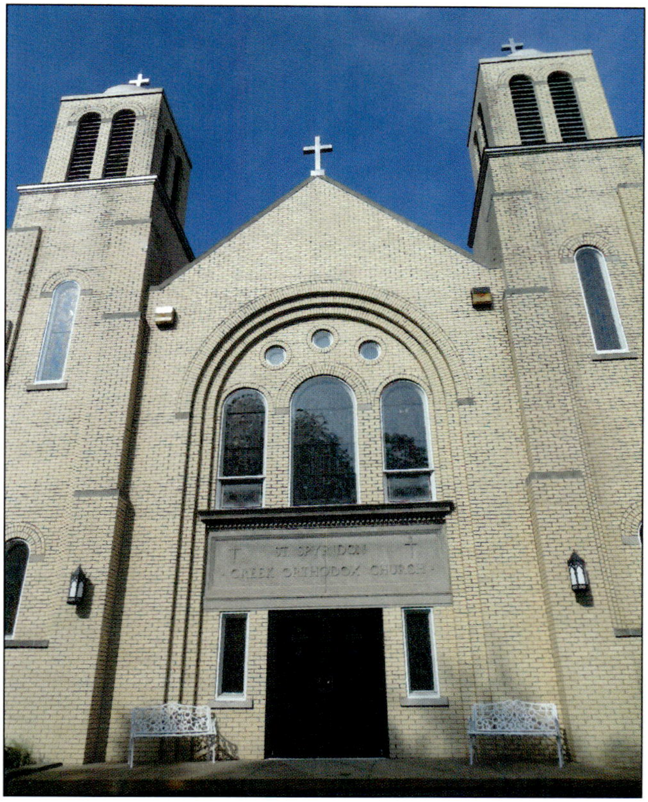

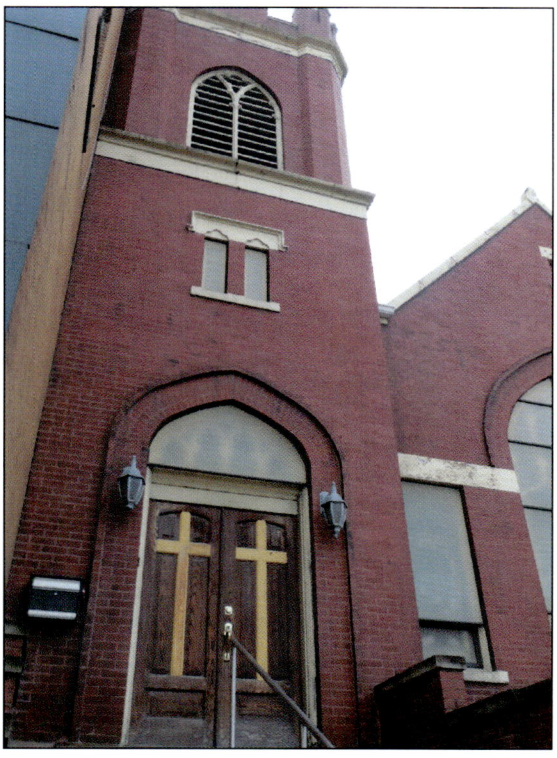

The First Christian Church is located on Sixth Street in downtown Monessen. One of the city's oldest church buildings, the sturdy brick edifice is nestled between commercial storefronts. The church proved convenient for those who attended and lived nearby. First Christian's congregation was established in 1900, and it has always been located downtown. (Courtesy of Karla Spangler.)

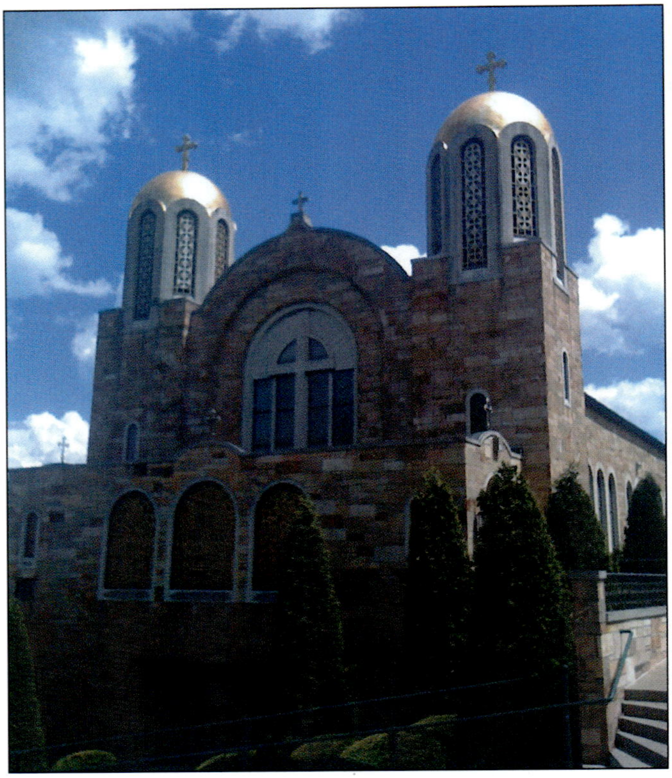

Located at the corner of McKee Avenue and Second Street is Assumption of the Blessed Virgin Mary Church, more commonly known as St. Mary's Byzantine Catholic Church. For over 100 years, the congregation has worshipped in the same location. The current building was dedicated in 1960 under Msgr. Andrew Parvensky. (Author's collection.)

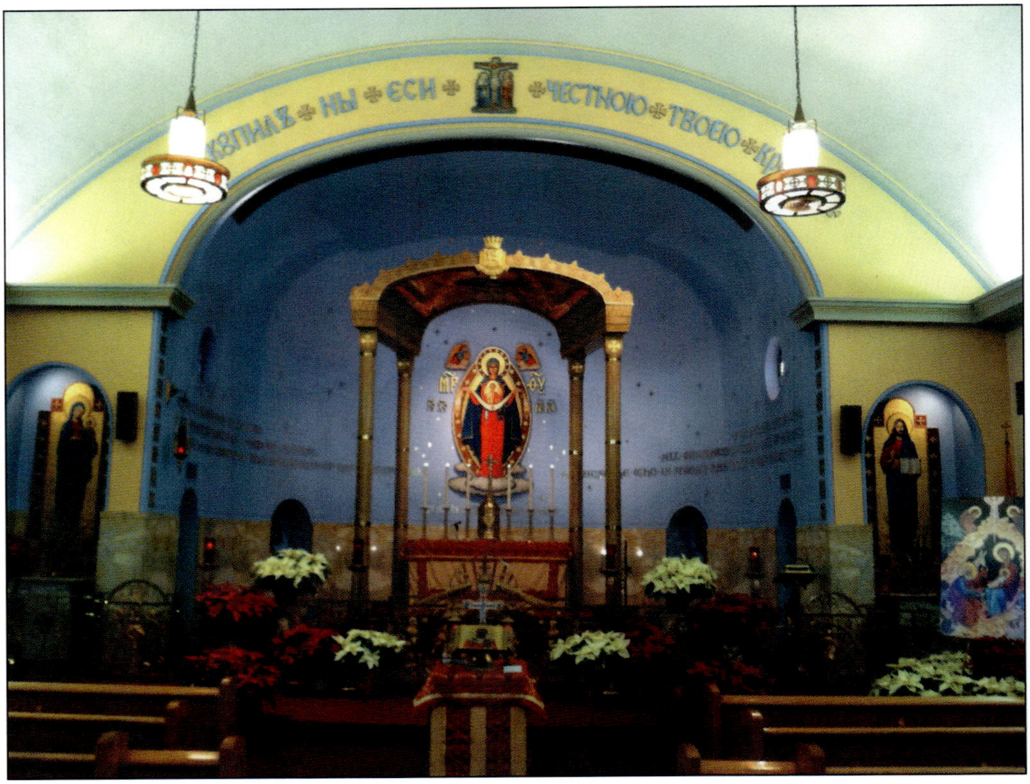

The colorful interior of St. Mary's, seen here at Christmastime, features a unique icon screen in front of the altar. The church is one of the more modern churches in the city and still has a stable congregation. The parish is made up of many people with Slovak and Carpatho-Rusyn (Ruthenian) descent. (Author's collection.)

The Hungarian Club, located on Parente Boulevard, is one of several ethnic clubs remaining in the city. Ethnic clubs were a way for immigrants to meet other people that spoke their language, shared their beliefs, and practiced their customs. They offered benefits such as insurance and various educational courses for new immigrants and residents alike. (Author's collection.)

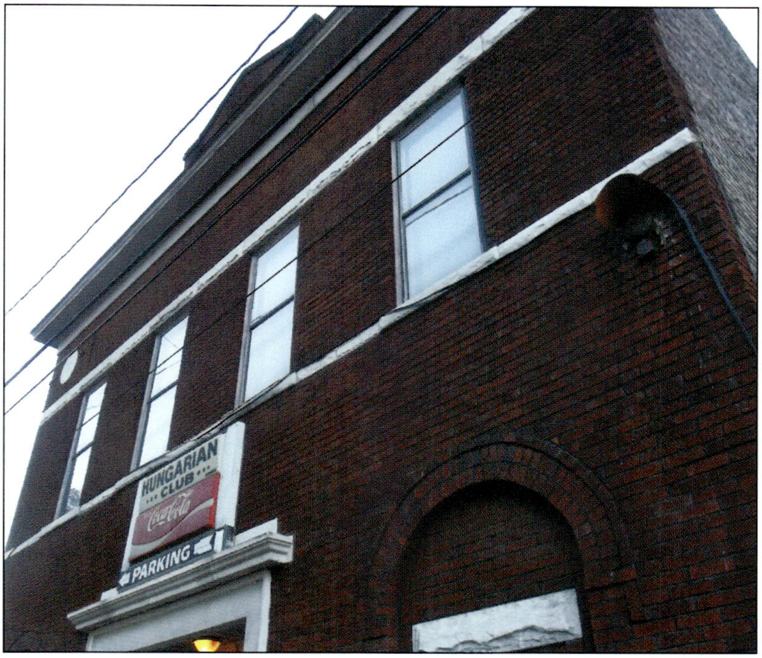

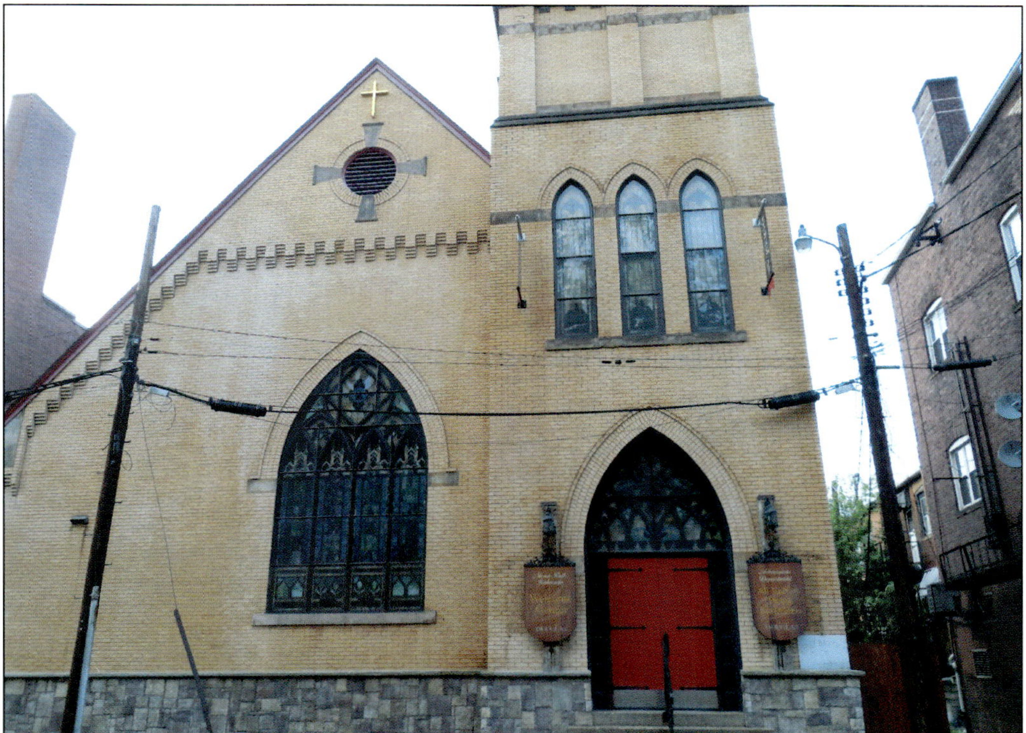

The First Baptist Church was another church that was located in the middle of the downtown area. First Baptist was built in 1909 and closed in the late 2000s. After it closed, Douglas Education Center purchased the church and made extensive renovations and restorations. (Courtesy of Karla Spangler.)

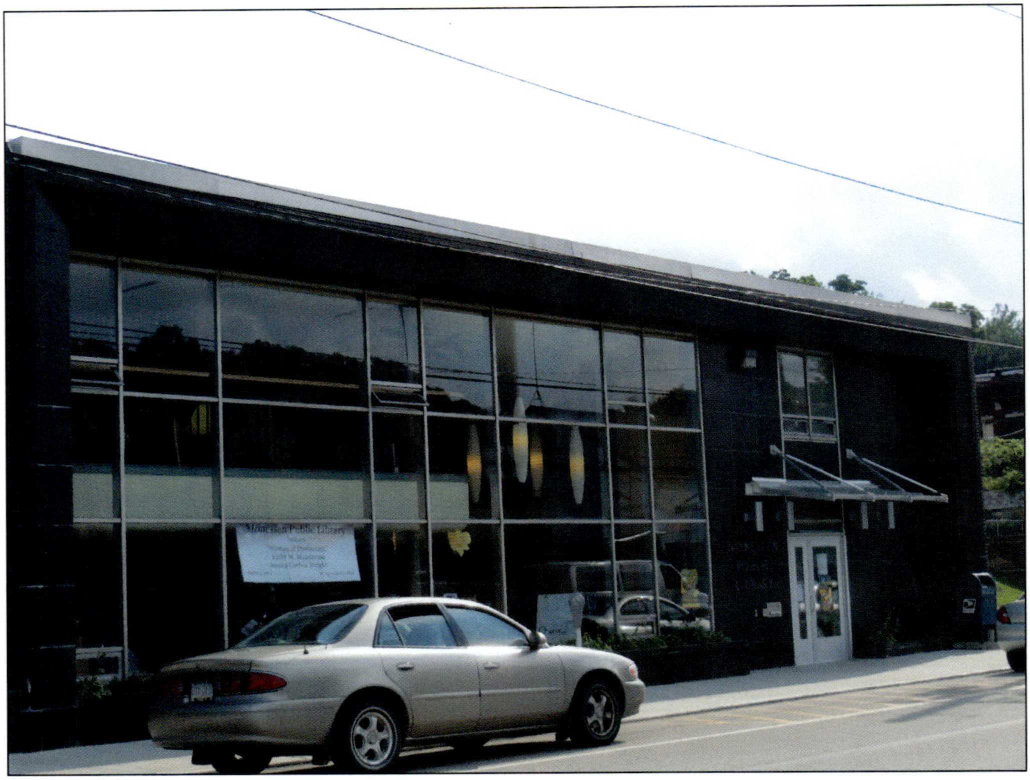

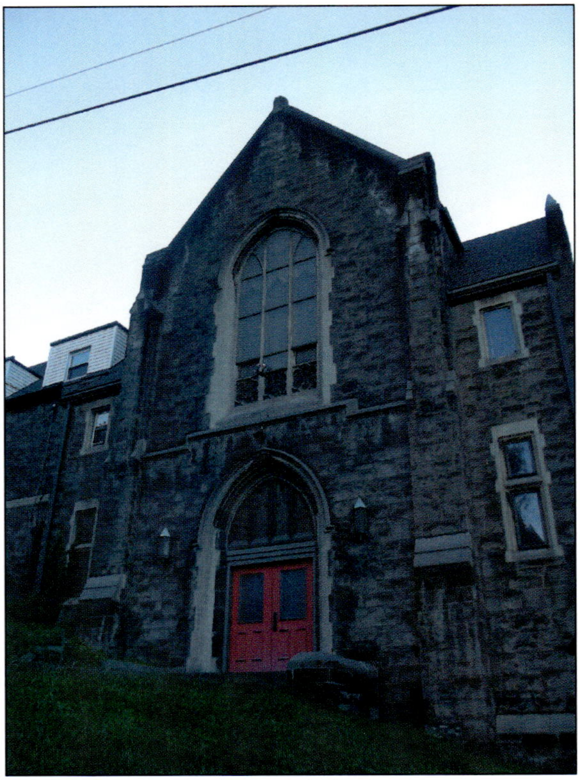

The Monessen Public Library served as a district center until 2009. It is located on Donner Avenue and now acts as a cultural center as well as a library. It was renovated in 2008, making the space more efficient and modern. Various exhibitions and events are held at the library, including activity sessions for children after school and during the summer. (Courtesy of Karla Spangler.)

The United Methodist Church is a large stone church built at the same location as its original structure, on the corner of Schoonmaker Avenue and Fourth Street. Its numbers have diminished throughout the years, like most other congregations in Monessen. The church was known for hosting a spaghetti dinner and craft market each year before the holiday season in order to raise money for their congregation. (Author's collection.)

One of the last auditorium-style buildings left in the city, Turn Halle is located at the corner of Donner Avenue and Second Street. It was home to the Monessen Turners, a German ethnic club for gymnastics. Turners were very popular in America in the late 19th and early 20th centuries.

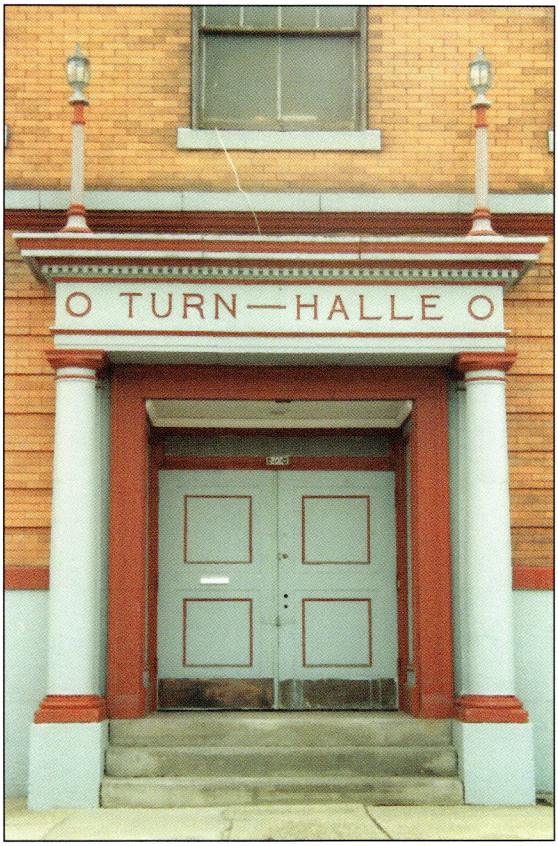

The New Italian Hall was located on Schoonmaker Avenue in downtown Monessen. The old building was originally the home to the Italian Society of Mutual Aid. Since then, the New Italian Hall closed and the building now houses Felicia's Restaurant and Lounge. This photograph from 1998 shows Monessen centennial banners lining the street.

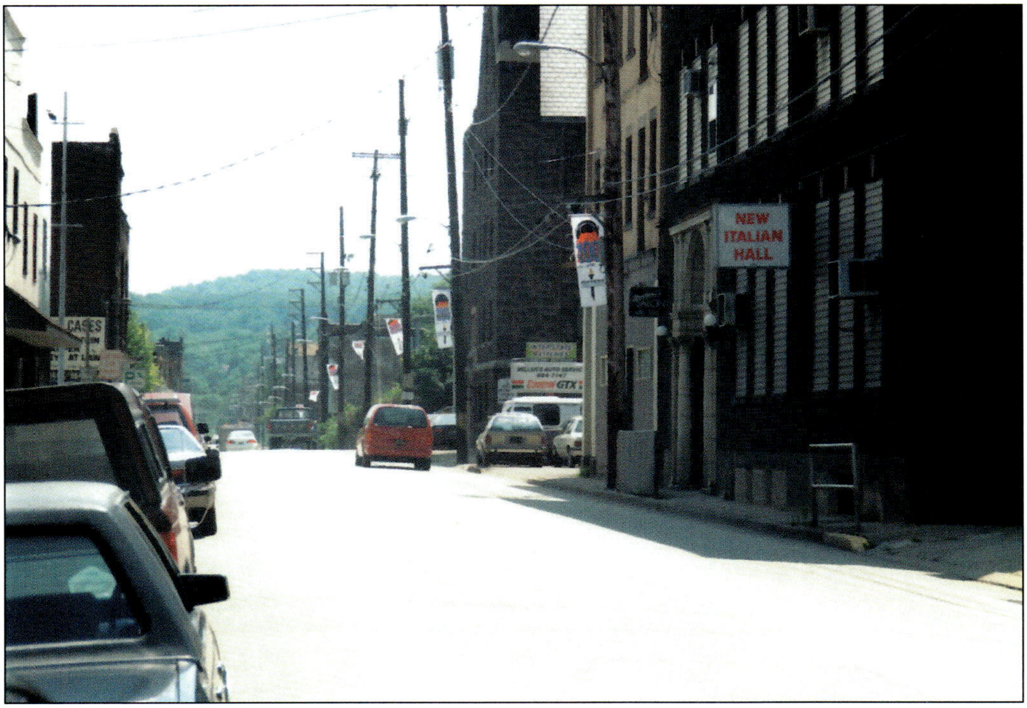

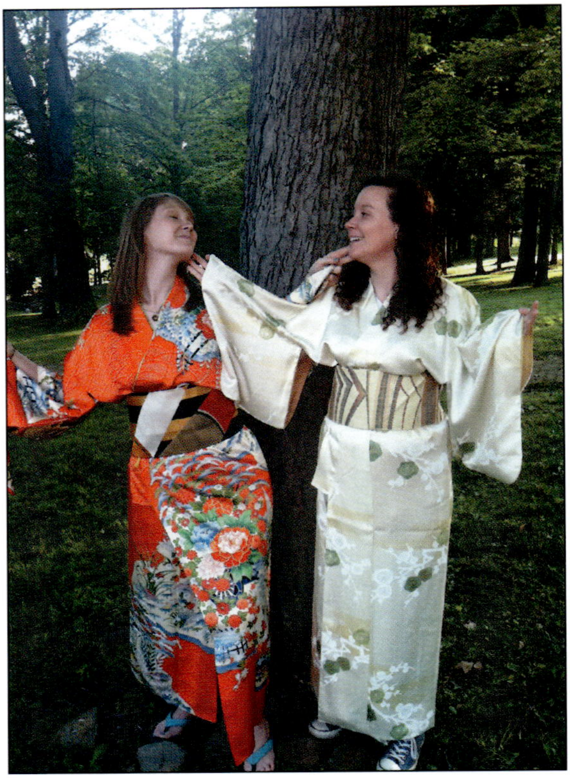

Jessica Show (left) and Karla Spangler (right) each model an authentic Japanese kimono at an event in Monessen City Park. Monessen is home to many nationalities, and although there is no recorded history of Japanese immigrants settling here, it is important to learn about various cultures of the world. Active Monessen citizens are currently making an effort to teach other citizens, especially the youth, about Japan and other cultures. (Author's collection.)

Castle Blood is a new attraction that came to the city several years ago. It moved to this location at the corner of First Street and Schoonmaker Avenue in 2014. The structure first served as a residence, then as a funeral home for many decades, and later it was left abandoned for nearly 10 years. The building is currently being refurbished and turned into a family-friendly, theatrical haunt. (Courtesy of Ricky Dick.)

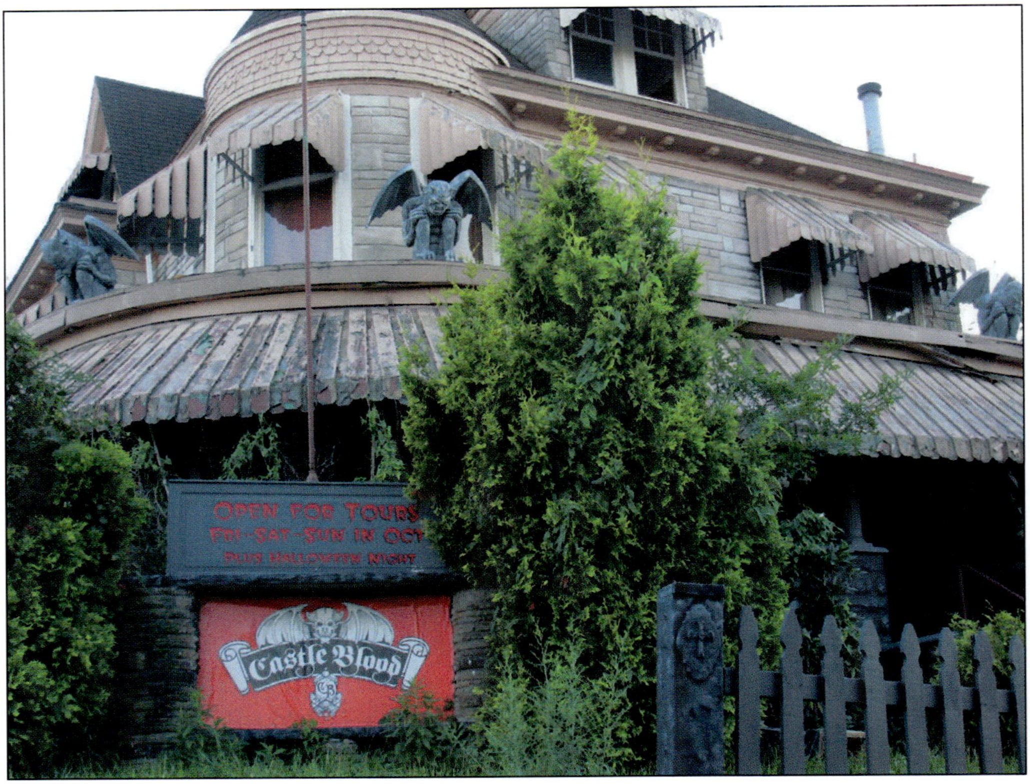

The Orchard Christian Fellowship is located on the corner of Eighth Street and Schoonmaker Avenue. The building originally housed St. Leonard's Roman Catholic Church, which was closed in the 1990s. The Orchard Christian Fellowship also operates the old parochial school next door, where it offers programs for the community. (Courtesy of Karla Spangler.)

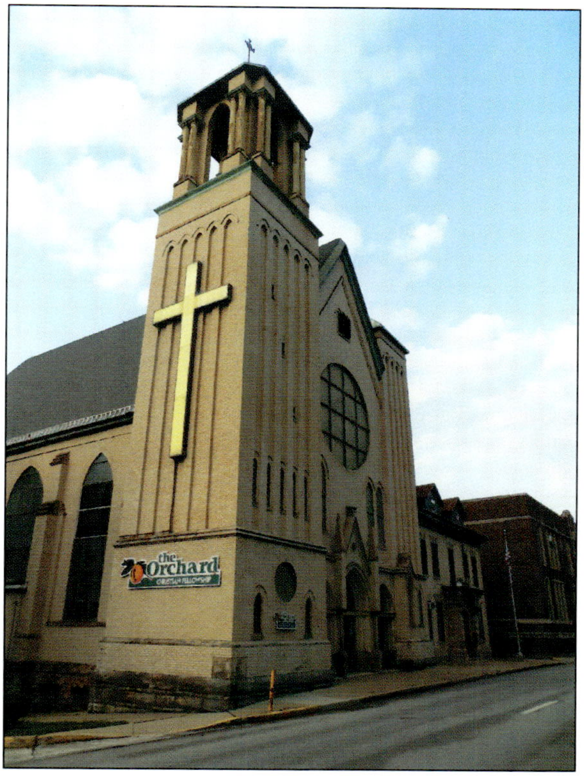

Pictured here is the interior of St. Nicholas Ukrainian Orthodox Church, located on Reed Avenue. The interior design of the old, brick building is original, and all the icons were painted by hand. The church bell is also original and hand pulled. (Author's collection.)

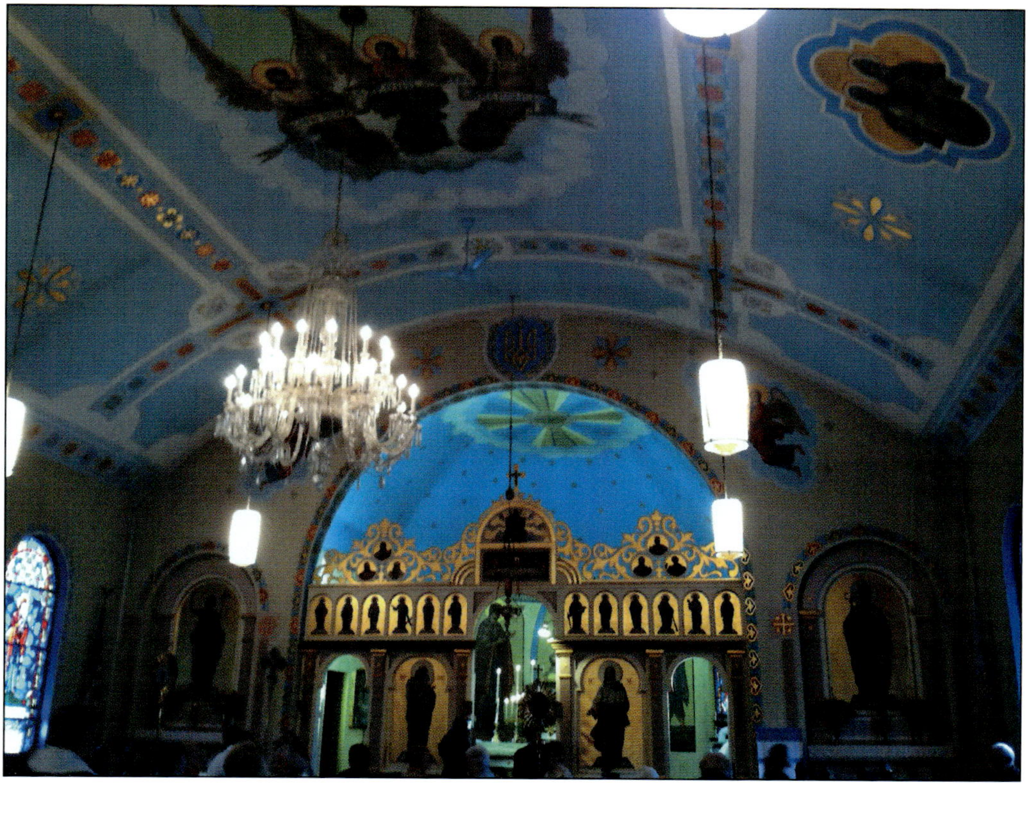

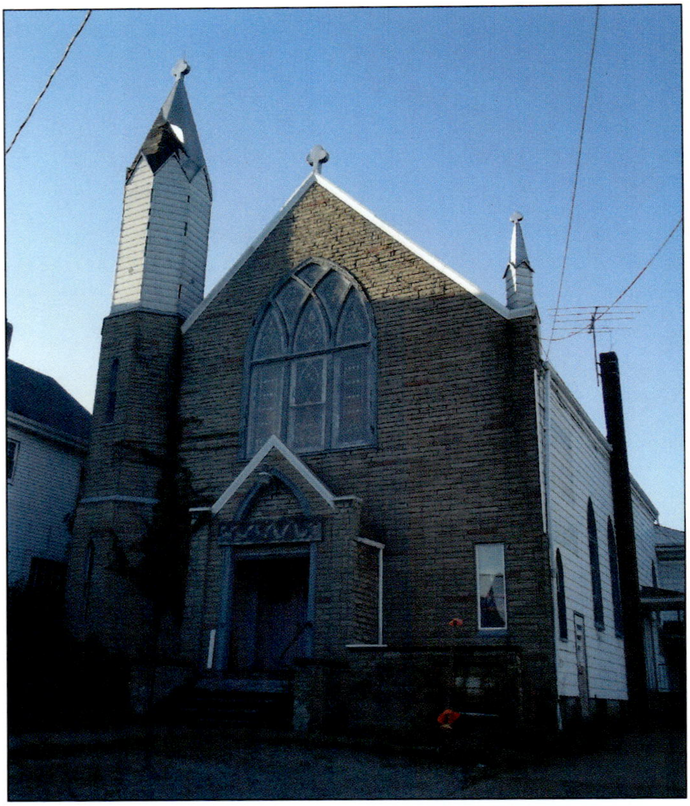

This photograph of St. Luke's Lutheran Church on Reed Avenue shows its age and the absence of a congregation for over 10 years. The church closed in the early 2000s and merged with St. Paul's Lutheran Church due to a declining congregation. The people of the church were mostly descended from Finnish immigrants. (Author's collection.)

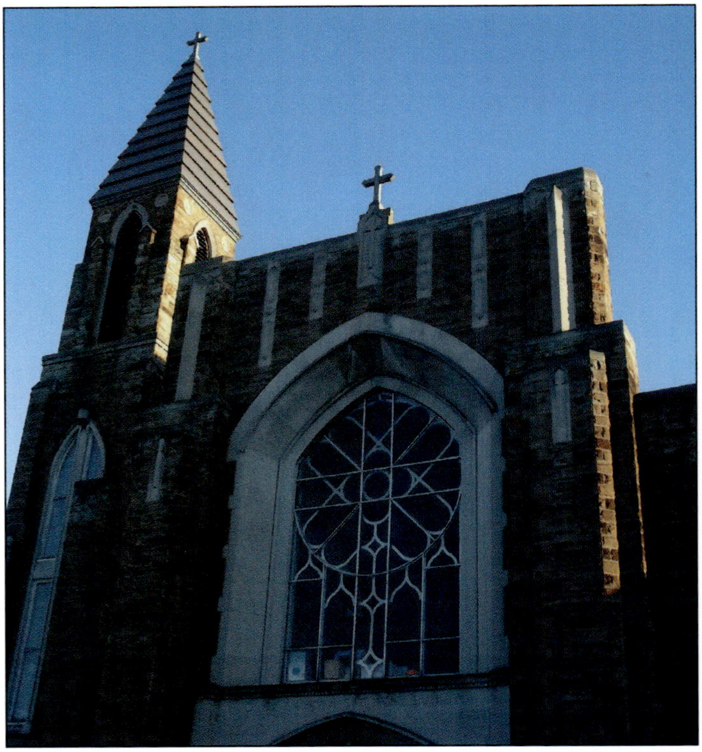

Another former church sits across the street from St. Luke's. Holy Name Church, once the city's Slovak Roman Catholic church, closed in 1991. It has had a much better fate, compared to its neighbor. The former stone church, which, unlike other churches nearby, is rather large, serves as an alternative learning and afterschool program center. (Author's collection.)

One of the city's Eastern Christian churches is St. Michael's Antiochian Orthodox Church, which is located on Patton Avenue. The building was constructed in the 1960s. It was originally known as St. Anthony of Padua Church, one of five Roman Catholic parishes that were closed during the 1990s. St Michael's moved into its current building from its former location on Ninth Street in 1992. (Author's collection.)

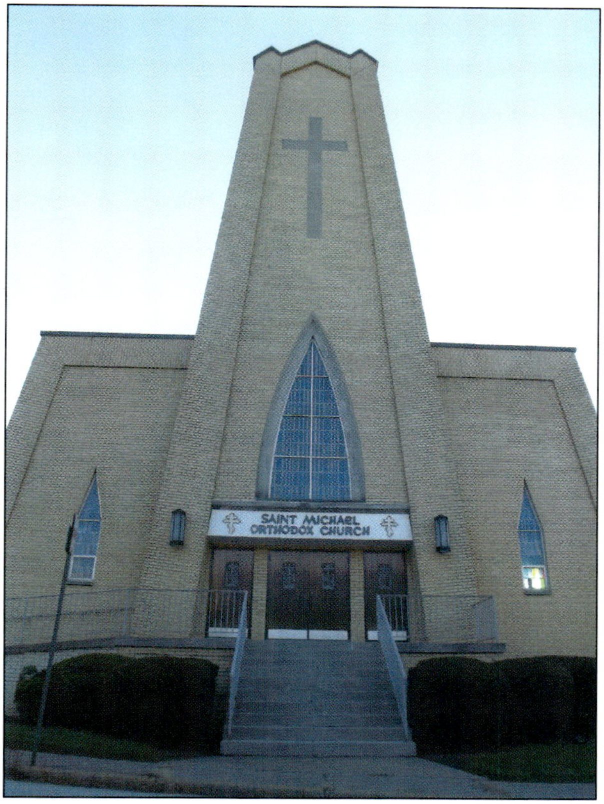

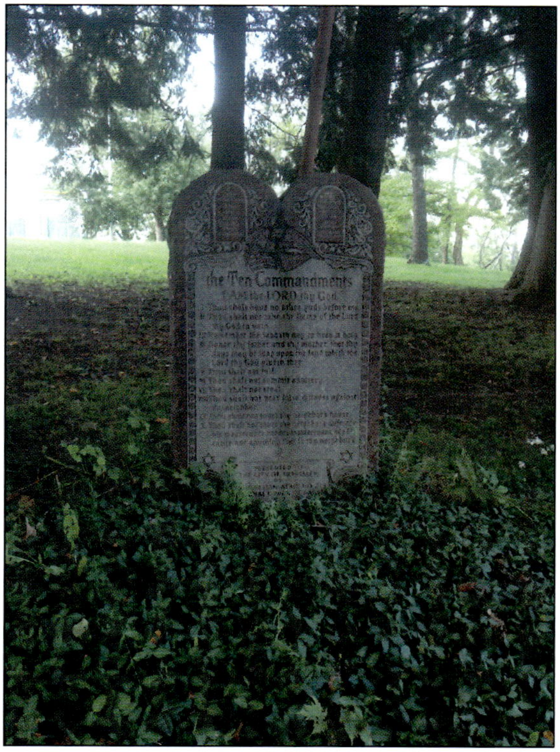

This plaque of the Ten Commandments located in Monessen City Park, near its baseball field, shows the city's religious roots. The Fraternal Order of the Eagles presented it to the city of Monessen to be displayed in the park. (Author's collection.)

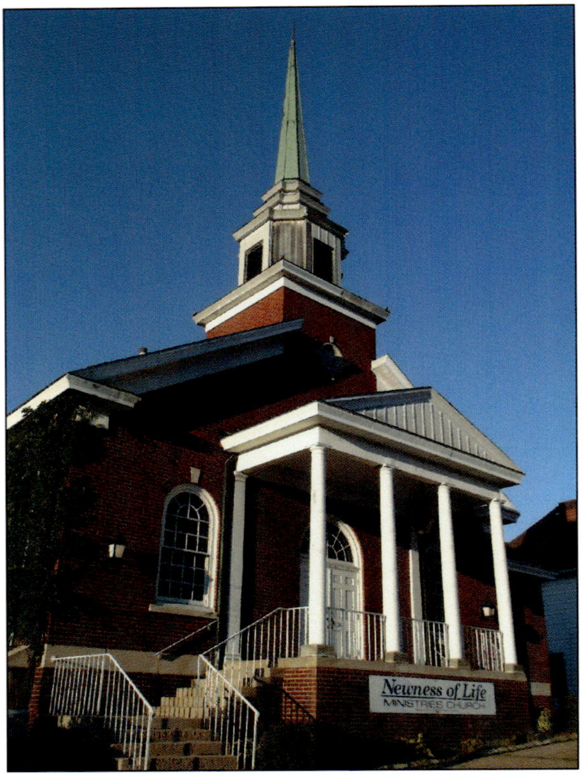

Newness of Life Ministries is a church that is located in one of Monessen's oldest neighborhoods. It sits at the corner of McKee Avenue and Sixth Street, next to Hillside Park, Monessen's oldest park. The structure was once home to the First Presbyterian Church of Monessen. (Author's collection.)

Temple Beth Am Synagogue was originally located on Schoonmaker Avenue in downtown Monessen, then known as the Kneseth Israel Synagogue. The Monessen and Charleroi synagogues merged together after breaking ground in 1952 for a new building on Watkins Avenue.

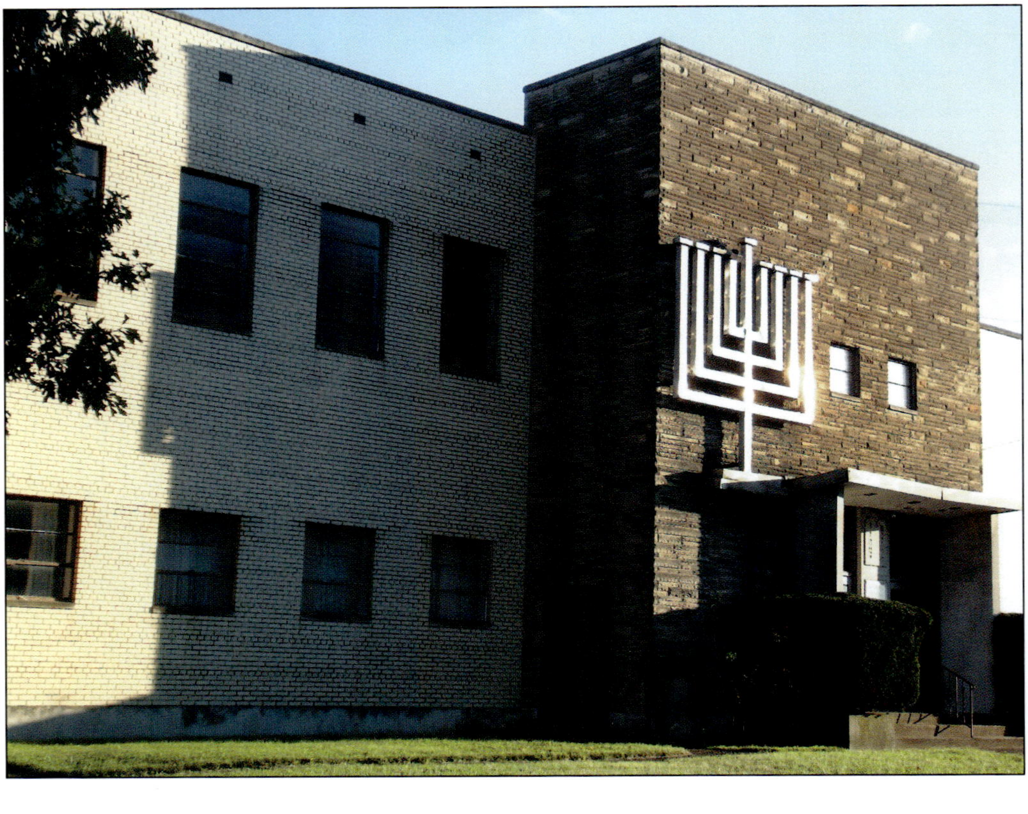

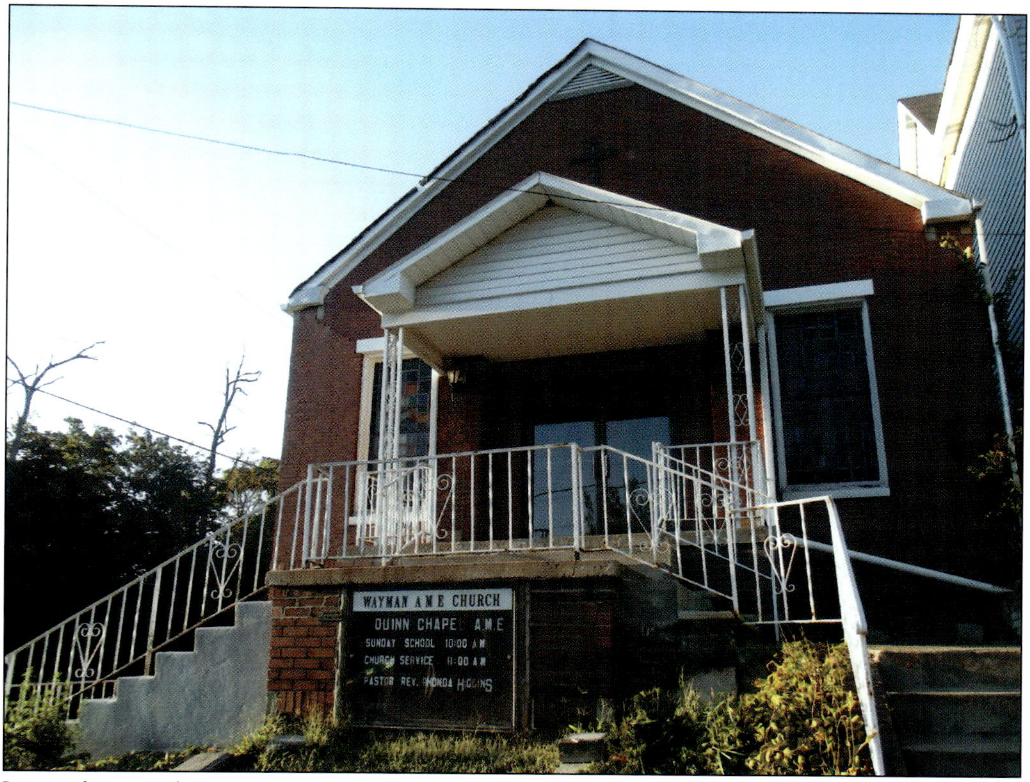

Located across the street from Gate of Heaven, Church of God in Christ is the Wayman AME church. It is located on the corner of Reed Avenue and McKee Way. Wayman AME is the oldest congregation in Monessen, and its original building is still used for worship services. (Courtesy of Jackie Pierce.)

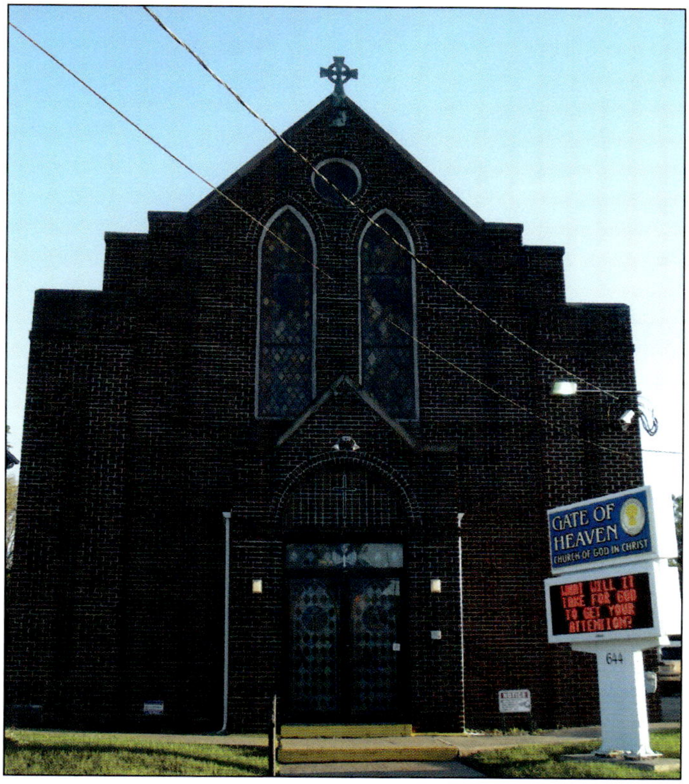

The Gate of Heaven, Church of God in Christ is a vibrant Monessen congregation. The church is located on Reed Avenue, near Ninth Street. The congregation of Trinity Episcopal Church originally used the building, which dates to about 1927. The church holds many events for their faithful community. (Author's collection.)

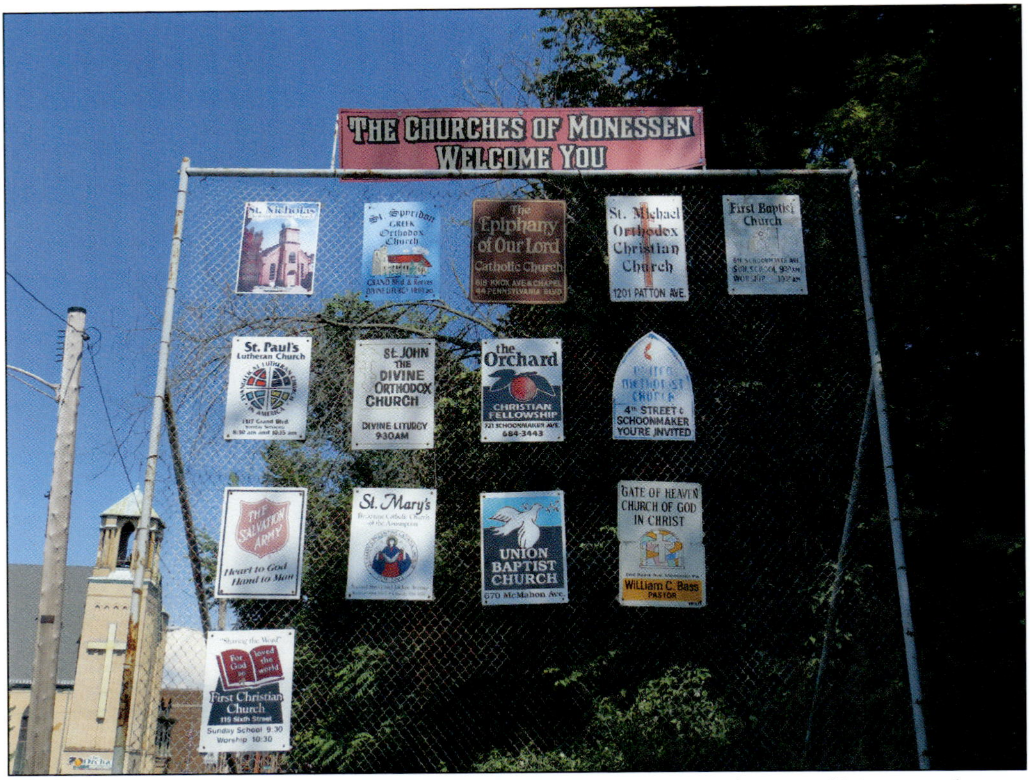

The city of Monessen has a total of 15 churches (not all represented on this sign). The sign welcomes motorists as they enter Monessen at Eighth Street from Westgate. Many motorists travel through Monessen each day and see this sign as they enter the city. (Courtesy of Karla Spangler.)

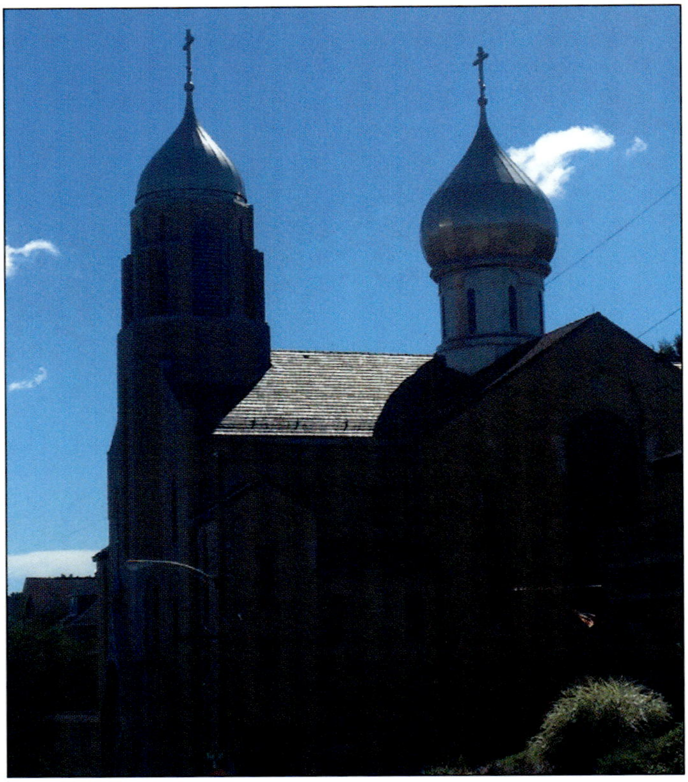

St. John the Divine Church is a Russian Orthodox church that is located at the corner of McKee Avenue and First Street. It is one of the many Eastern Christian churches that are in Monessen. The icons in the church's interior were hand painted.

Three

The Fall of Steel

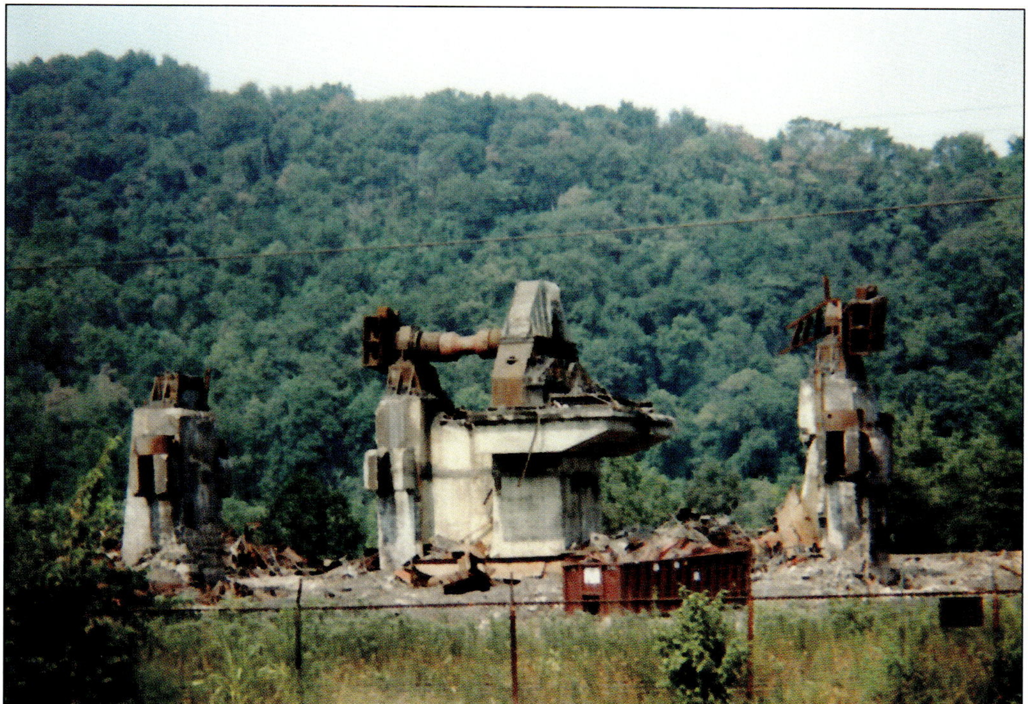

Pictured here are some of the Pittsburgh Steel blast furnaces in the process of being torn down. Pittsburgh Steel remained in Monessen until 1986, when cheaper labor was found in other countries. Many factories in the cities and towns within the Mon Valley suffered the same fate as the Monessen plant.

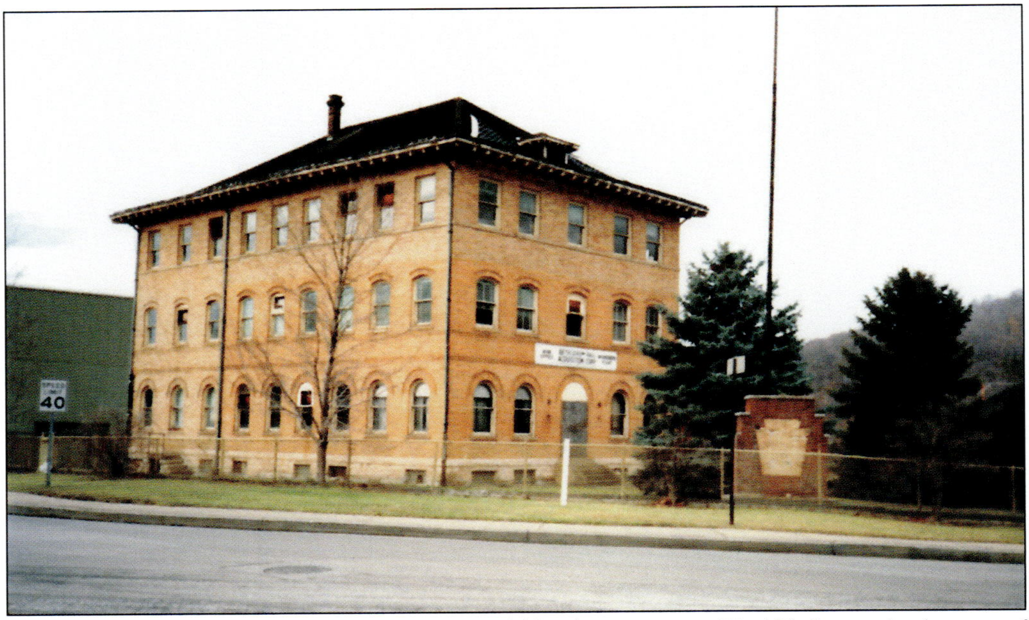

The Pittsburgh Steel office building was a beautiful brick structure on Twelfth Street. At the time of its construction, there was an entire neighborhood spanning five blocks near it. Progress in the mid-20th century made way for an expansion of Route 906, eliminating the entire neighborhood.

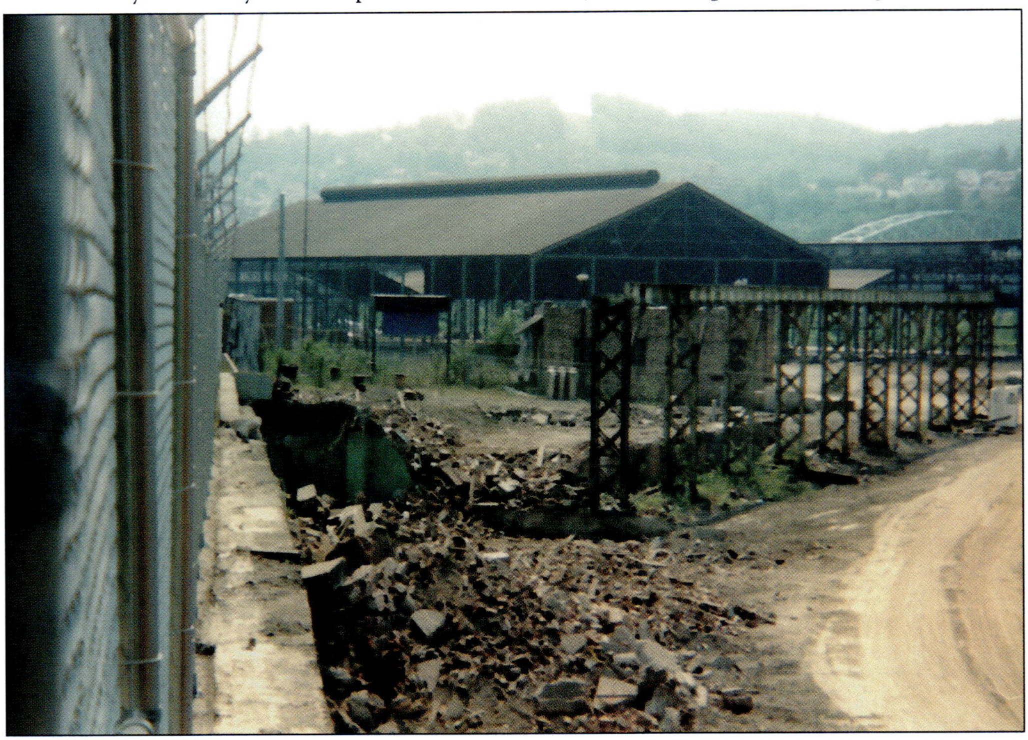

These buildings are situated where Wireton once stood. Wireton was a neighborhood of company houses in Monessen that was built near the mill. Part of the neighborhood was demolished when Pittsburgh Steel expanded and constructed these buildings, and the rest was demolished when Route 906 was extended due to heavy mill traffic.

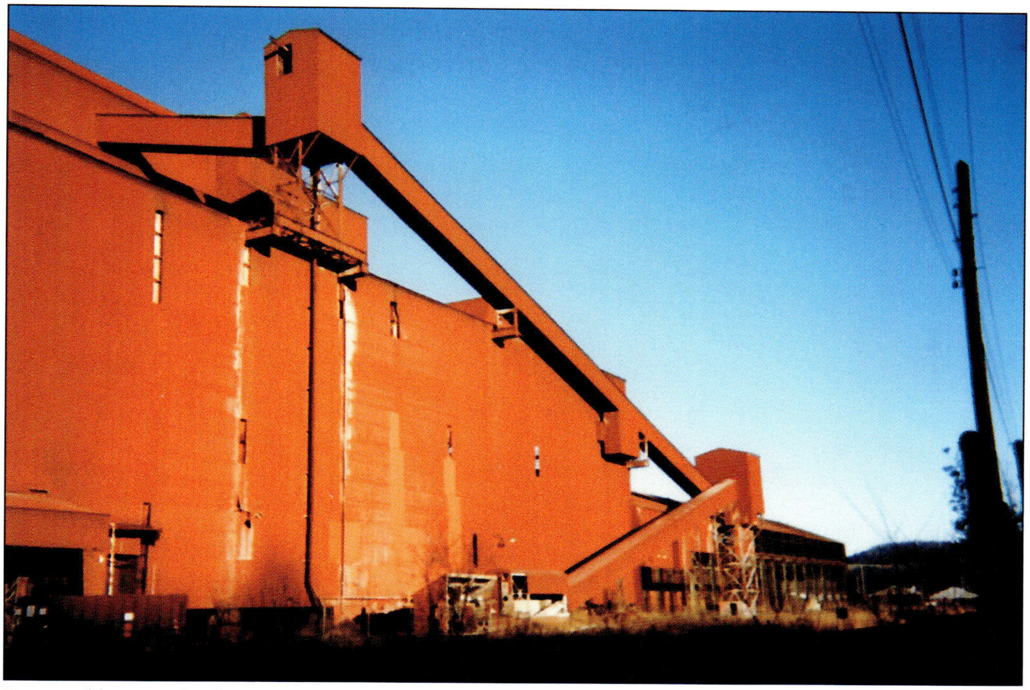

Pictured here is the basic oxygen furnace (BOF) near Third Street before it was demolished. The BOF towered over the commercial district of the city. It was responsible for turning pig iron into steel with the use of oxygen. This process is still a vital part of steelmaking today.

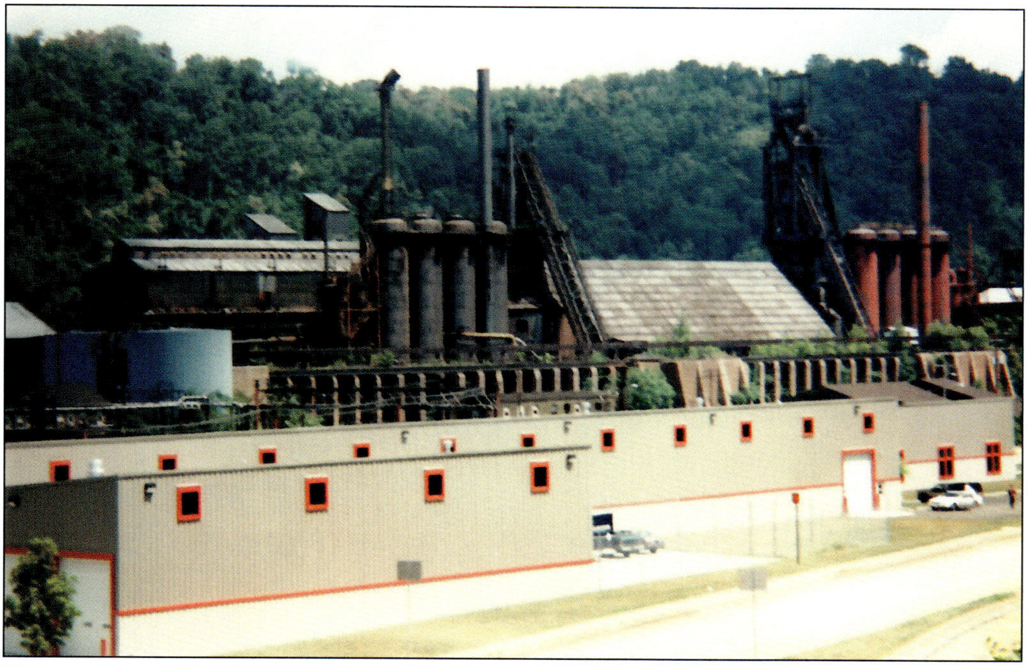

This view shows the blast furnaces of Pittsburgh Steel, which were torn down with the rest of the derelict plant. The blast furnaces were used during the smelting process of steel production. The process of smelting is done by converting an ore into a finished, base metal. This photograph was taken before demolition in 1996.

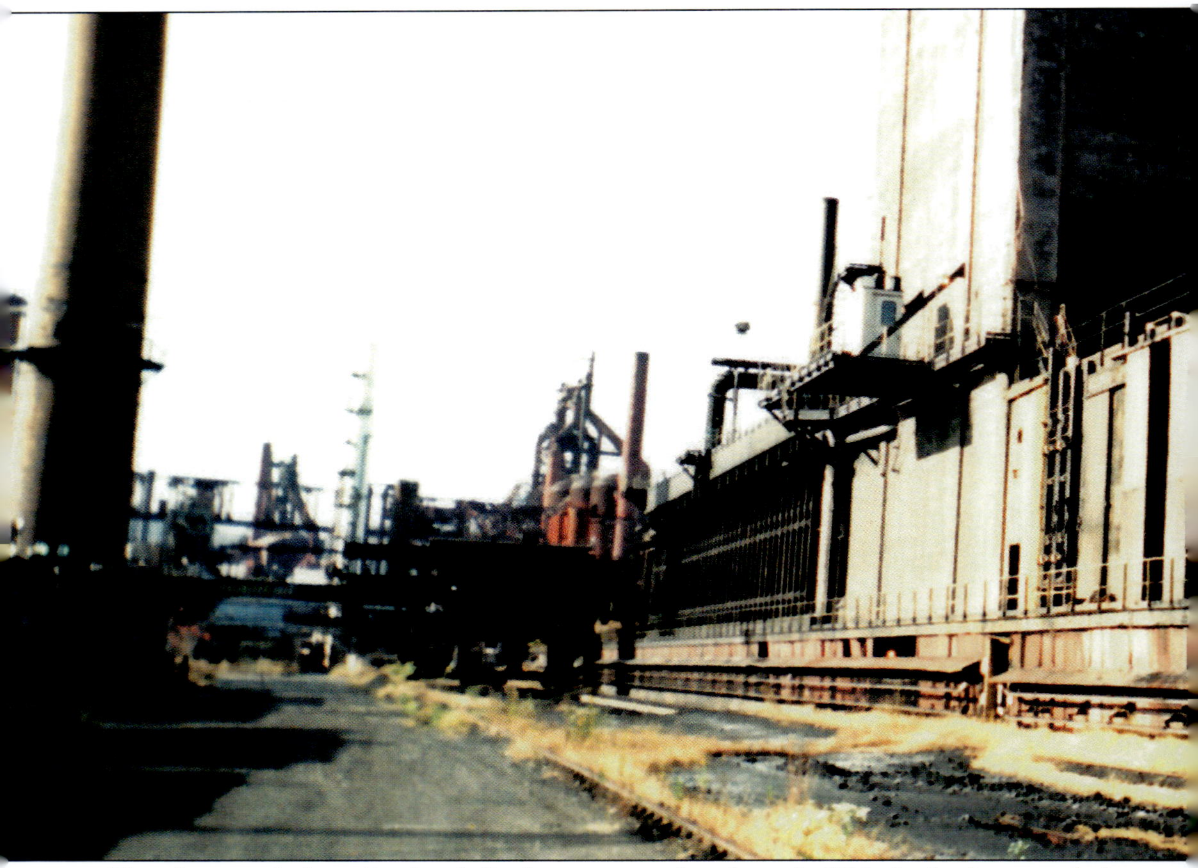

This photograph shows Pittsburgh Steel as it appeared in the early 1990s. In the foreground, the coke works can be seen. The coke works is still in operation today but is owned by a different company. In the background are the blast furnaces. The portion of the mill, spanning from the

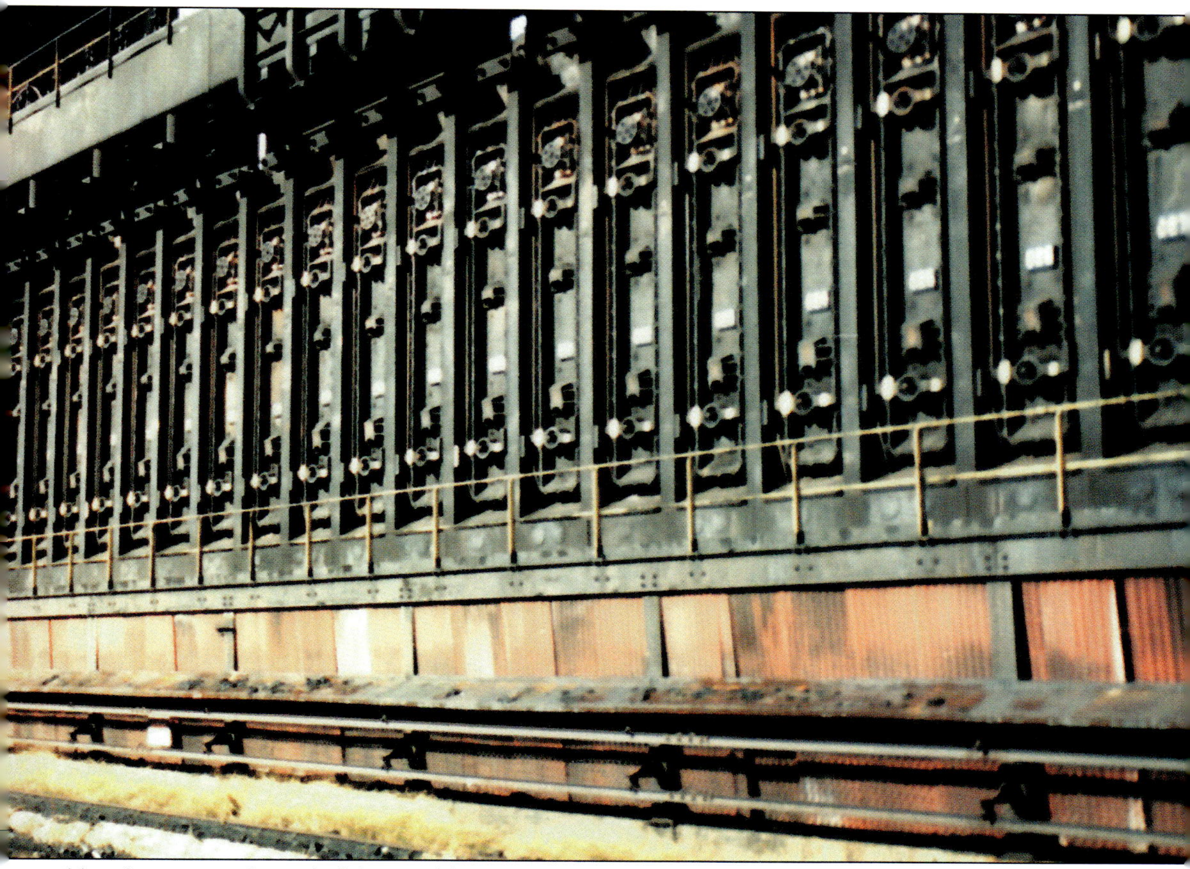

blast furnaces to the end of the city (about seven blocks), was demolished due to its 10-year vacancy. In its heyday, Pittsburgh Steel employed nearly 3,000 people at its Monessen plant. It was a major source of income for the citizens and the city as well. It ceased operations in 1986.

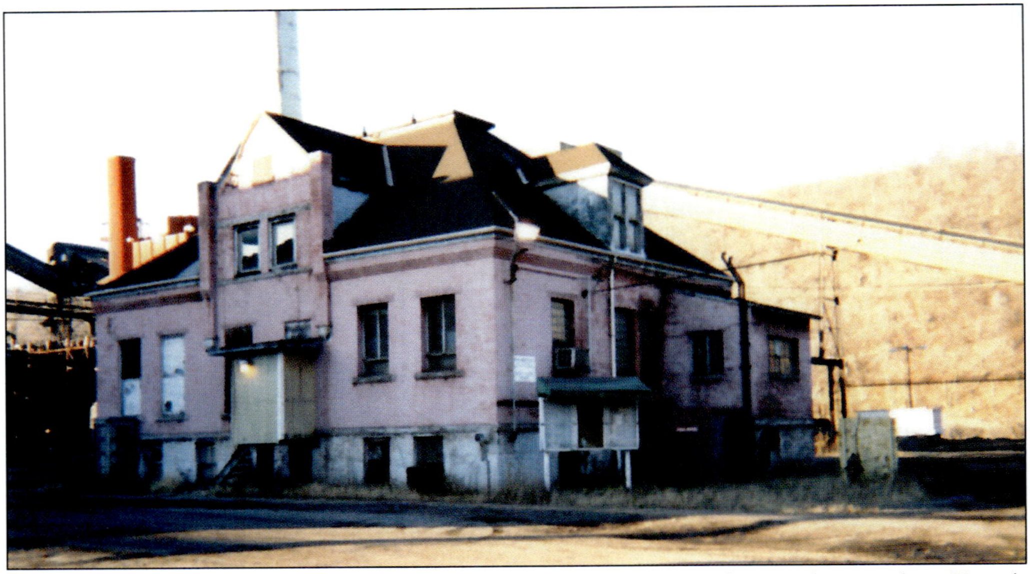

One of the office buildings on the property of the coke plant complex can be seen from Fourth Street. William Henry Donner, one of Monessen's founders, constructed this building in the late 19th century. The pink building, as it is known, served as Donner's office and headquarters for his National Tin Plate Company. The office was only a few blocks away from his home, which was located on Parkway.

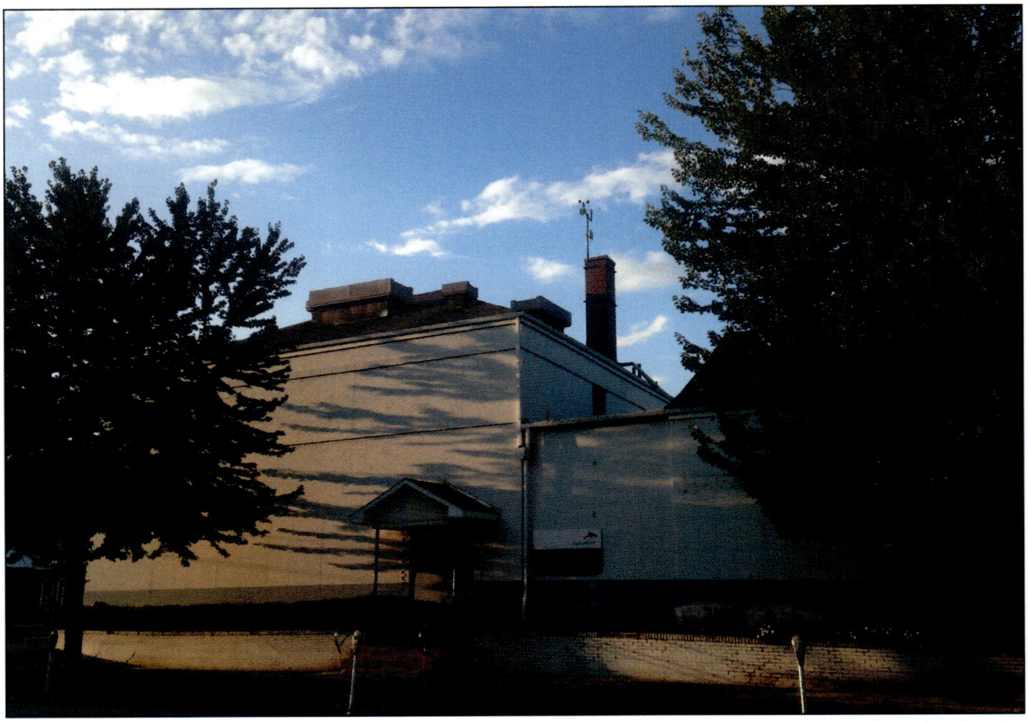

This building, which is located at Fourth Street and Donner Avenue, once served as the freight train station. The station was heavily used throughout Monessen's history, especially during the mid-20th century. It is now the office building for ArcelorMittal, the company that operates the coke works in the city.

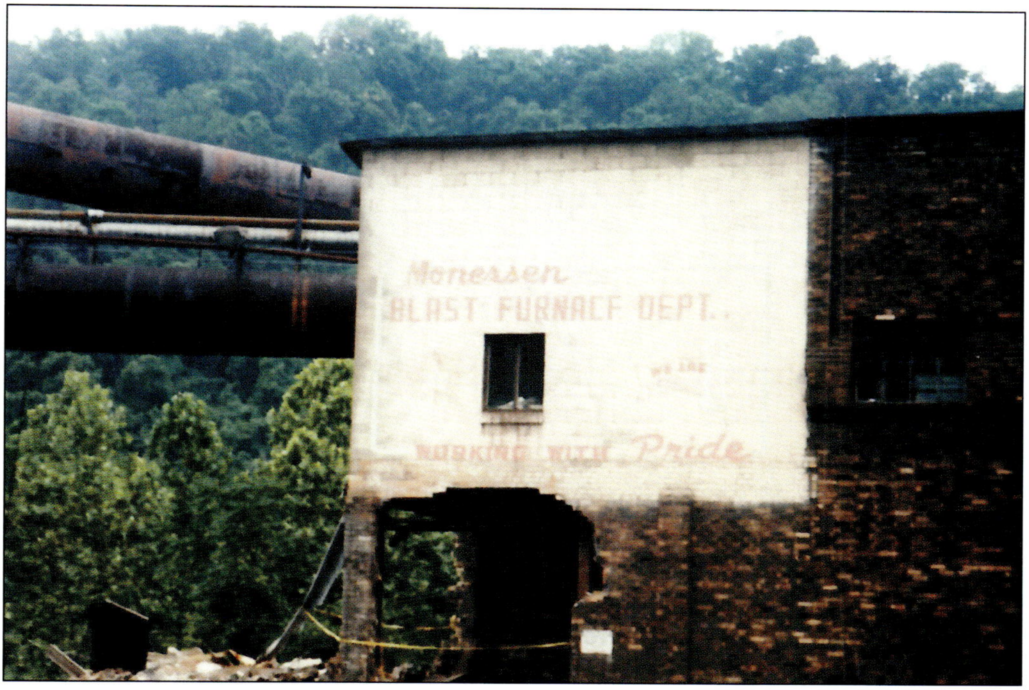

Pictured here is a painted sign on one of the buildings near the blast furnaces of the Monessen plant of Pittsburgh Steel. It reads "Monessen Blast Furnace Dept . . . Working with pride." Working in the blast furnaces was one of the most demanding jobs at the mill. This building has since been demolished.

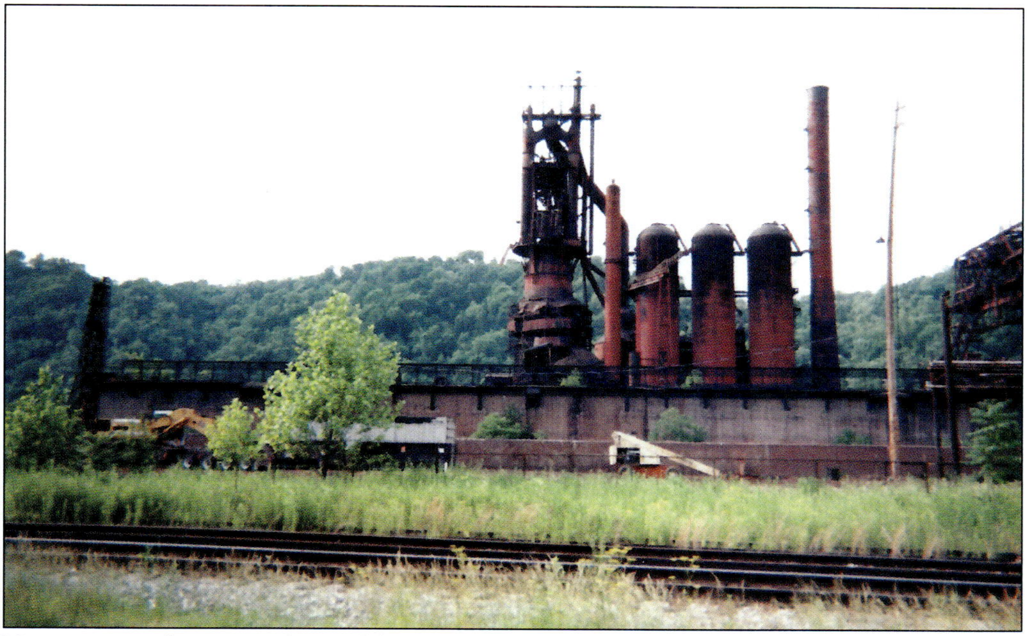
Here is an up-close view of one of three blast furnaces at the Monessen plant. This was the last remaining portion of the inactive mill to be demolished. After its closing in 1986, film crews came to Monessen to film scenes for *Robocop* at the abandoned mill. The burnt-out industrial architecture was perfect for their film.

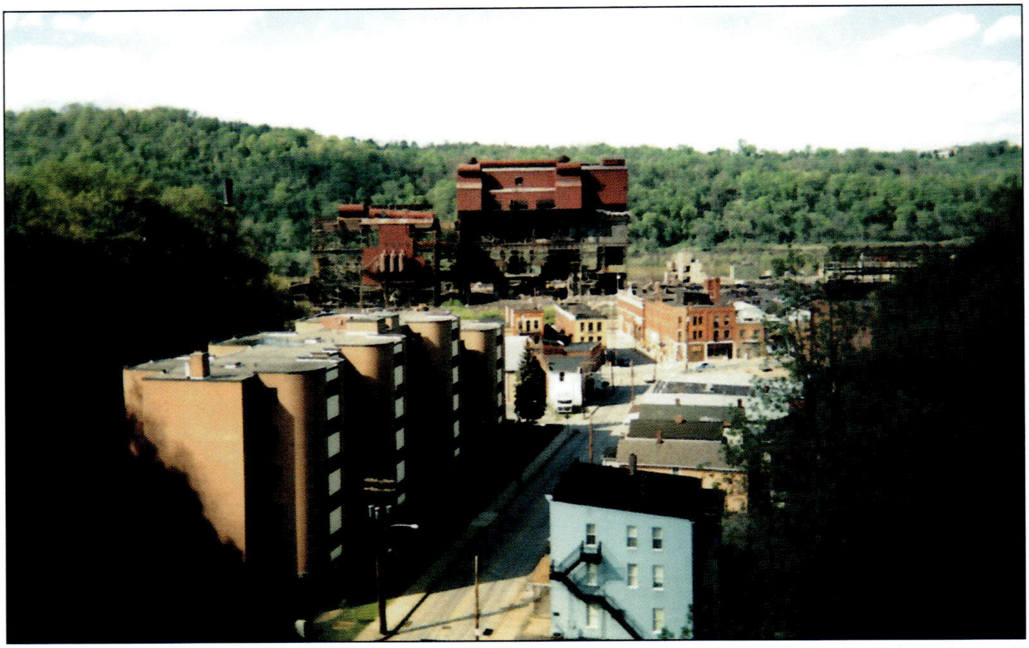

The BOF can be seen from the Reed Avenue Bridge. It was the largest building within the mill complex as well as the largest structure in Monessen at the time of its demolition.

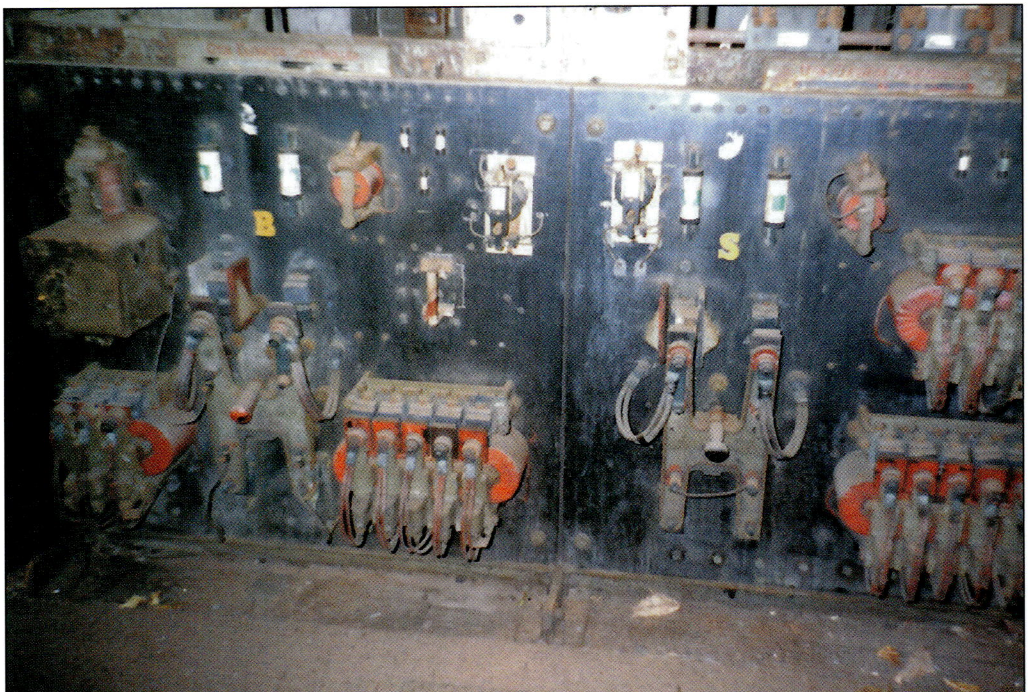

These controls were part of the No. 2 blast furnaces at Pittsburgh Steel. They were in the skip control house, which no longer exists. Otis Elevator Company manufactured the controls, and they were used in the blast furnace until it was closed in the 1980s. The photograph is dated from 1994.

Four

HARD TIMES

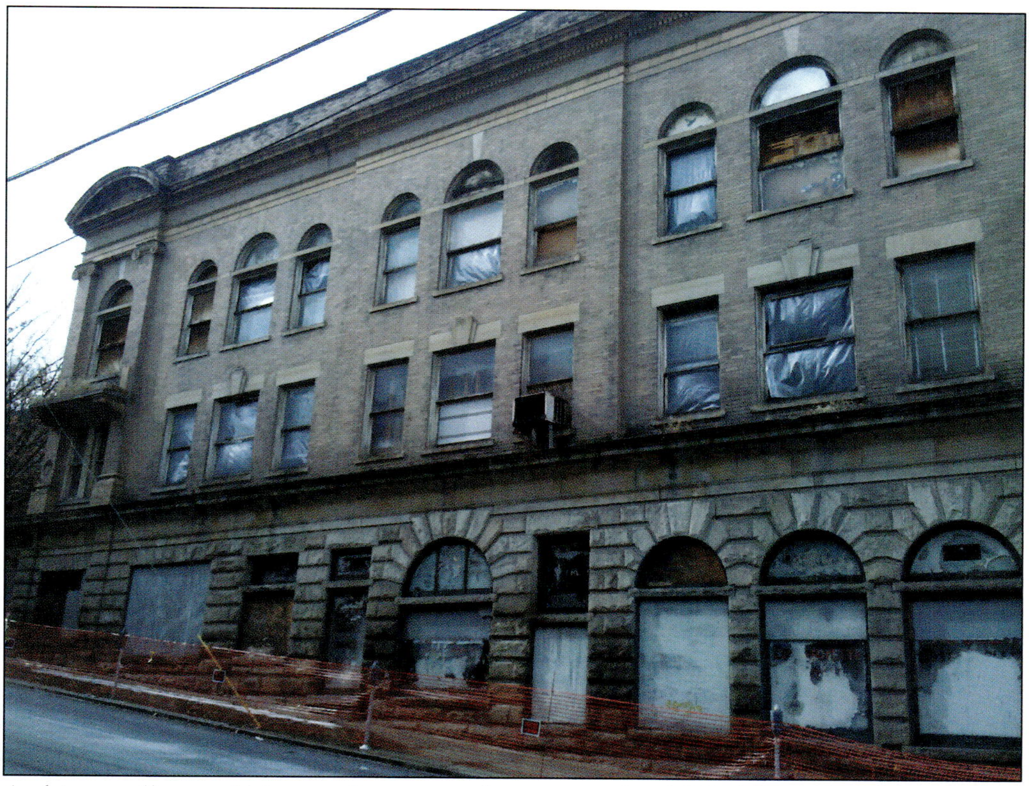

Architecturally one of Monessen's most prized structures, the old Health Mart Building has seen better days. It has been vacant for several decades due to the lack of jobs and stagnant economic growth in the city. It was once a beautiful building that housed the Monessen Bank and Trust Company. Following that, the building was home to the Masons, as well as numerous doctors' offices. (Author's collection.)

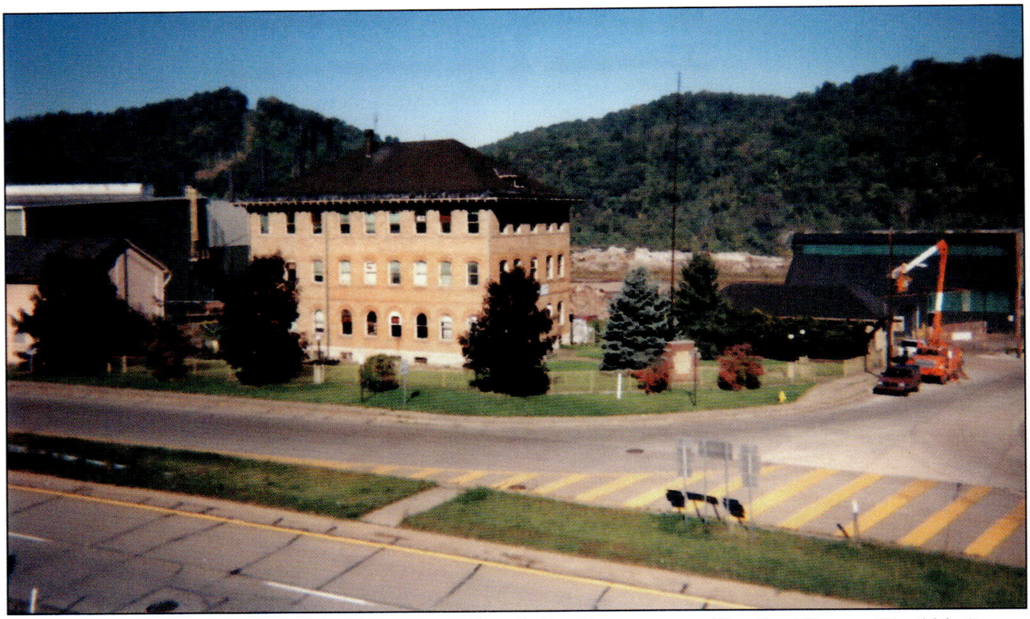

Pictured here is a side view of the former Pittsburgh Steel company office building at Twelfth Street in the Westgate section of the city. The photograph was taken from the Twelfth Street steps. Behind the building are other structures that were part of the mill, most of which were demolished.

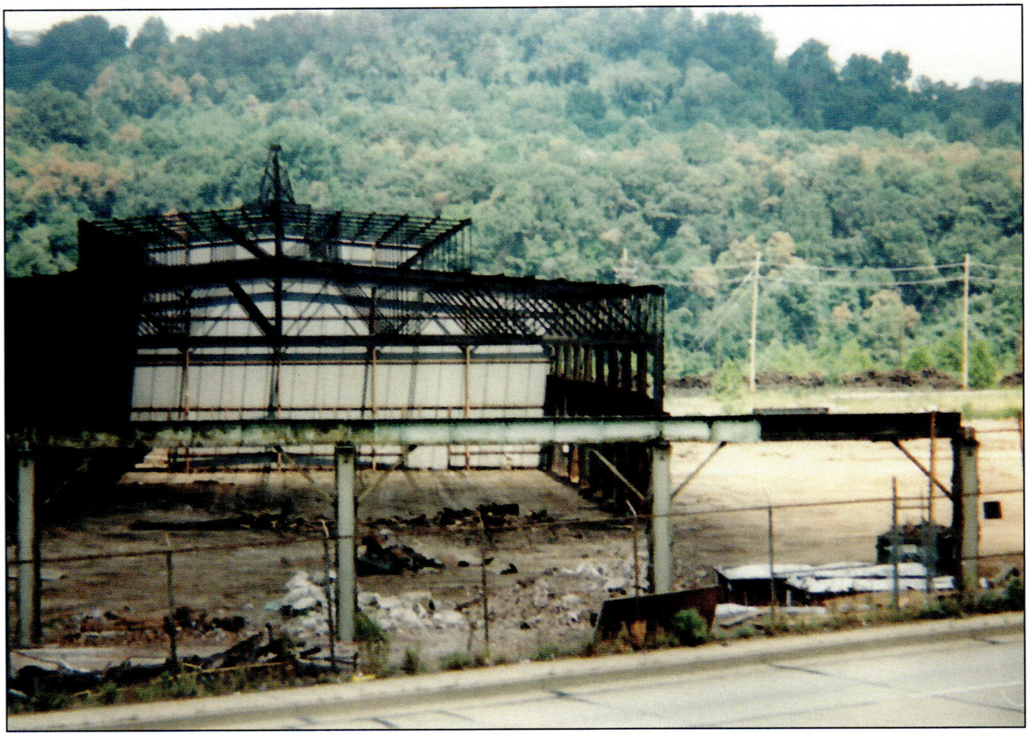

Many of the structures from Pittsburgh Steel were demolished in the mid-1990s. Much of the land that was used by the mill still sits vacant today. After 10 years of disuse, the structures were not salvageable and had to be torn down. This structure was near the office building at Twelfth Street.

Standing in the middle of the block on Donner Avenue is one of the oldest buildings in Monessen. The building once housed a J.C. Penney store, but it is now home to a taxidermist. During more prosperous times in the middle of the 20th century, the third floor was home to the Getodo Club, one of the most successful gambling joints in the eastern part of the country. (Author's collection.)

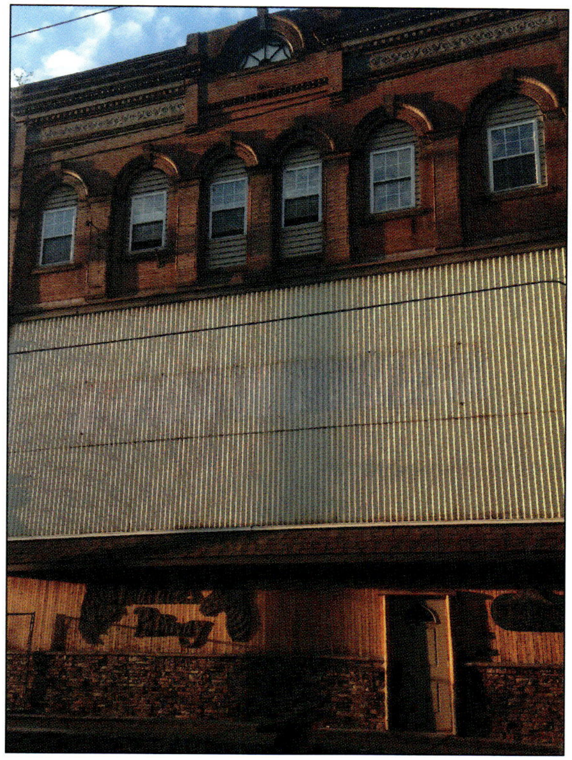

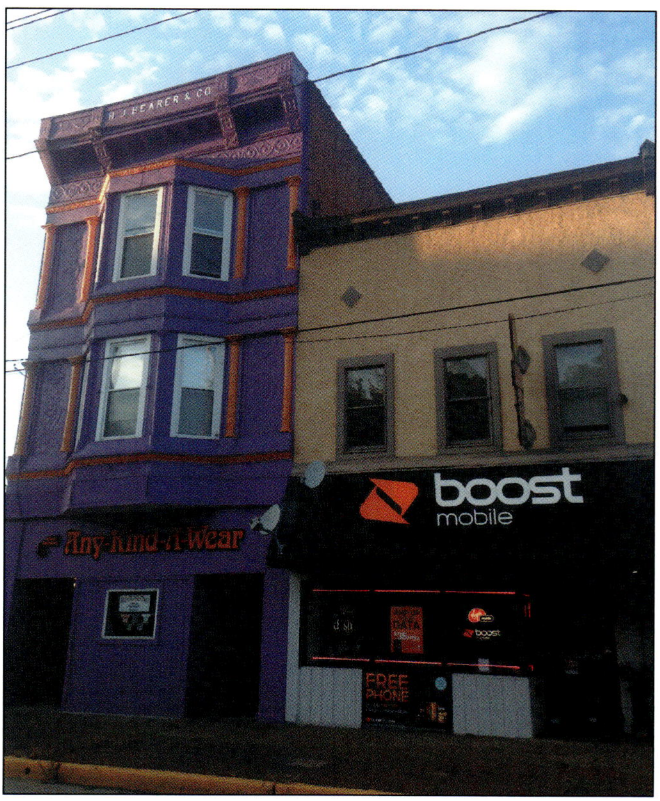

Fortunately, not all of the structures in the downtown district have been vacated. These two businesses between Fourth and Fifth Streets on Donner Avenue have revived their buildings. The purple building is the only one in the city with a tin-plated front. (Author's collection.)

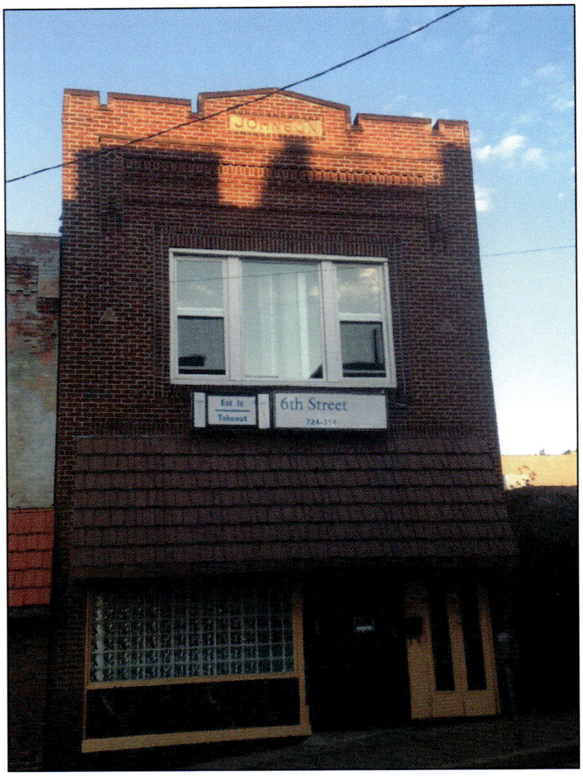

Once a poplar place to visit when Monessen was at its height, the Johnson's Restaurant building sits vacant on Sixth Street. Johnson's Restaurant served meals in the city for years. They were famous for their drop-cakes and butterscotch rolls. (Author's collection.)

An old stone fire pit remains unused at Monessen City Park. The park used to have many events such as bonfires and concerts and offered bicycle rentals. This overgrown fire pit tells the story of a Monessen that has seen better, more successful days. The park has a number of areas like this one; many of them remain unused. (Author's collection.)

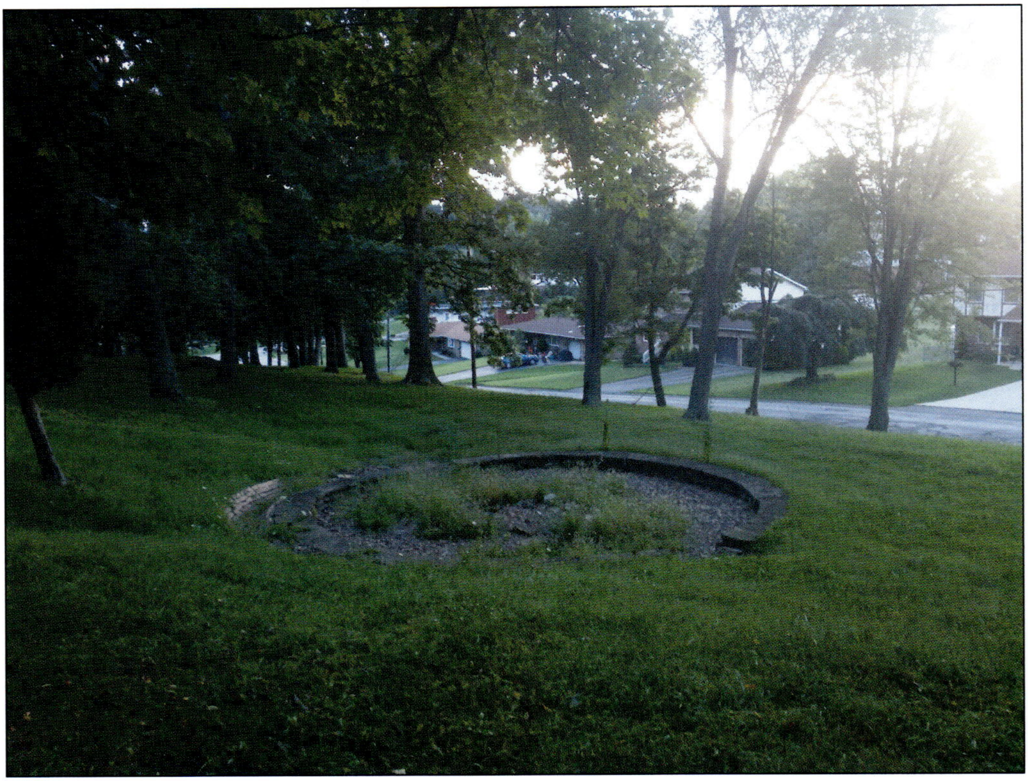

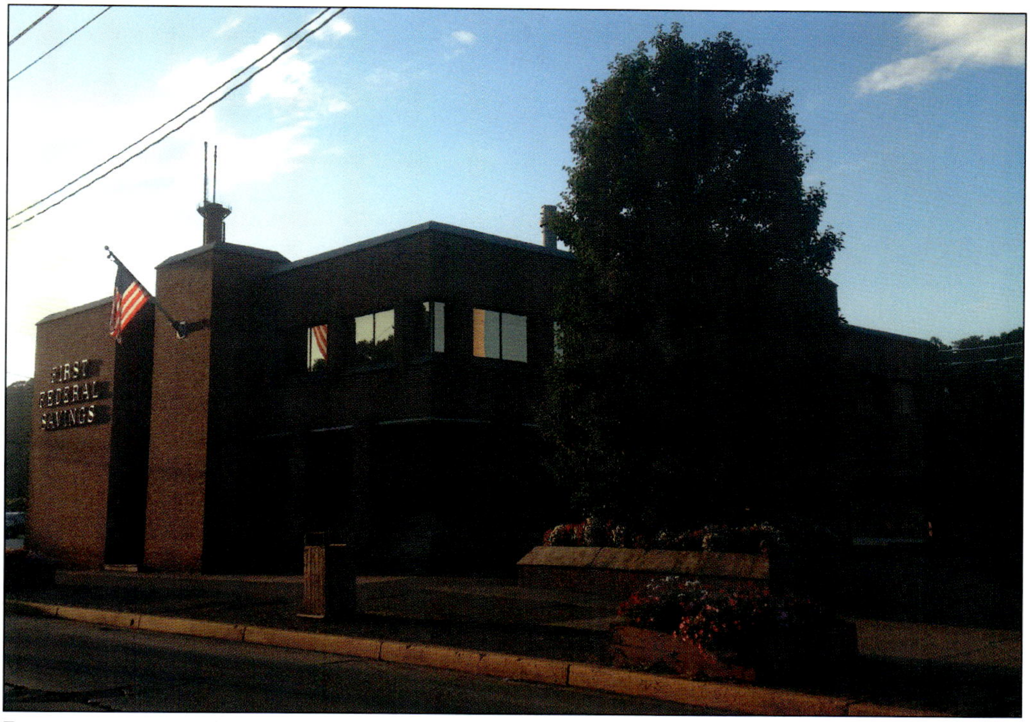

Despite Monessen's shaky economy, First Federal Bank has had its headquarters in Monessen for over 90 years. The bank was originally located on Sixth Street and Schoonmaker Avenue. In the 1960s, it moved down one block to its current location on Donner Avenue. (Author's collection.)

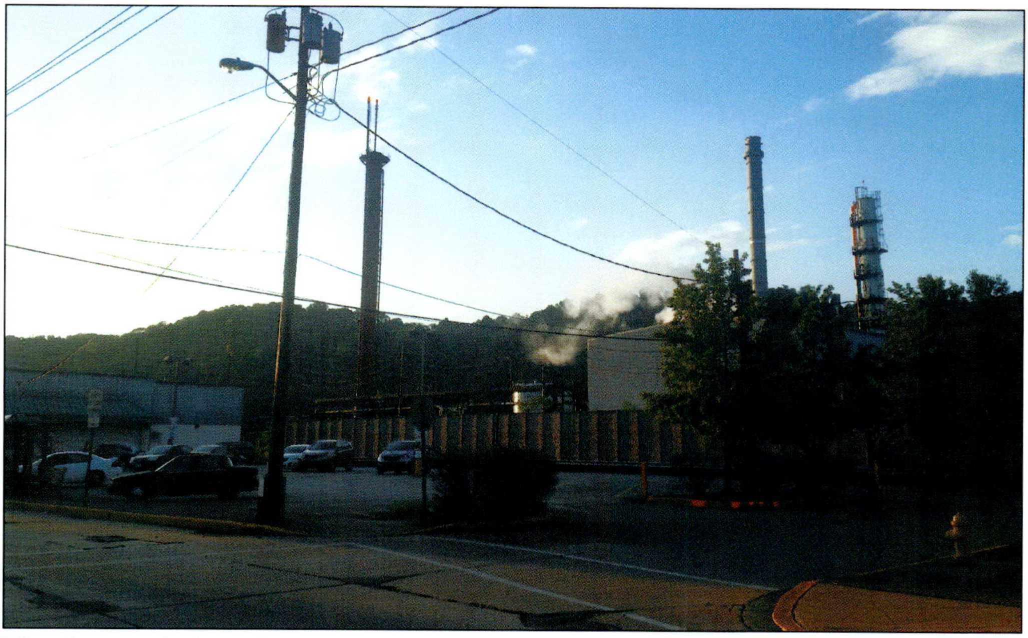

This photograph shows the remaining portion of the mill still in operation at the same intersection as First Federal Bank. In this parking lot, Pres. John F. Kennedy gave a speech to a crowd of 25,000 in 1962. Streets were packed, and there was a sea of people throughout the entire downtown area. (Author's collection.)

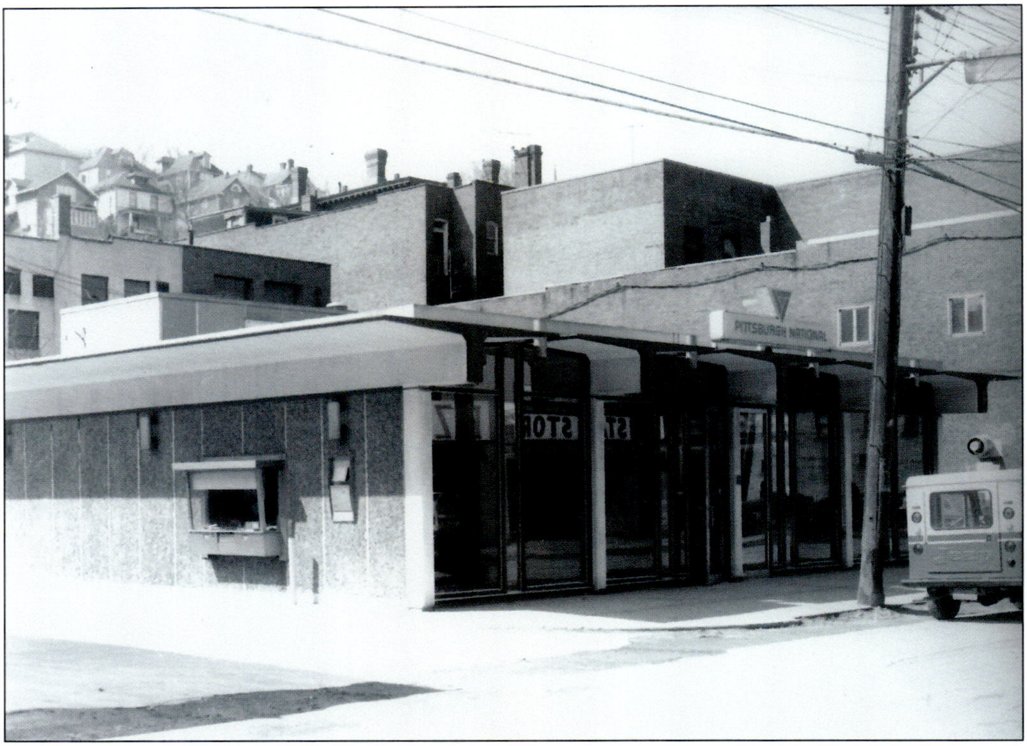

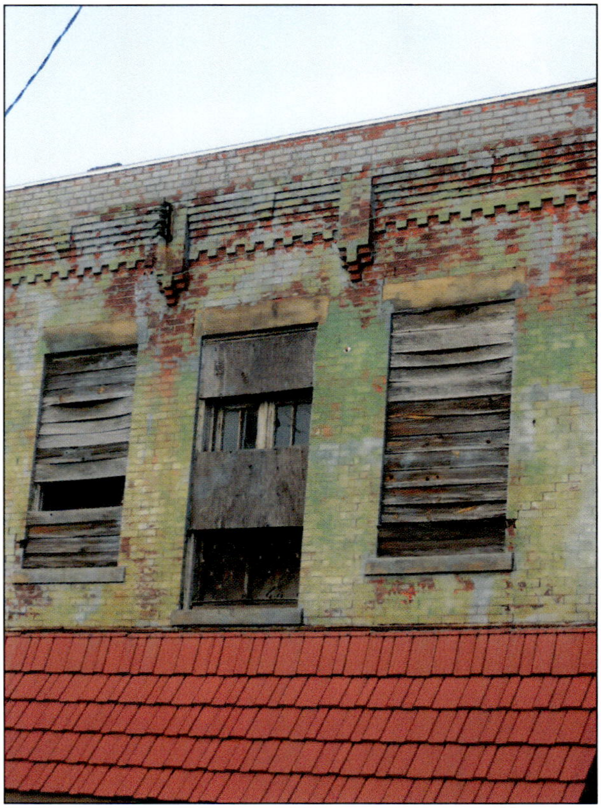

The Pittsburgh National Bank is pictured here on Donner Avenue. This building served as a bank until the early 2000s, when it was Pittsburgh National Company. It currently houses a medical program that is part of Douglas Education Center. The building was constructed in the 1960s as part of an effort to modernize Midtown.

Pictured here is the upper level of a large commercial building in the downtown area. Many buildings in the city have become abandoned due to population decline and lack of economic activity. (Courtesy of Karla Spangler.)

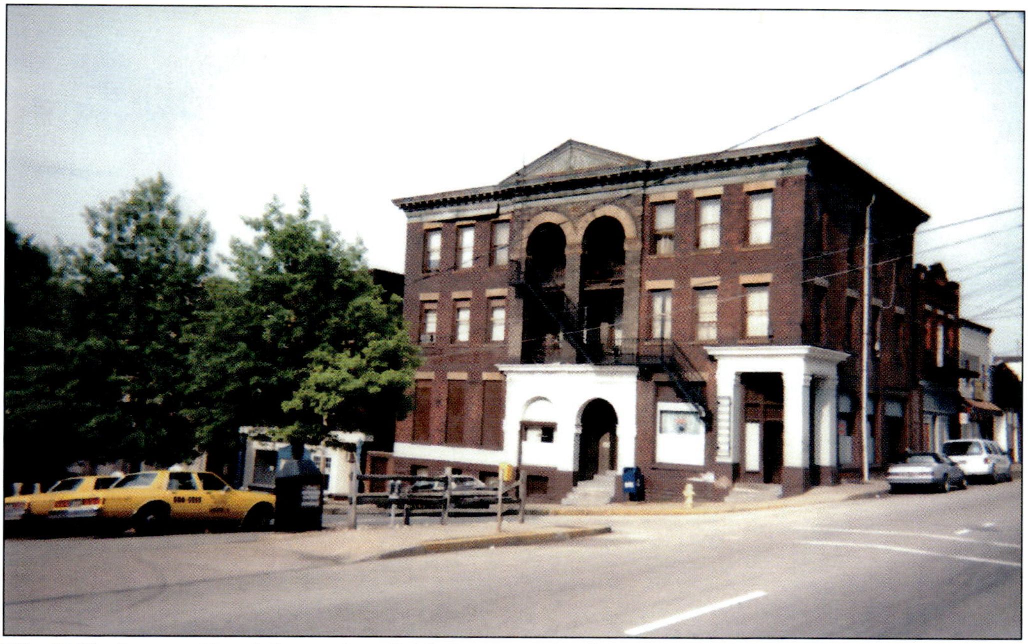

The Fifth Avenue Hotel, located on Fifth Street and Schoonmaker Avenue, was once one of the nicest hotels in the city. The building was constructed in 1900 and served as a hotel, restaurant, and bar for many years. It is the only hotel structure remaining in the city and one of the last remaining commercial buildings from the turn of the 20th century.

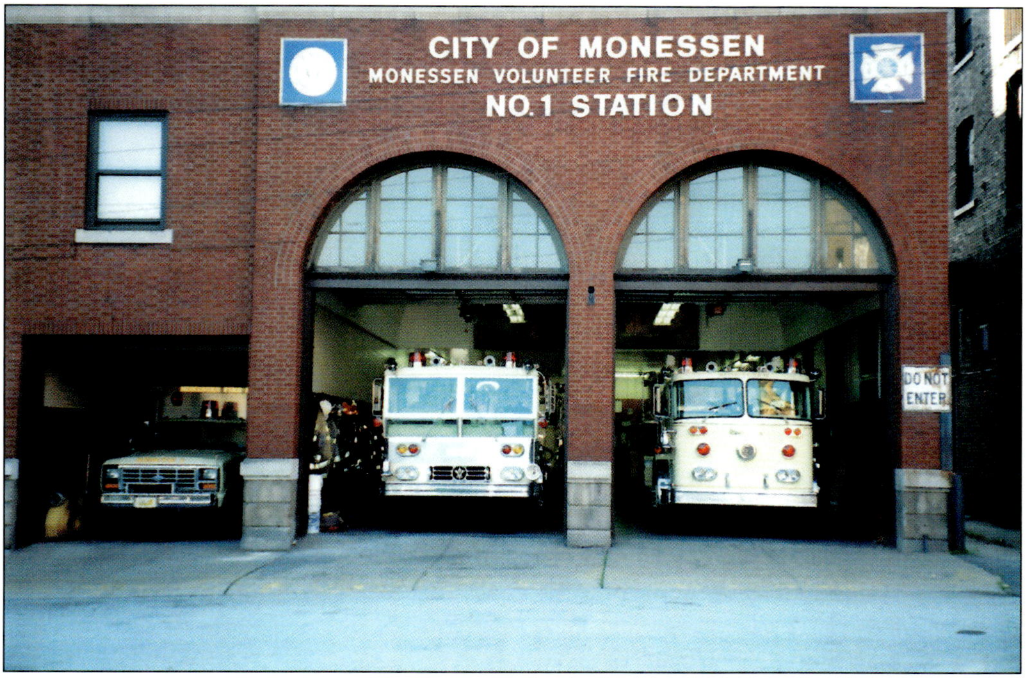

Monessen fire trucks are parked in the old fire station bays. The Monessen Fire Department No. One used this Third Street facility until 2012, when the new public safety building was completed across the street. The move marked the third time in city history that the municipal building was moved.

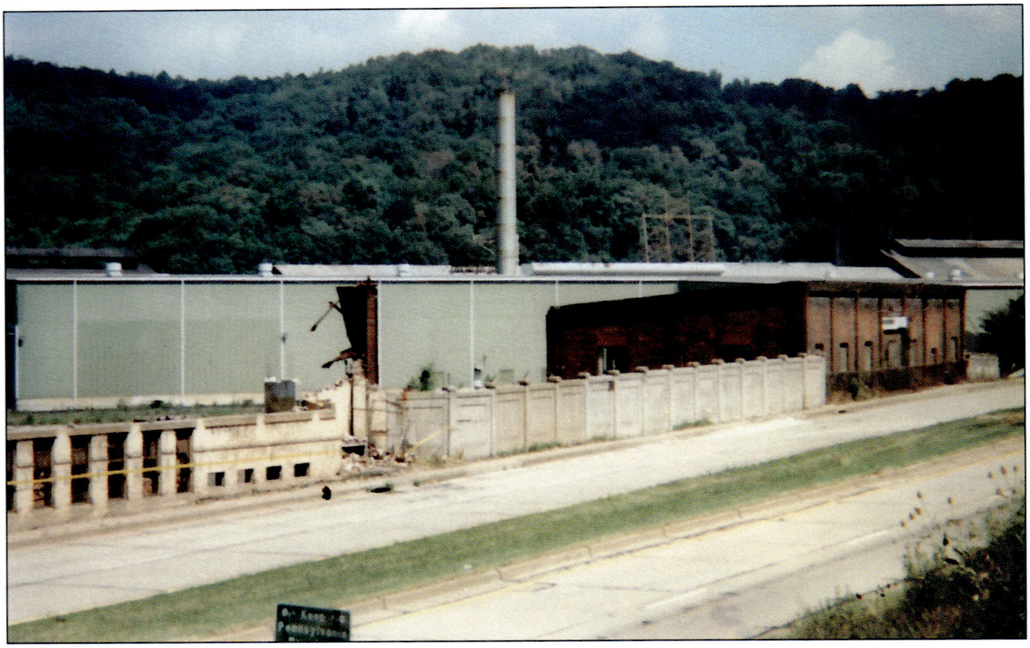

Pictured here is the derelict rail mill of Bethlehem Steel Corporation's works in Monessen, as it stood in 1998. By this time, parts of the mill were being demolished. The large green building was salvaged since it was newer; it is currently occupied and still standing today as part of the Riverfront Industrial Park II.

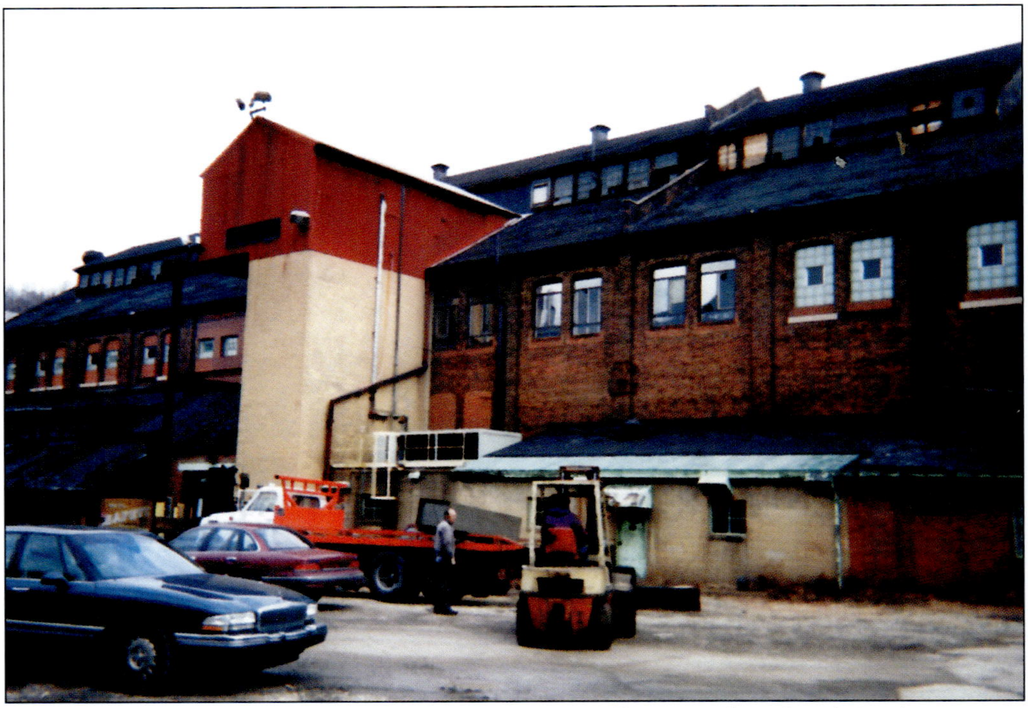

This brick structure was another building that was originally a part of Pittsburgh Steel's operation in Monessen. This building was located in the Westgate section of the city, near the rail mill, and was among those torn down in the late 1990s.

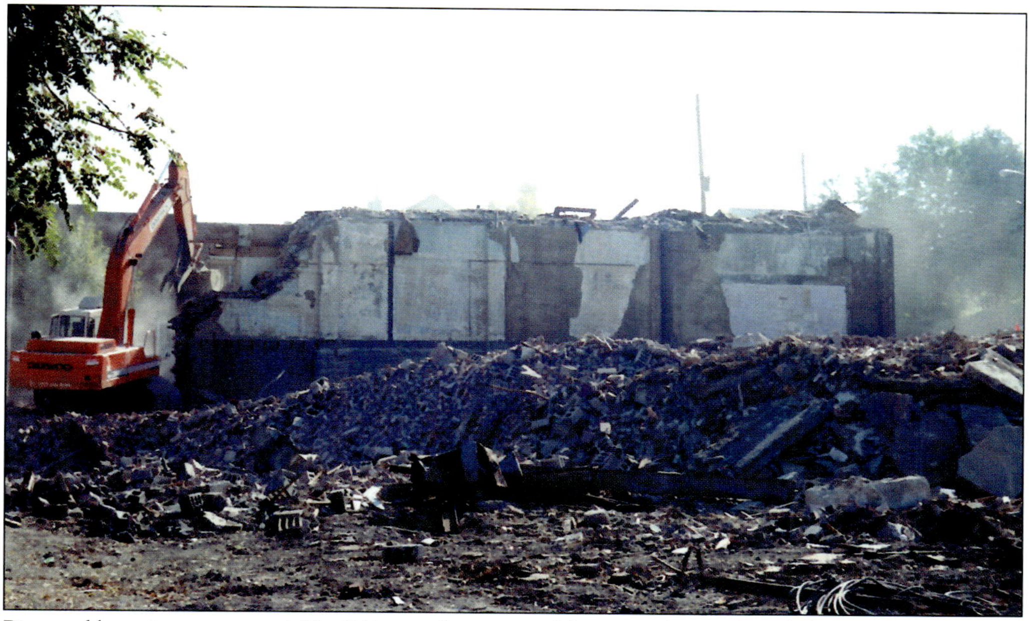

Pictured here is a commercial building in downtown Monessen being demolished. Many buildings were demolished throughout the entire city in an effort to clean up the area and attract developers. The problem got out of hand as the decades progressed, and the city continued to have more vacant properties than they could manage.

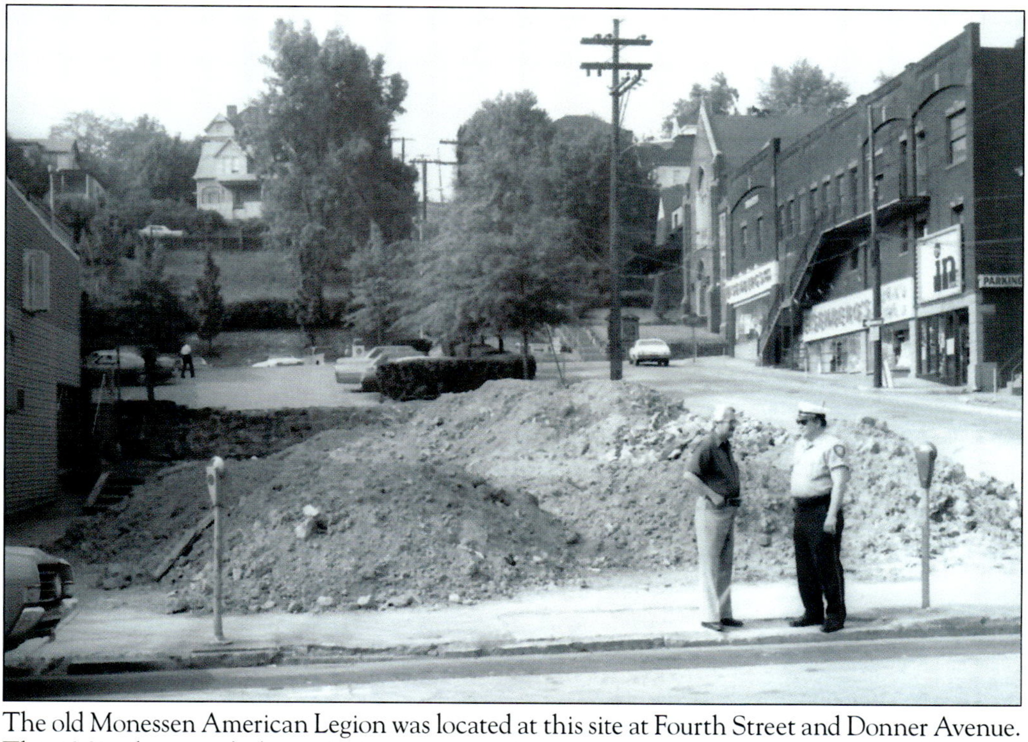

The old Monessen American Legion was located at this site at Fourth Street and Donner Avenue. This 1960s photograph shows the lot after the building was demolished. Originally, the Monessen Borough Building was located here, before operations were moved to its new location at Third Street when the city charter was obtained.

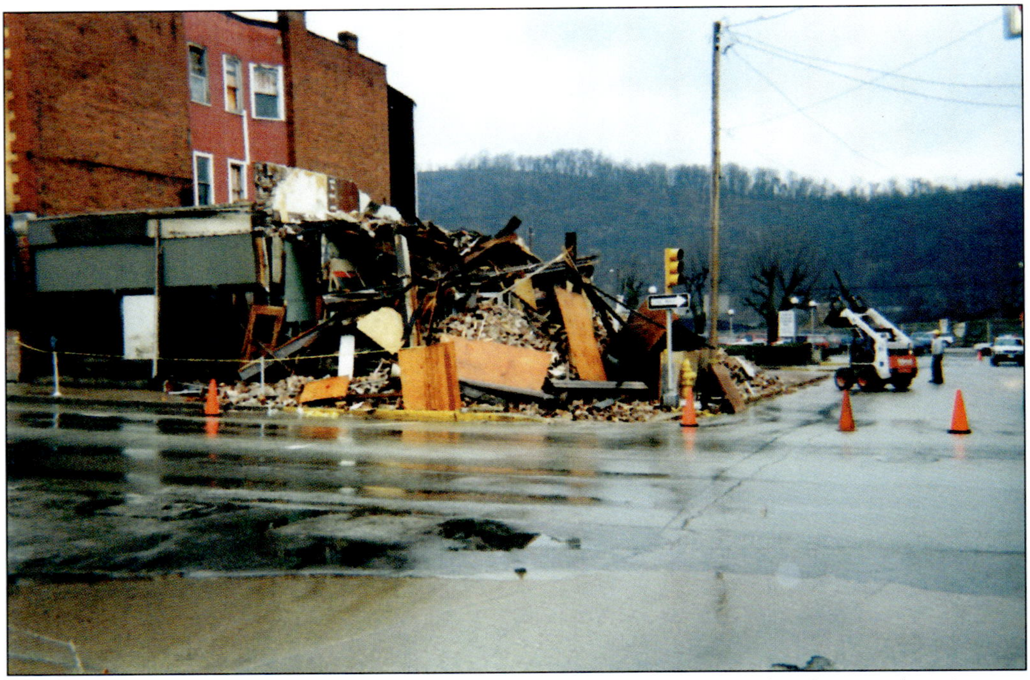

The old Sherwin-Williams building at the corner of Third Street and Schoonmaker Avenue stood vacant for many years before it was demolished in the late 1990s, after the business moved to the Westgate section of the city.

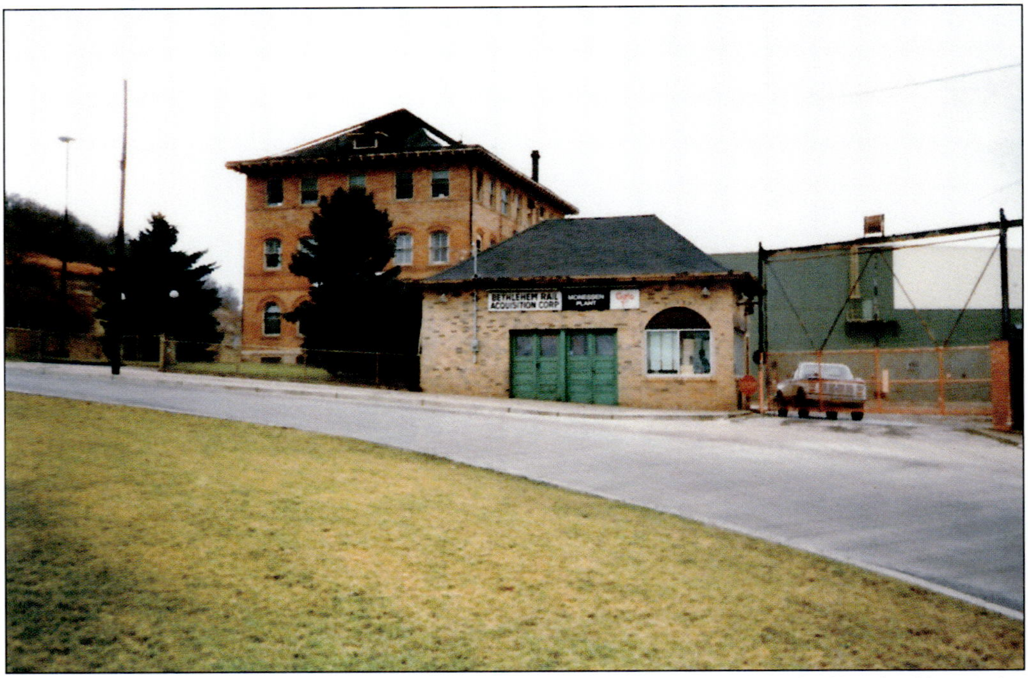

Pictured here is another view of the former Pittsburgh Steel gatehouse and office building. The site was located on Twelfth Street as part of Bethlehem Rail before closing in the 1980s. The building fell into disrepair and was demolished. The gatehouse is still used today and serves the company that is housed in the former rail mill.

Five

A New Century, a New Era

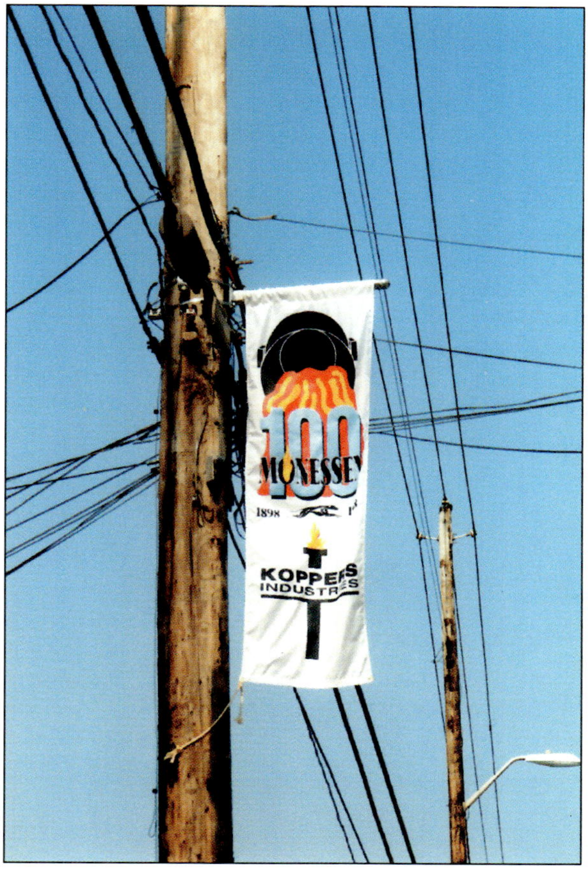

Pictured here in 1998 is a banner marking the 100th anniversary of the founding of the city of Monessen. Festivities, ceremonies, and special events were held throughout the entire year. The banners were sponsored by Koppers, which was a company that ran the coke plant, the sole industry that remained in the city.

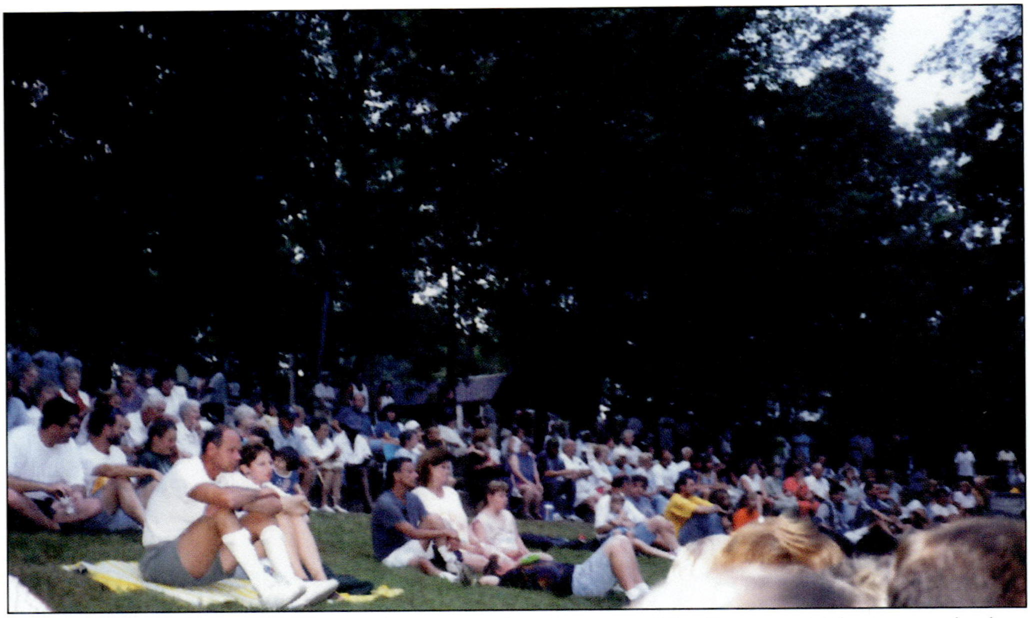

A crowd of people enjoys a musical event at the Monessen City Park amphitheater in the late 1990s. Some knew the amphitheater as the bandstand. It was a common venue for musical acts, large and small, to perform at each weekend. The amphitheater continues to host performances that are free to the community.

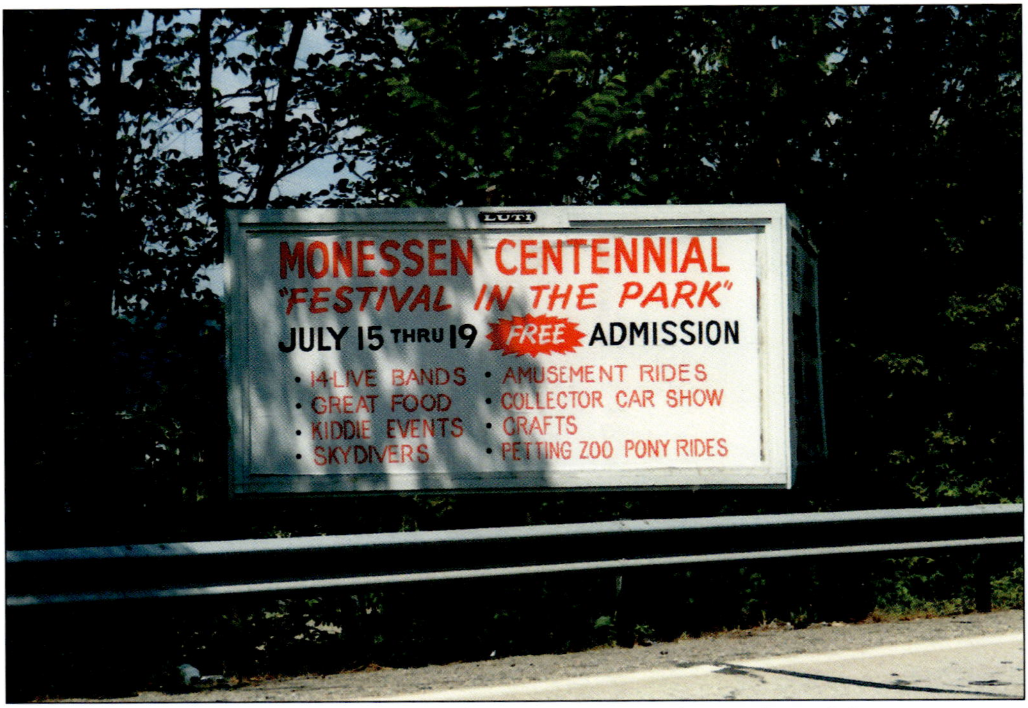

Many festivities were held in Monessen during its centennial year. One of these events was a festival at Monessen City Park. It featured food, games, concerts, and pony rides; there was fun for everyone. The four-day event was attended by hundreds of people from Monessen and nearby communities.

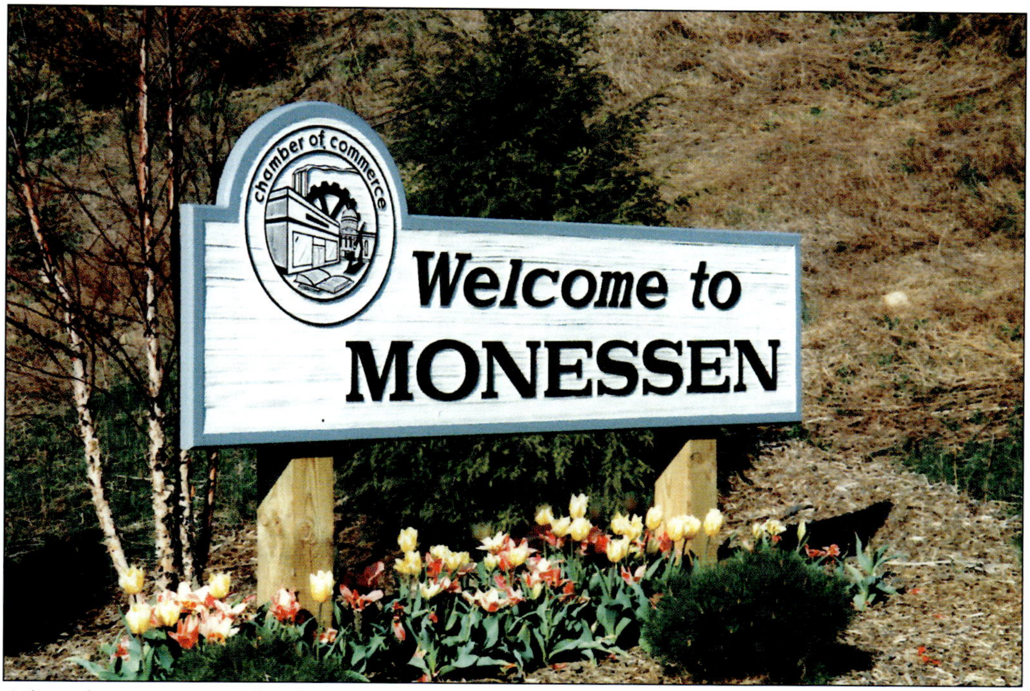

A brand-new sign with landscaping was erected along Route 906 heading towards the Westgate section of Monessen in the late 1990s. The sign continues to welcome drivers who are entering the city. There is an older, larger welcome sign on the opposite end of the city, at Eastgate.

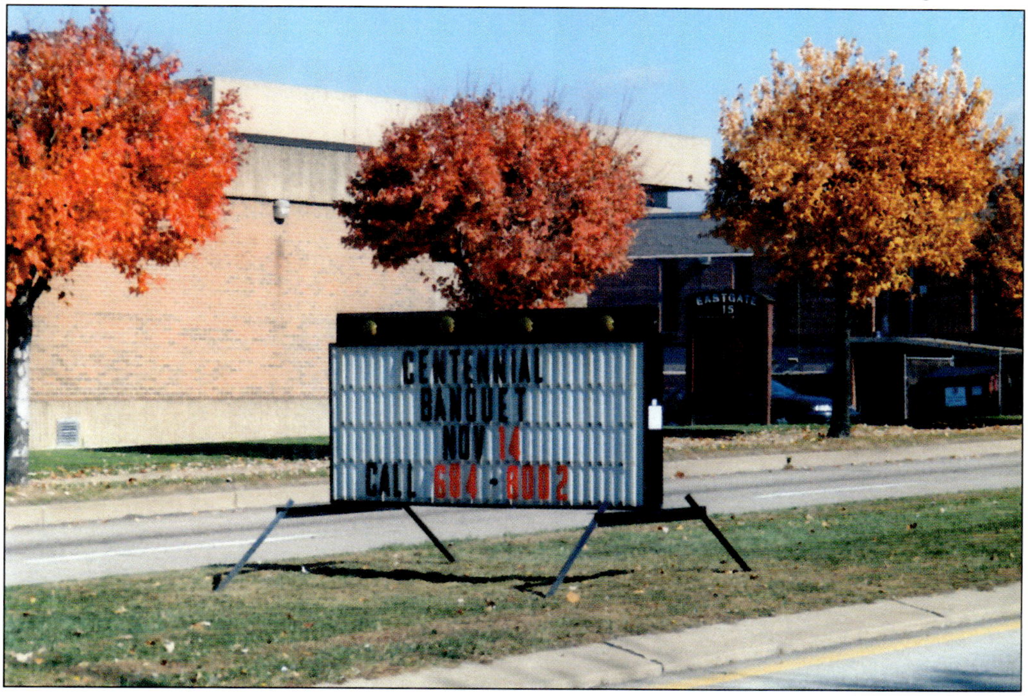

Throughout the year, the city held many events celebrating its 100 years of existence. One of these events was its centennial banquet. The banquet was held at the Firemen's Social Club in one of the complexes in the Eastgate section.

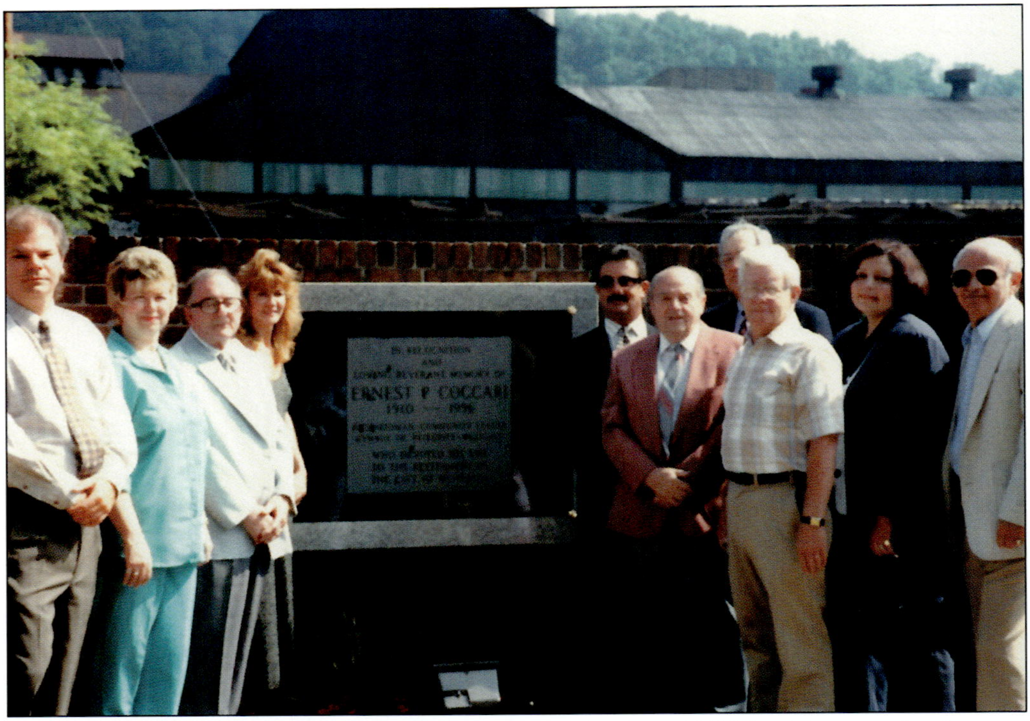

In the mid-1990s, citizens gather for a photograph in front of the newly dedicated memorial to Monessenite Ernest Coccari. Coccari was a businessman and politician, and he served on the Monessen Chamber of Commerce. He was also part of the Frankie Barr Orchestra, which played with many well-known musicians.

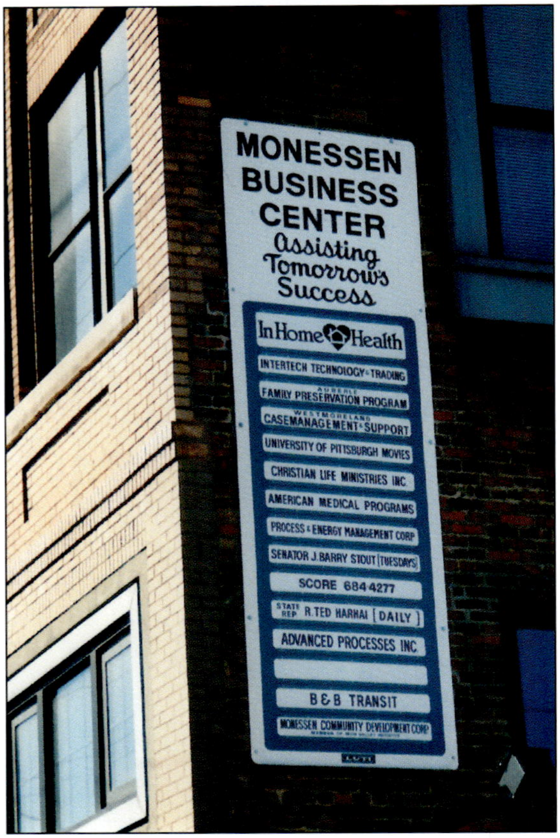

The Monessen Business Center was located in a large commercial building on Donner Avenue. It was a business incubator in the 1990s, intended to help spur economic activity in the city and attract small businesses. Due to mismanagement and a deteriorating city infrastructure, the project was disbanded.

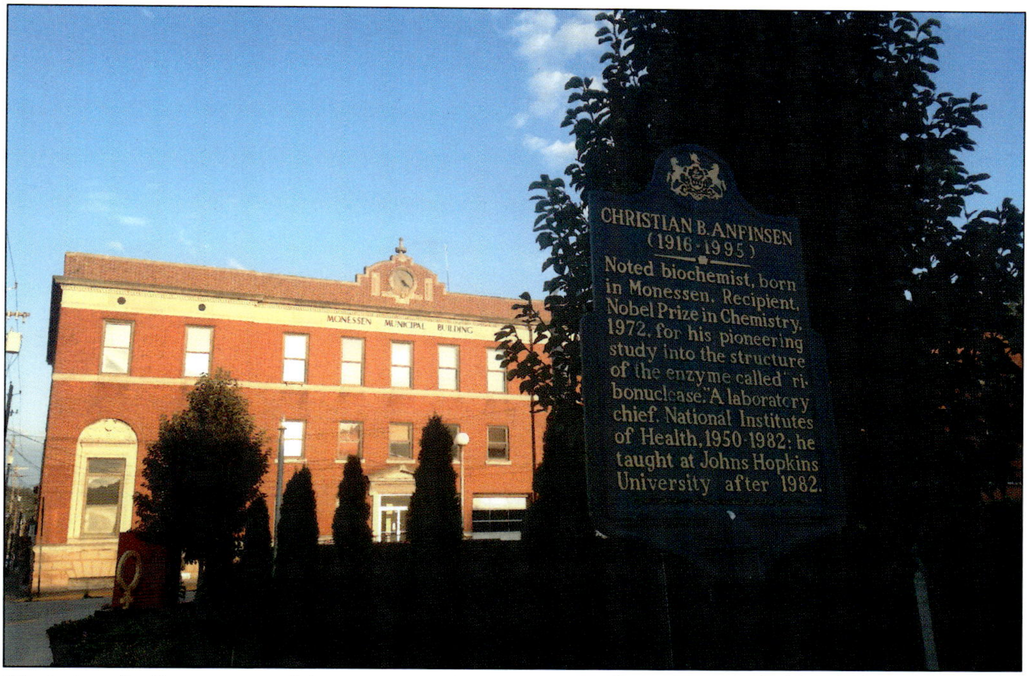

Christian Anfinsen was a Monessenite who went on to become a Nobel Prize laureate for his study of ribonuclease. He also penned Anfinsen's dogma, a microbiology postulate relating to ribonuclease. This marker was dedicated in 1998 during Monessen's centennial year. The former, vacant Monessen Municipal Building can be seen in the background. (Author's collection.)

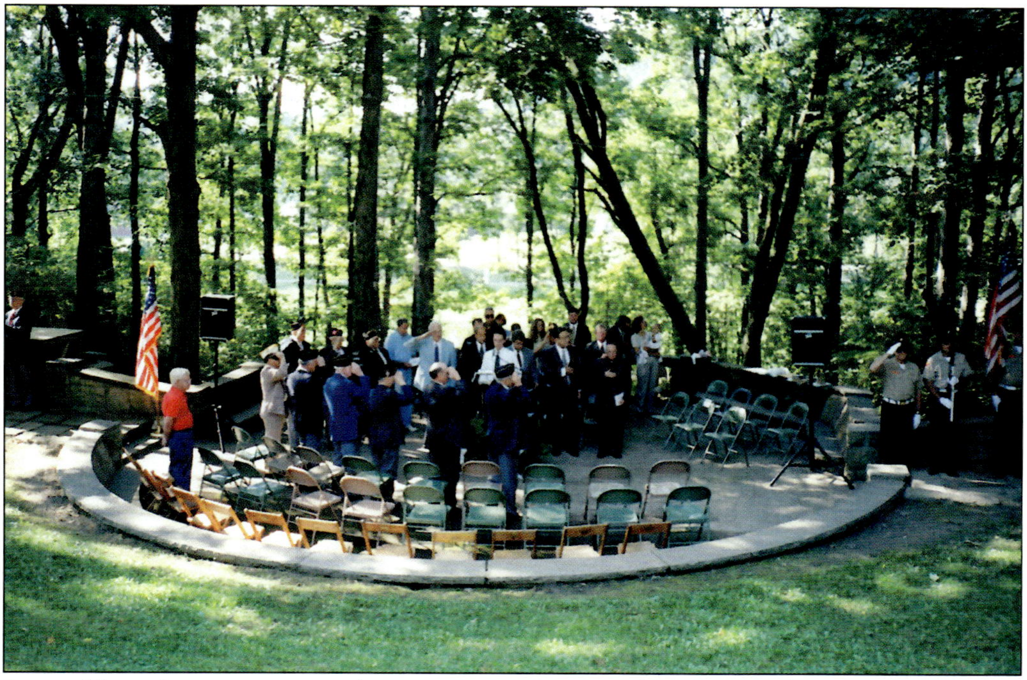

Pictured here during a centennial ceremony are Monessen dignitaries and veterans saluting the American flag. This event was held to honor those who have served in the military. Until 2013, this was one of the last major events held at the amphitheater in the city park.

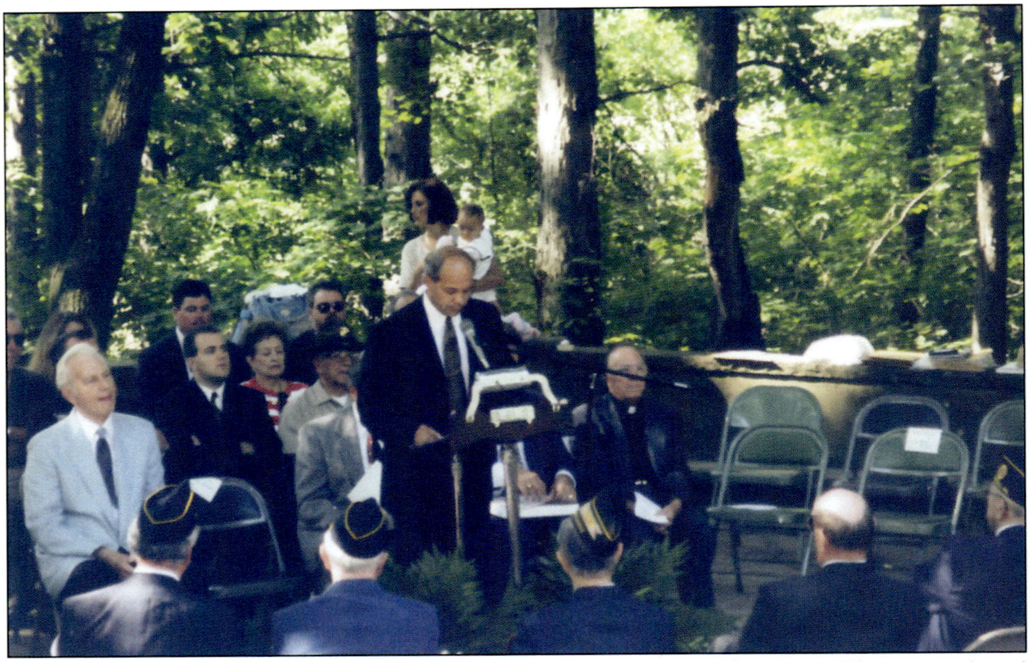

Pictured here is former mayor Ted Harhai giving remarks to citizens and veterans. They are gathered at the Monessen City Park amphitheater as part of a centennial ceremony. Harhai served two four-year terms as mayor of the City of Monessen before he became a state representative.

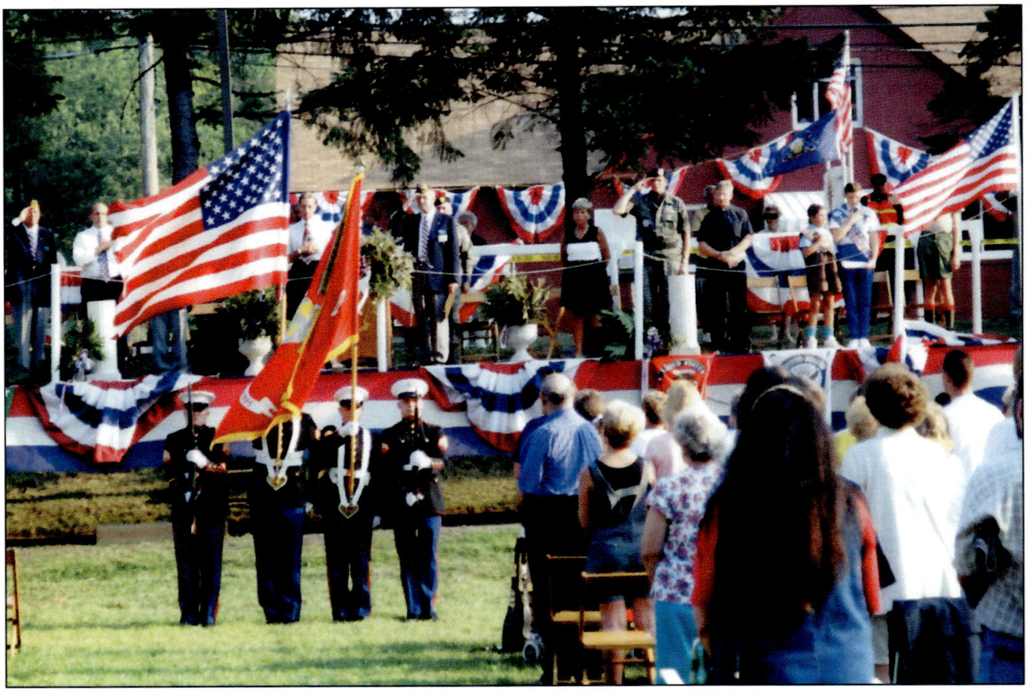

Citizens and veterans look on as the colors are posted. This was part of a ceremony at Monessen City Park in 1998. As part of the centennial celebration, the traveling Vietnam Memorial Wall made an appearance in Monessen. The event attracted many people from the area to view the wall and remember their loved ones.

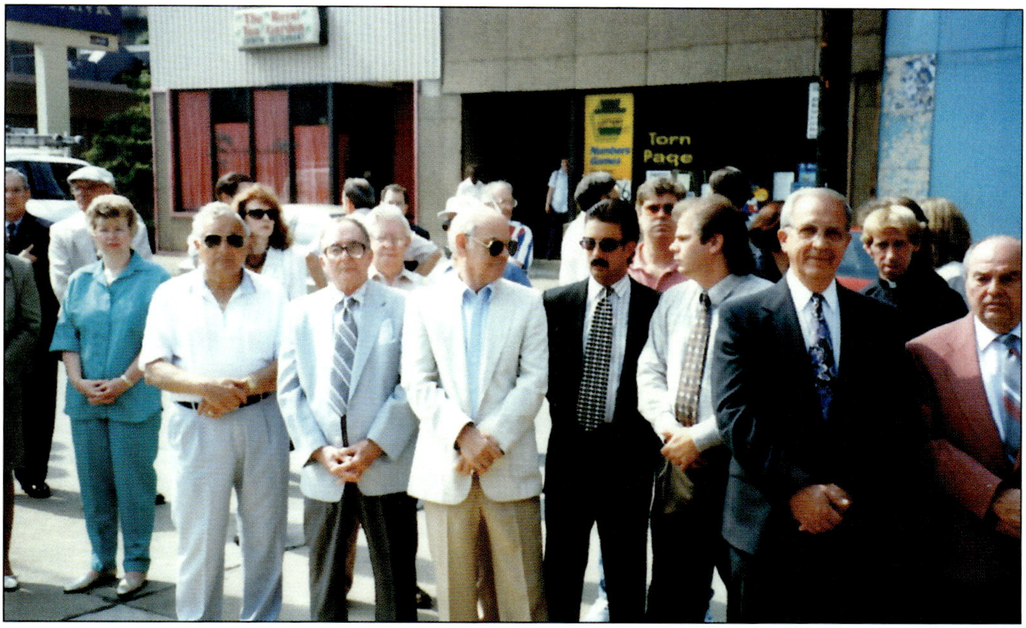

A crowd of citizens gathers in downtown Monessen to honor Ernest Coccari. Coccari served as executive director for the Monessen Chamber of Commerce for 11 years. He selflessly loved his city and wanted to see it thrive. A plaque in his honor and memory can be found on Donner Avenue near Fifth Street in the heart of the commercial district.

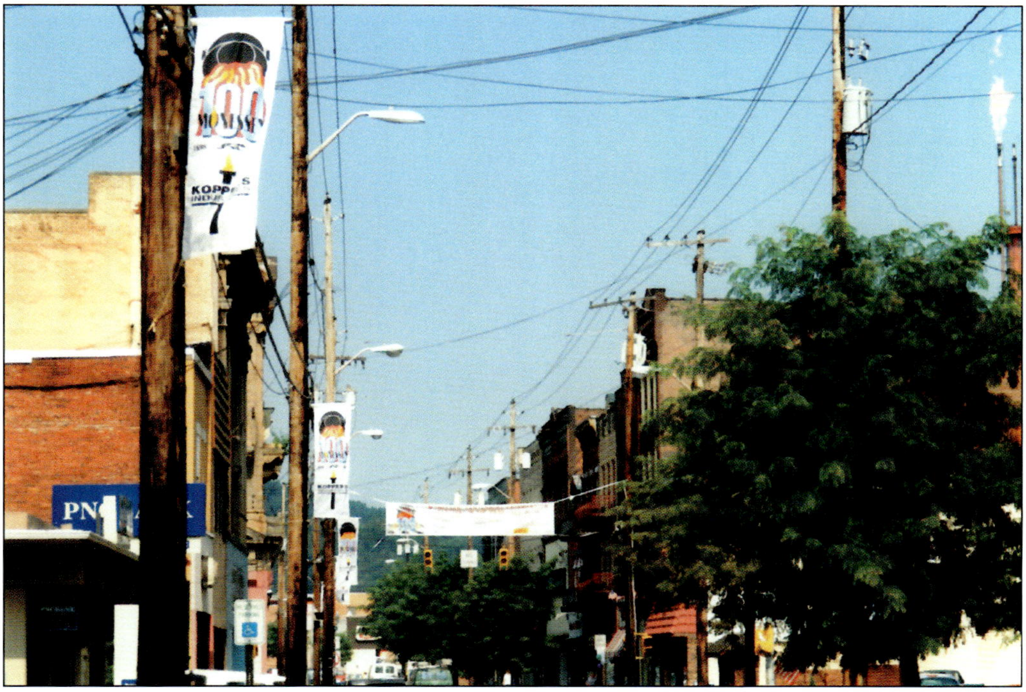

A more thriving downtown can be seen in this photograph from 1998. Donner Avenue looks alive as the city prepares itself for the public eye. Unlike now, most of the buildings in downtown are still inhabited, and there are still some businesses there. Many businesses left after the turn of the 21st century, when the economy continued to worsen.

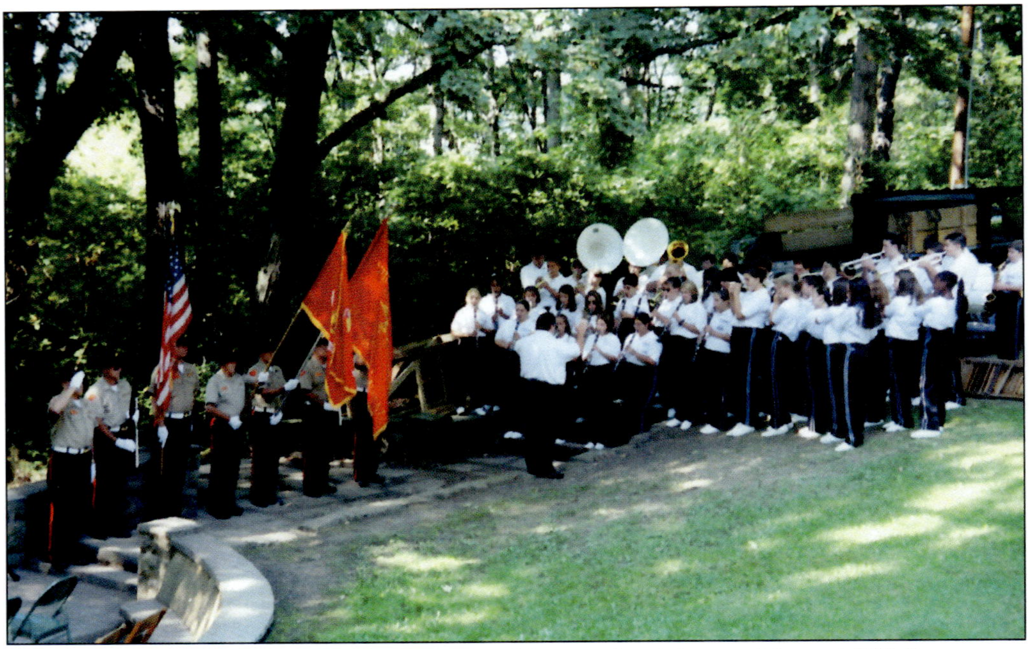

Veterans gather at Monessen City Park as part of the traveling Vietnam Memorial Wall ceremony in 1998. The wall continues to travel throughout the country reminding people of servicemen and women's sacrifices.

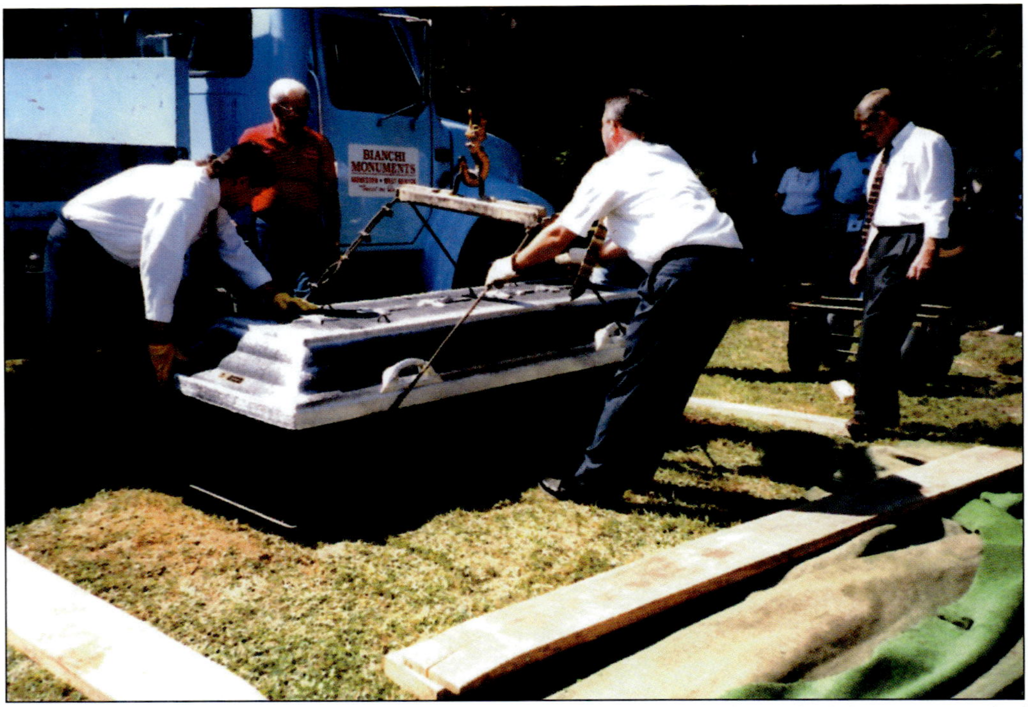

Crews worked in Monessen City Park to install a time capsule, which marked the centennial of the city in 1998. Various city leaders, dignitaries, and citizens buried items that reflected upon how they felt as Monessenites. The time capsule still stands in the city park, and there is no date on the stone that marks when it should be opened.

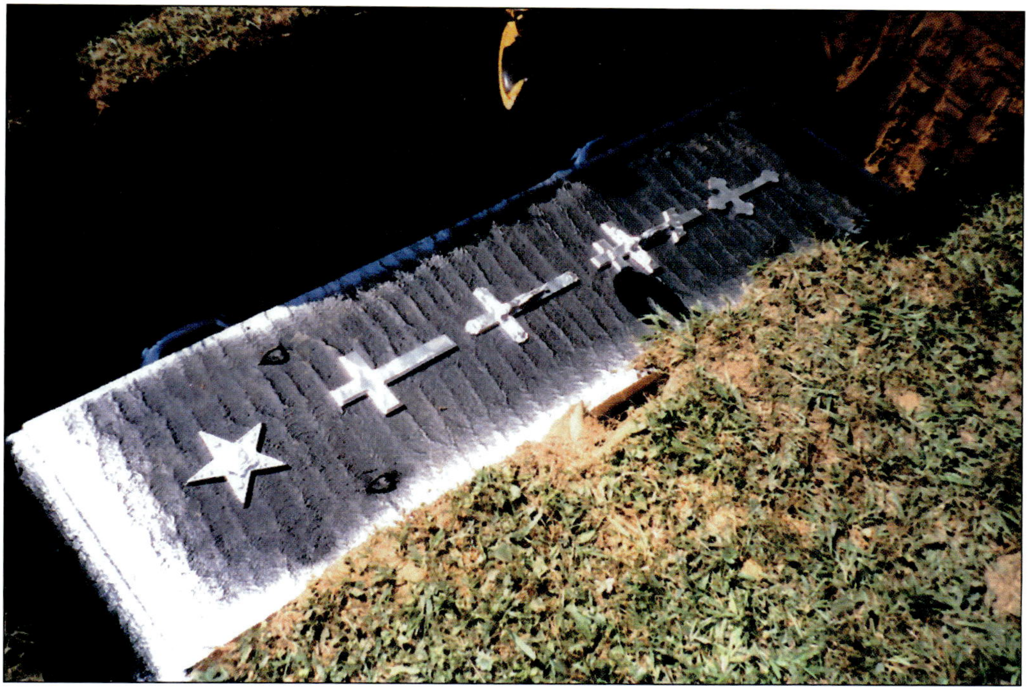

The time capsule that was installed at Monessen City Park is very large. Many mementos reflecting the city were placed into it before it was sealed. The top of the capsule has a Star of David and crosses of varying styles, representing the array of faith communities in the city.

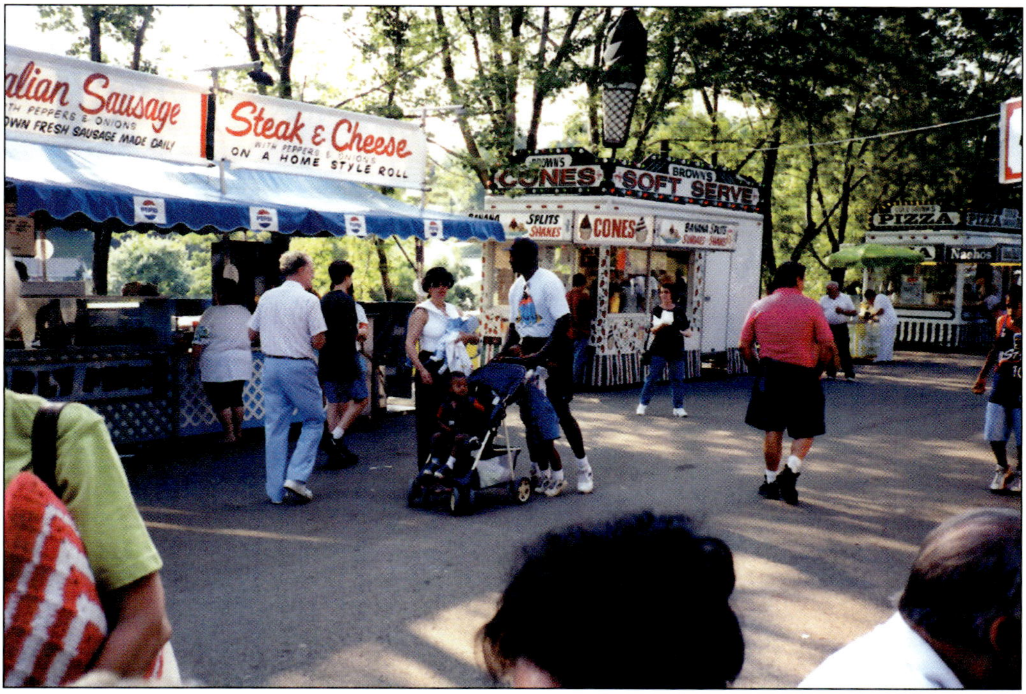

Community members enjoy strolling through the festival at the park in 1998, marking 100 years since the city was established. The festival had many activities and a lot of food to choose from. The event was well attended by many people, young and old alike.

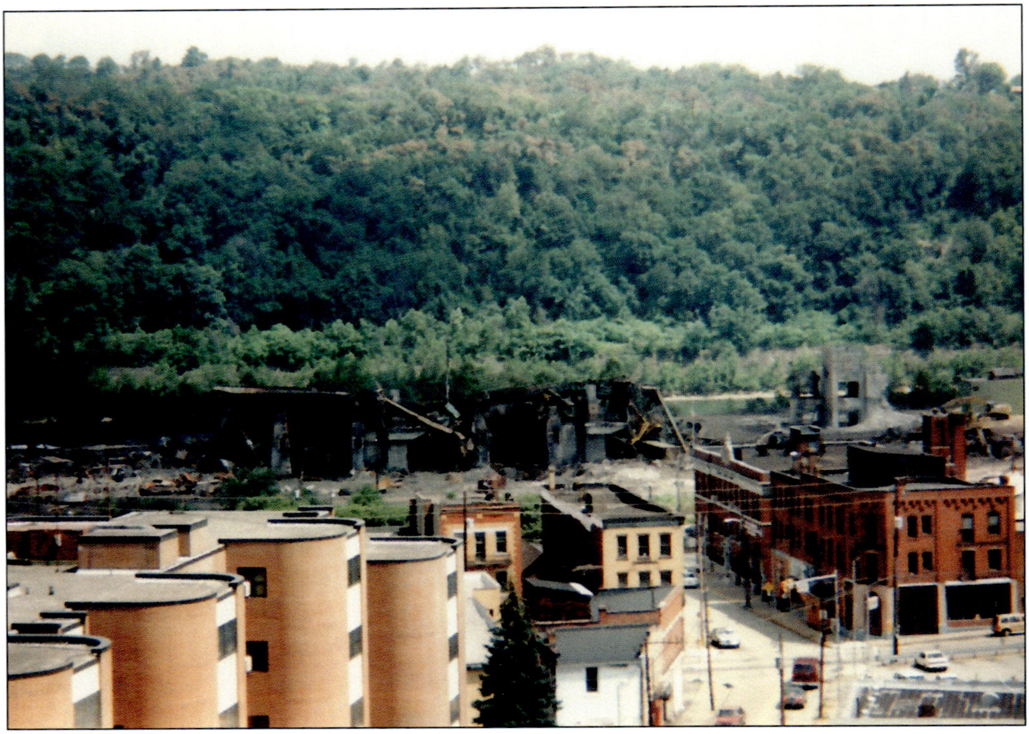

The BOF was torn down, along with many other structures that were part of the mill, in order to revitalize and beautify the city. Also pictured here are the former Monessen Municipal Building to the right and Valley Manor high-rise to the left.

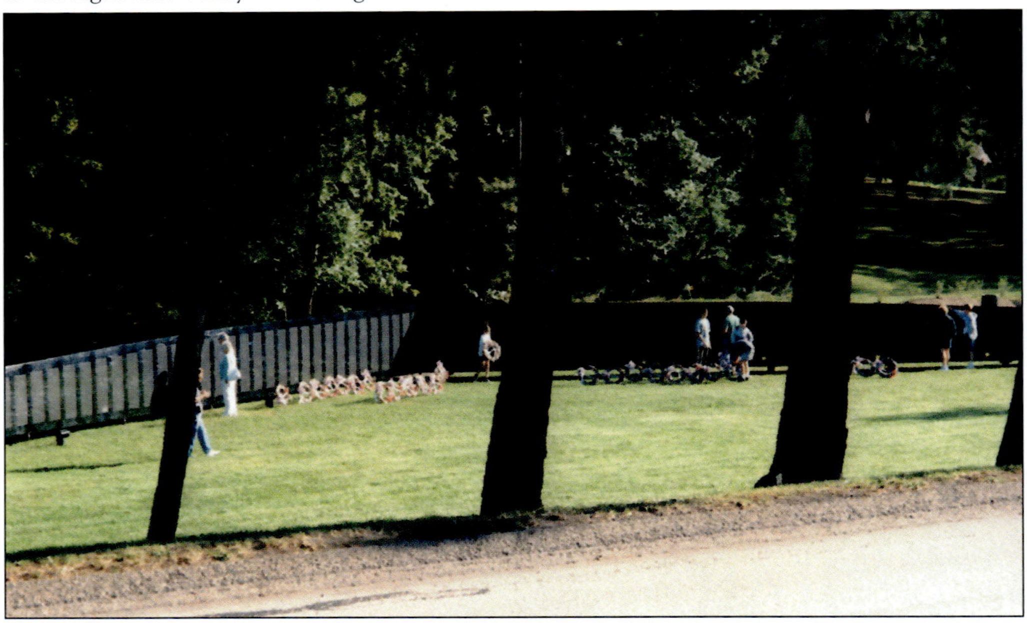

In 1998, visitors pay their respects at the traveling Vietnam Memorial Wall at Monessen City Park. The wall could be seen from Grand Boulevard. It stayed in the city for three days before it continued its circuit throughout the country. The wall continues to travel to various cities throughout the country.

A banner marking the 105th Western Pennsylvania Firemen's Convention can be seen hanging above Donner Avenue at Fifth Street. The convention travels from city to city each year. The large parade and events brought local fire departments and their families to the city.

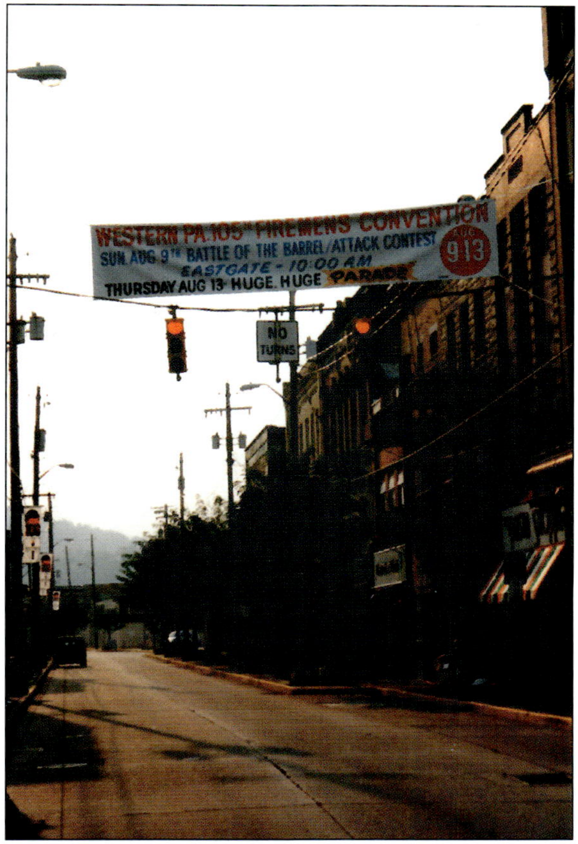

The sign at the intersection of Tyrol Boulevard and Eastgate Avenue welcomes visitors to the city. This 1998 photograph shows an advertisement for the firemen's convention and parade held that year. The sign, which is sponsored by the Monessen Chamber of Commerce and various other organizations and businesses, still welcomes people to the city each day.

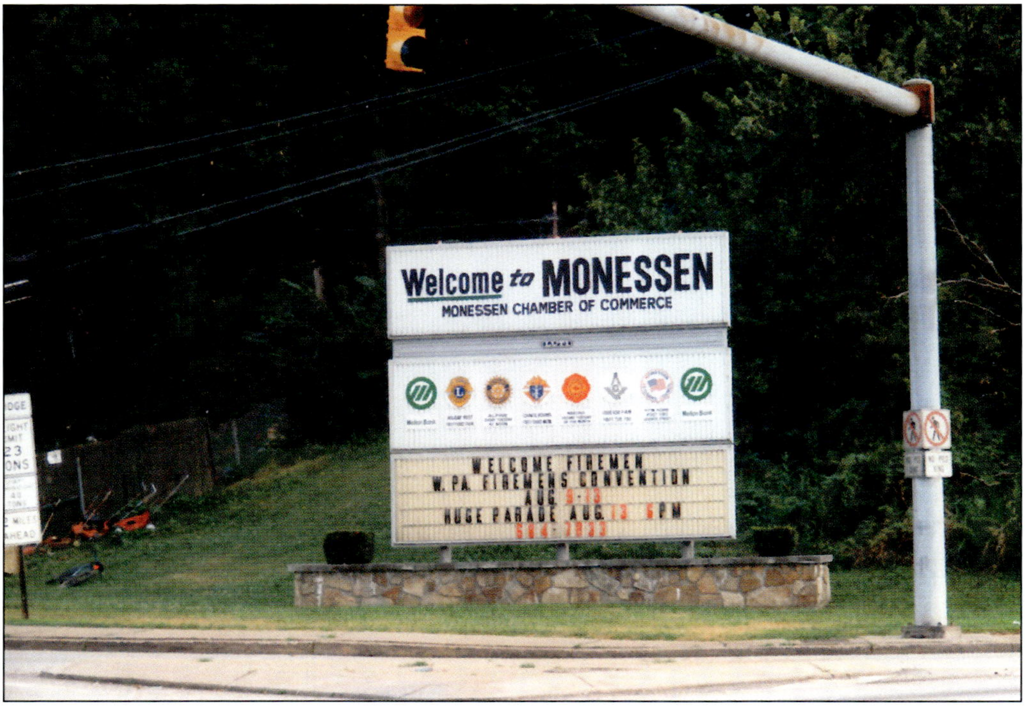

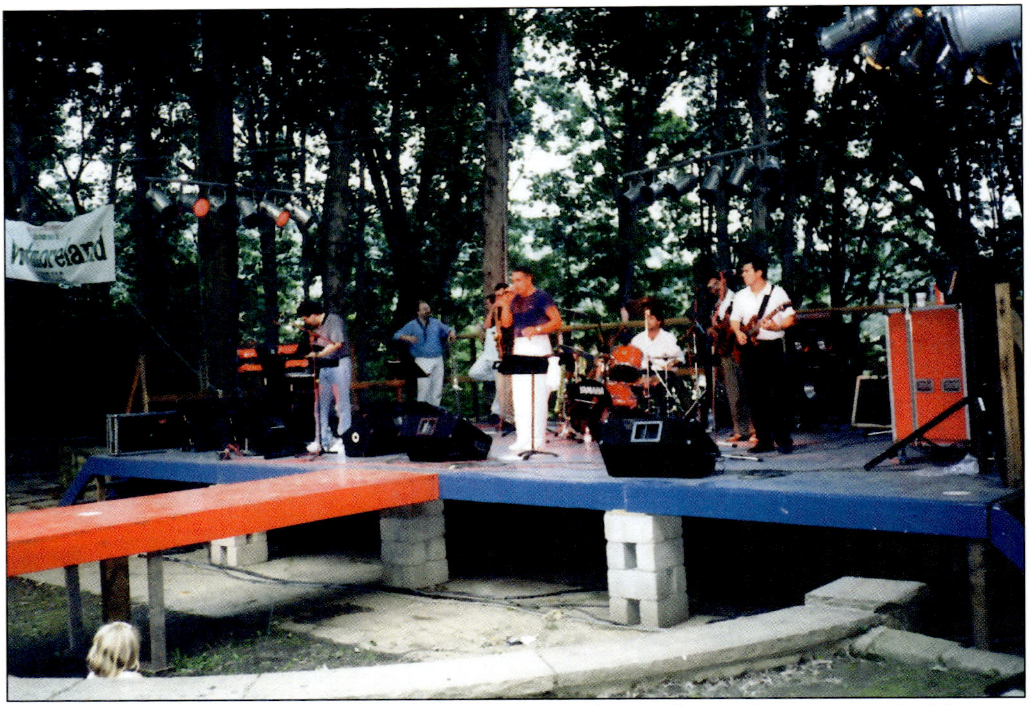

A band performs at the old Monessen City Park amphitheater during the centennial celebration in 1998. A wooden stage and catwalk were built on top of the old stone structure to allow the band to have more room to perform. The stage remained for the duration of the centennial festivities that year.

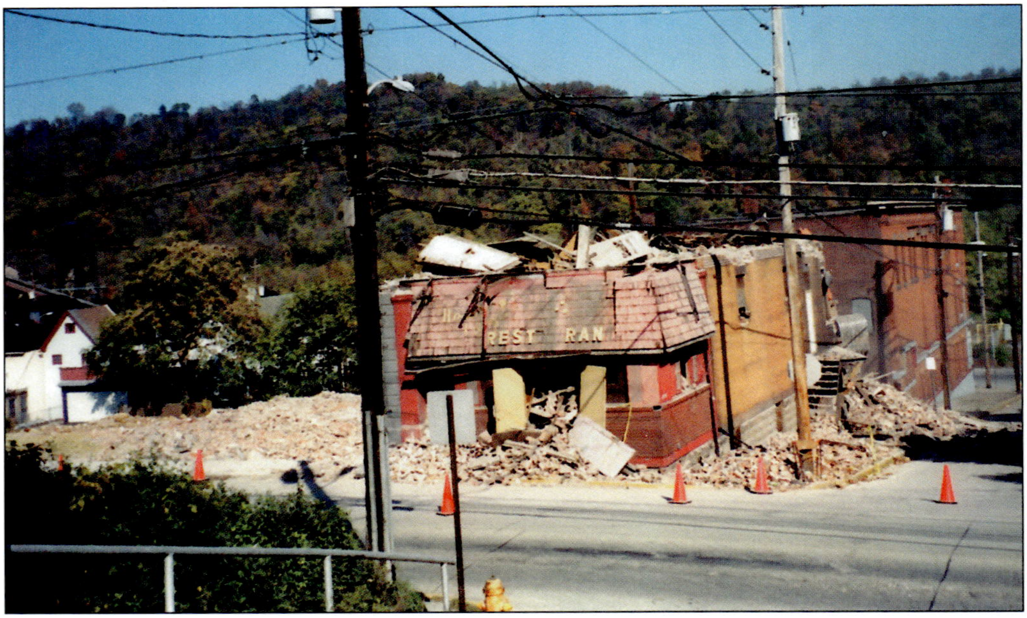

A building is demolished in downtown Monessen at the corner of Second Street and Schoonmaker Avenue in an effort to clean the city and rid it of its growing amount of abandoned properties. This commercial building housed a restaurant until the 1980s, when it became too hard to keep small businesses alive in the city.

Six

Pushing for a Renaissance

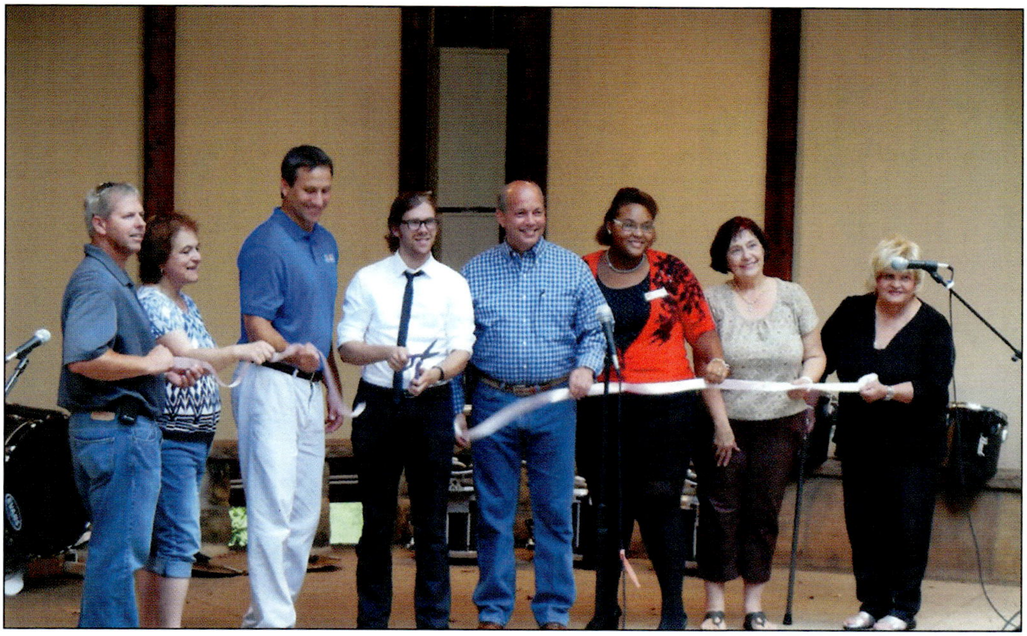

Members of the Monessen Amphitheater Committee cut the ribbon to the newly renovated amphitheater. The amphitheater at Monessen City Park was built in the early 1930s, and it was renovated in 2014. Pictured here with the committee are Westmoreland County commissioner Ted Kopas (with scissors) and state representative Ted Harhai (fifth from left). (Author's collection.)

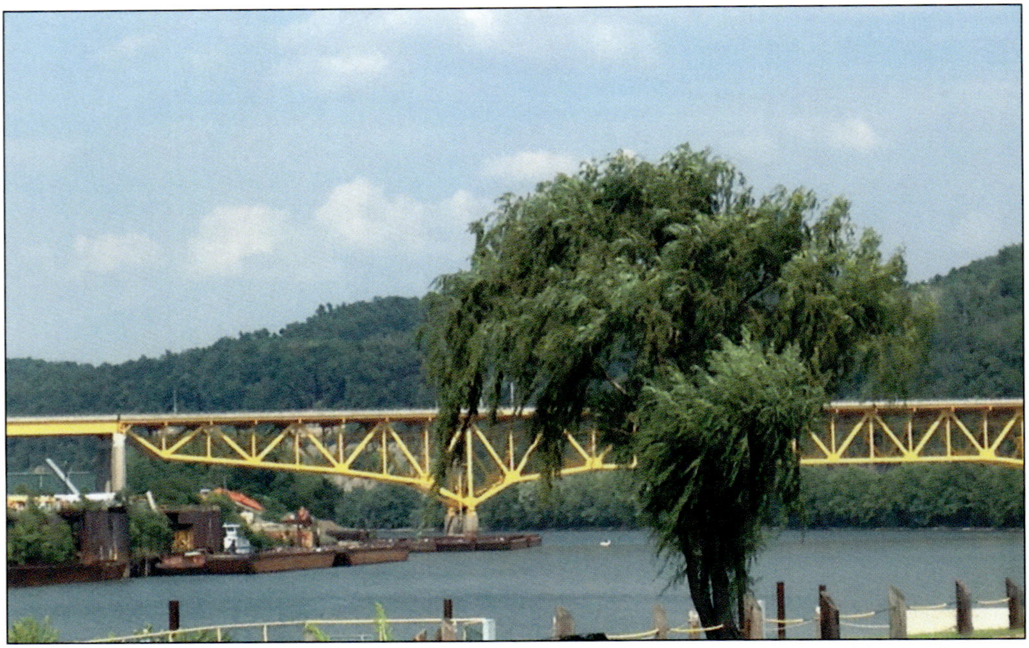

The Donora-Monessen Bridge, now named after Stan Musial, a native of the neighboring Donora, Pennsylvania, can be seen from the Herman Mihalich Boat Launch in Monessen. The boat launch, which has a small park attached, is named after the late state representative and is situated along the Monongahela River in Monessen's Eastgate section.

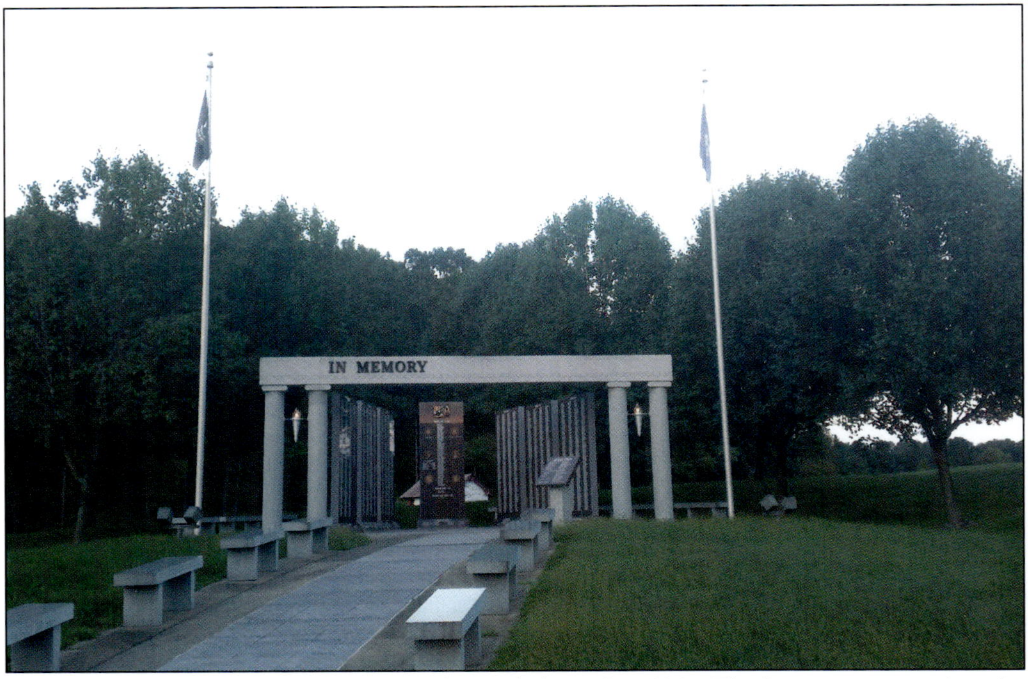

The war memorial at Monessen City Park was dedicated in 2001. The large monument has the names of all those who served in the various wars from World War I forward. Many community organizations and citizens also purchased brick pavers and benches to honor their loved ones. (Author's collection.)

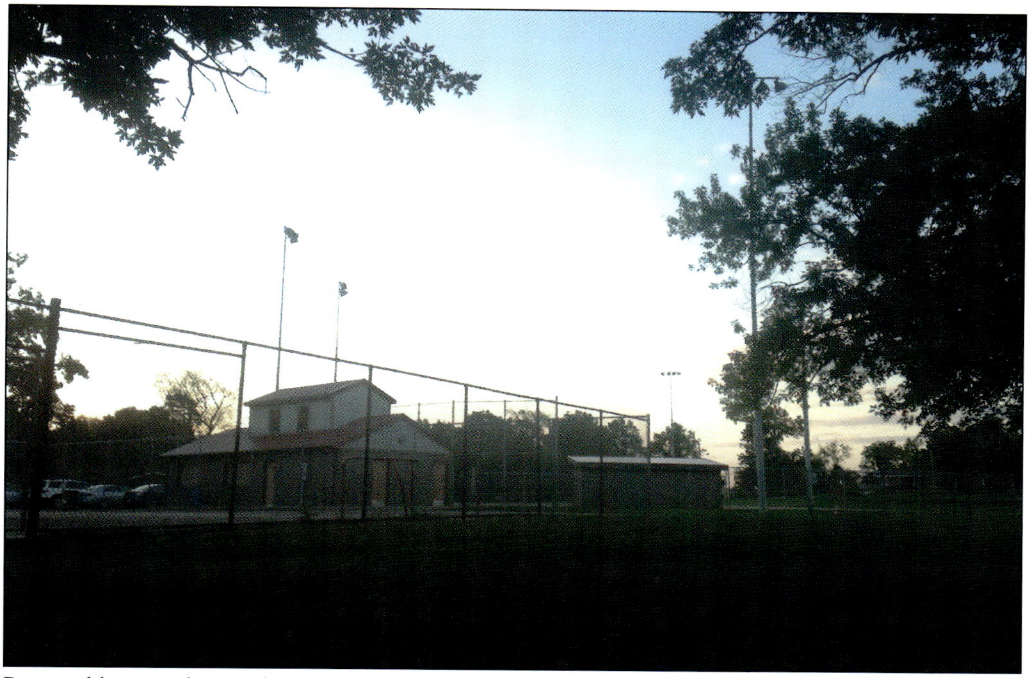

Pictured here is the newly constructed baseball field house at Monessen City Park. To the right of the field house is the Monessen City Park baseball field. In the early 2010s, the ballpark was renovated, and new lights were installed. Many youth baseball groups play and practice at the park in the summer. (Author's collection.)

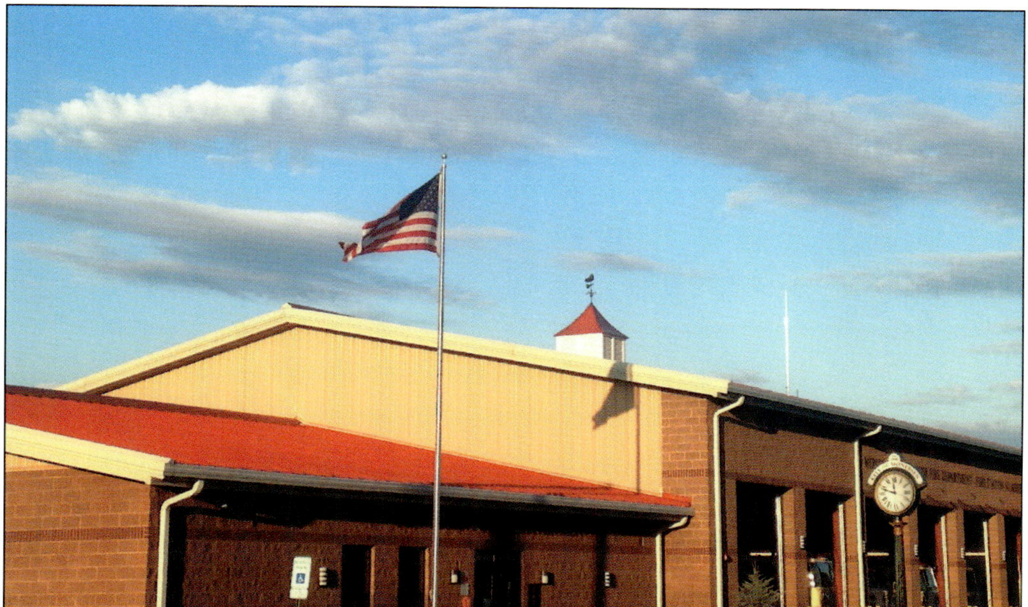

The recently built Monessen Public Safety Building is home to the fire department and the police force. The structure, which was completed in 2012, is located across the street from the previous municipal building, which is currently unoccupied. The Brown Street clock can be seen in front of the building. (Author's collection.)

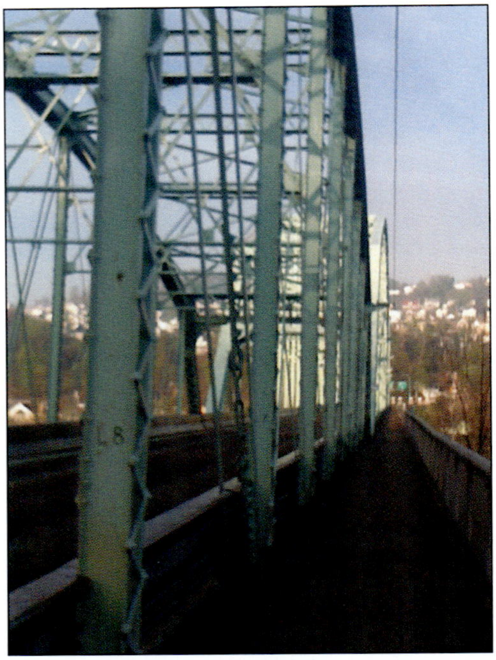

The Charleroi-Monessen Bridge was a Pennsylvania Petit truss bridge that was built in the early 20th century. Due to structural deficiencies, the bridge was demolished and rebuilt. This is a photograph of the former structure as it stood before demolition. It was in the National Register of Historic Places.

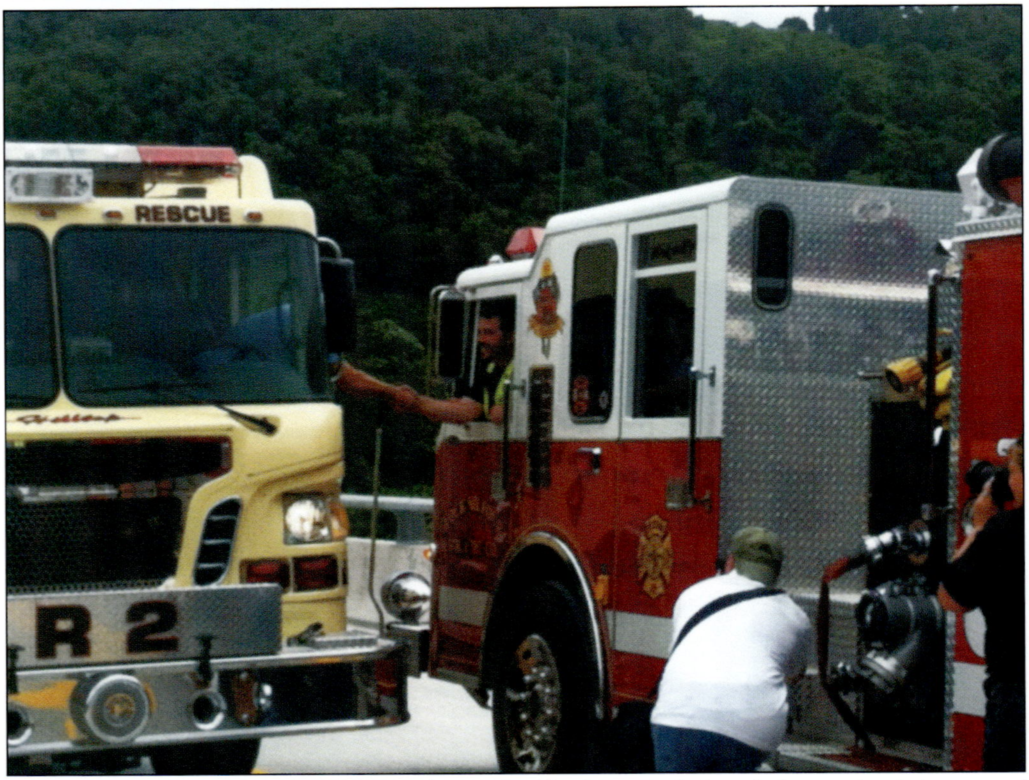

Firemen of Monessen and a neighboring borough, Charleroi, shake hands during the dedication of the bridge. After its demolition, the Charleroi-Monessen Bridge was renamed the John K. Tener Bridge, after the former Pennsylvania governor. The new bridge was dedicated on June 29, 2014, with celebrations on both sides of the bridge. (Author's collection.)

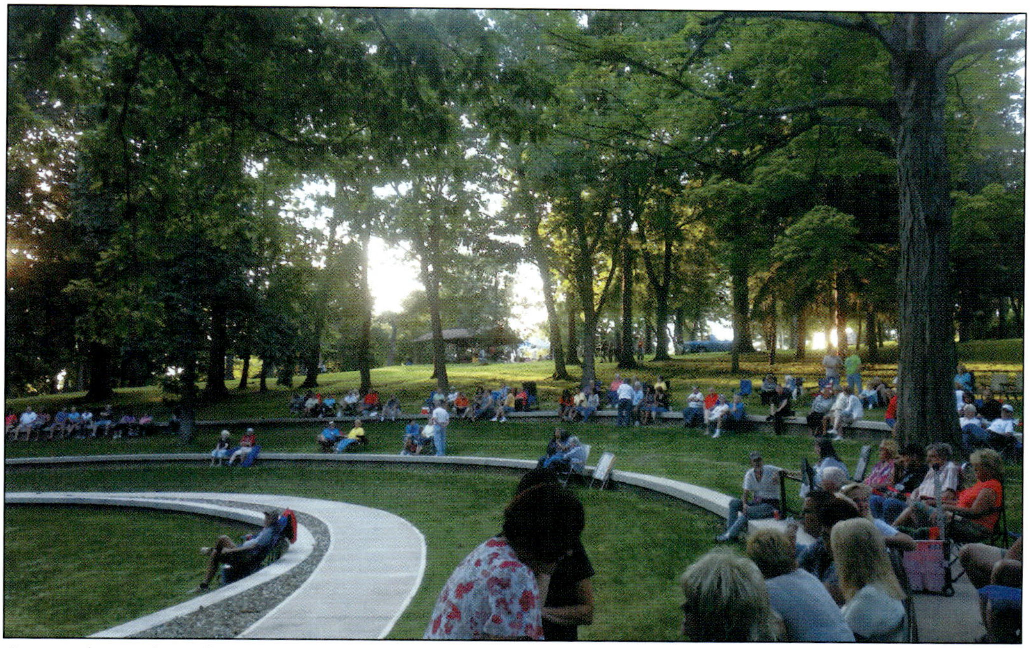

A crowd is gathered at Monessen City Park amphitheater for one of its inaugural events. Since its renovation was completed, the amphitheater has held many concerts and performances featuring a variety of genres and styles. It is the hope of the amphitheater committee that the venue spurs economic activity in the area. (Author's collection.)

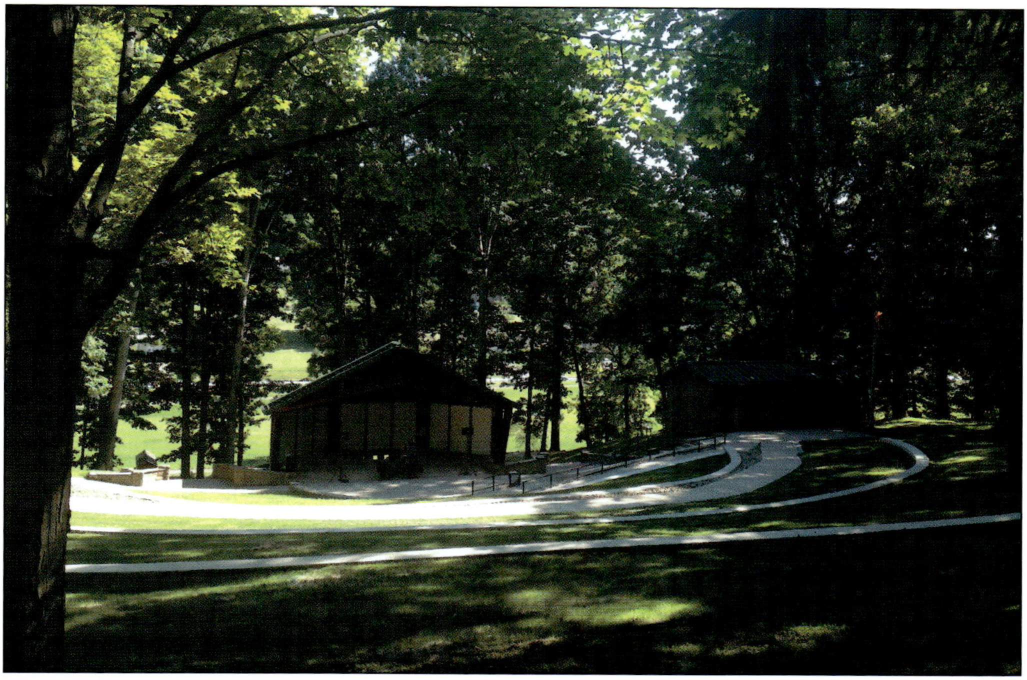

The newly renovated amphitheater at Monessen City Park boasts a beautiful setting among the trees. People gather at the park for various concerts and events. They are able to bring a chair or a blanket and enjoy the atmosphere of the park. The amphitheater's original design was a Works Progress Administration (WPA) project. (Author's collection.)

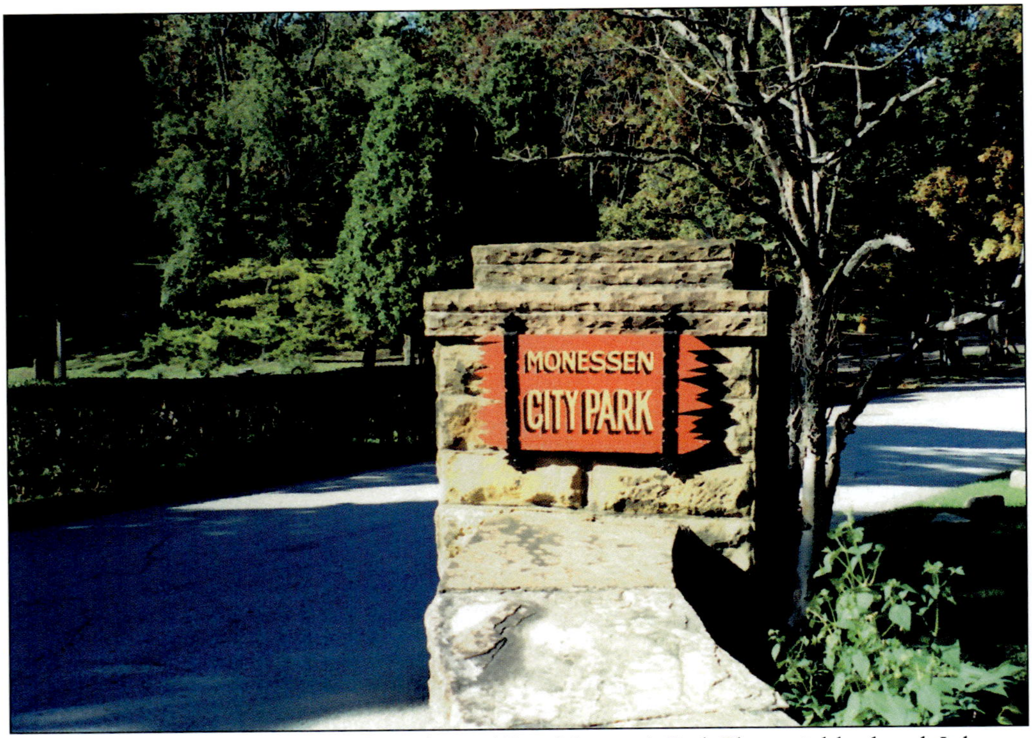

Monessen City Park is a large park in the middle of the city's Park Plan neighborhood. It boasts tennis courts, playgrounds, an amphitheater, various memorials, a baseball field, and many scenic paths. The park is still used by many citizens today. It has been an asset to the city of Monessen since the early 1930s.

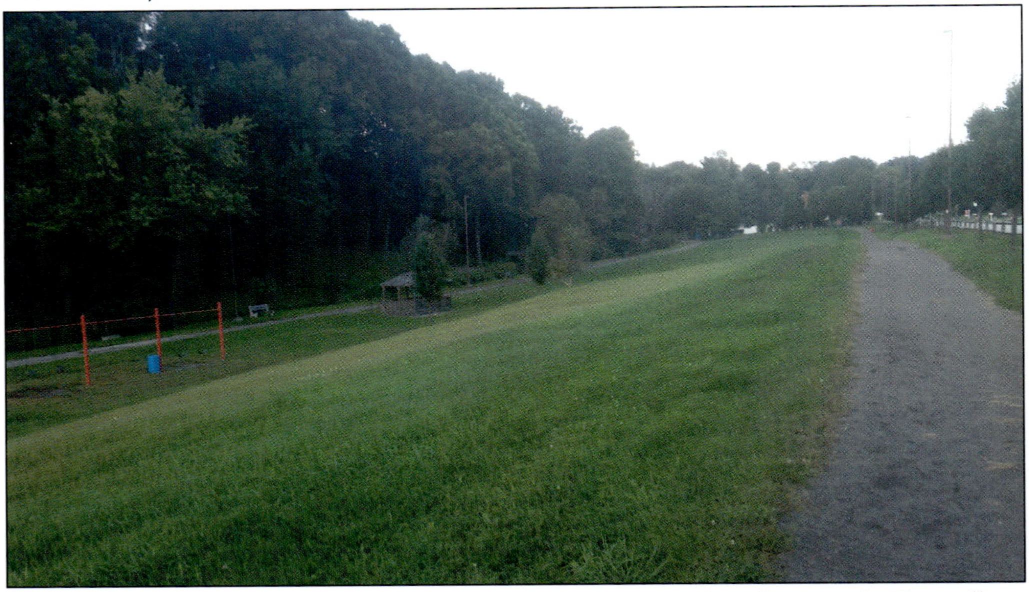

Joggers are able to enjoy the amenities at the Monessen City Park walking track. The walking track is the most-used part of the park. Around the track is the war memorial dedicated to all Monessenites who have served the country. There are also several benches, rest areas, and a pavilion.

Several miles of scenic paths cross through the upper portion of Monessen City Park. Many of the paths were discovered over the last few years. At least one mile of pathways still remains covered with grass and soil. The paths wind through the park in a formal, circular pattern. (Author's collection.)

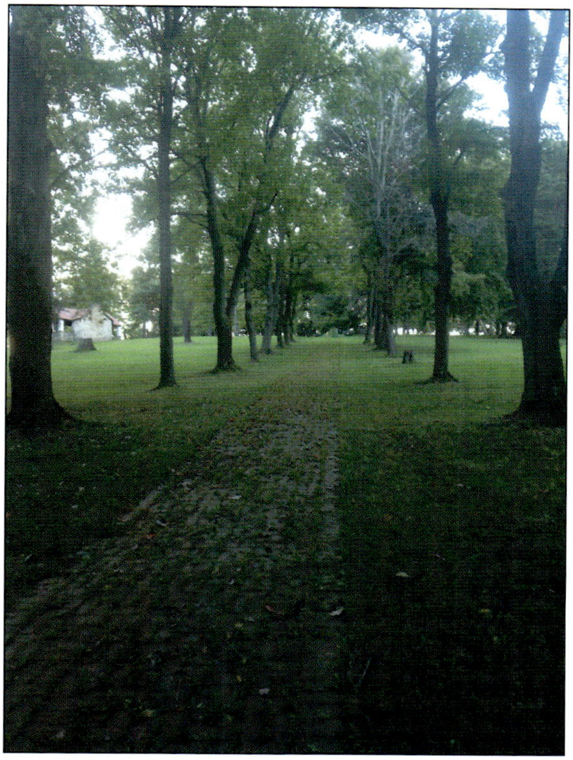

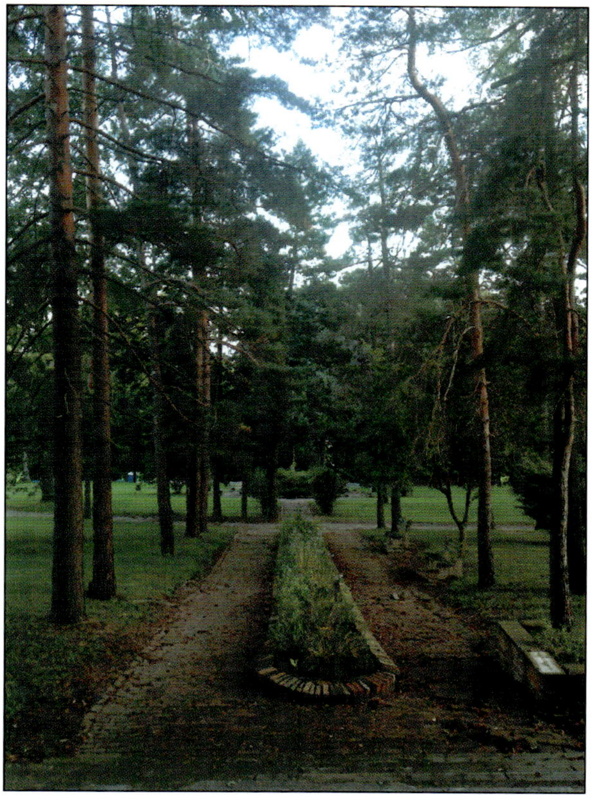

The brick paths that wind through the upper portion of Monessen City Park were a WPA project. Many amenities in the park, such as pavilions, barbeque areas, and the Monessen City Park amphitheater were also WPA projects. Many of the paths are lined with trees, like this one, which is located at the top entrance to the park. (Author's collection.)

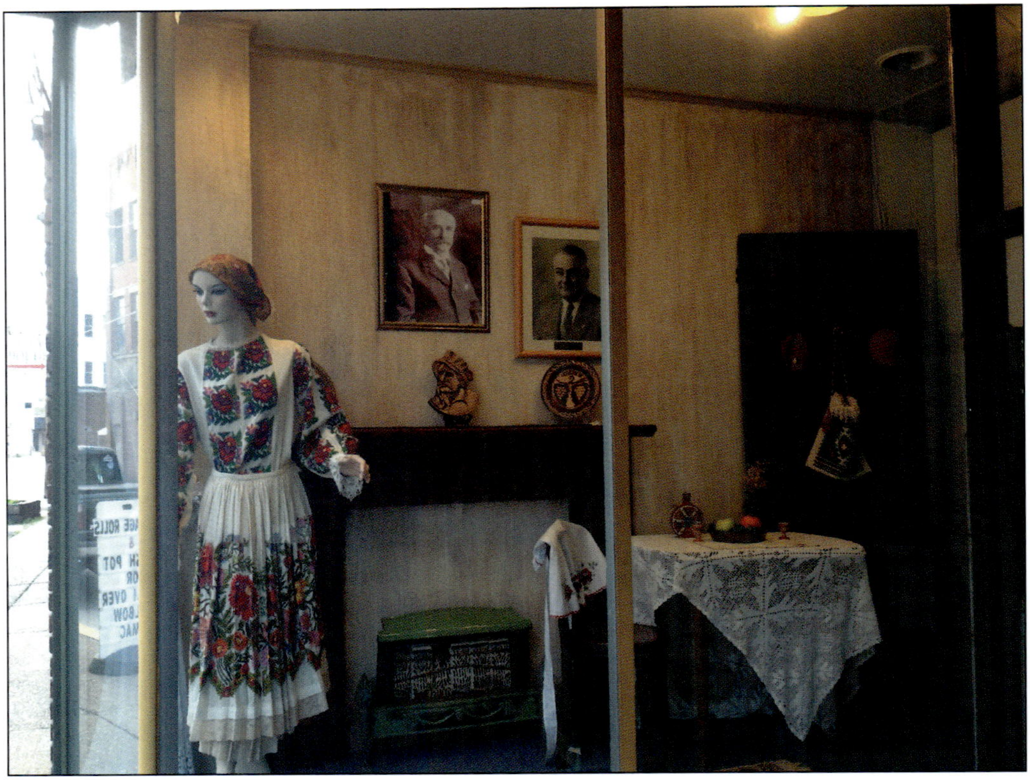

The front windows at the Monessen Heritage Museum are always decorated. The Greater Monessen Historical Society decorates the windows of the museum to reflect their newest exhibit or a major holiday. This small act is reminiscent of when all of the shop windows in downtown Monessen were filled with decorations and items to purchase. (Courtesy of Karla Spangler.)

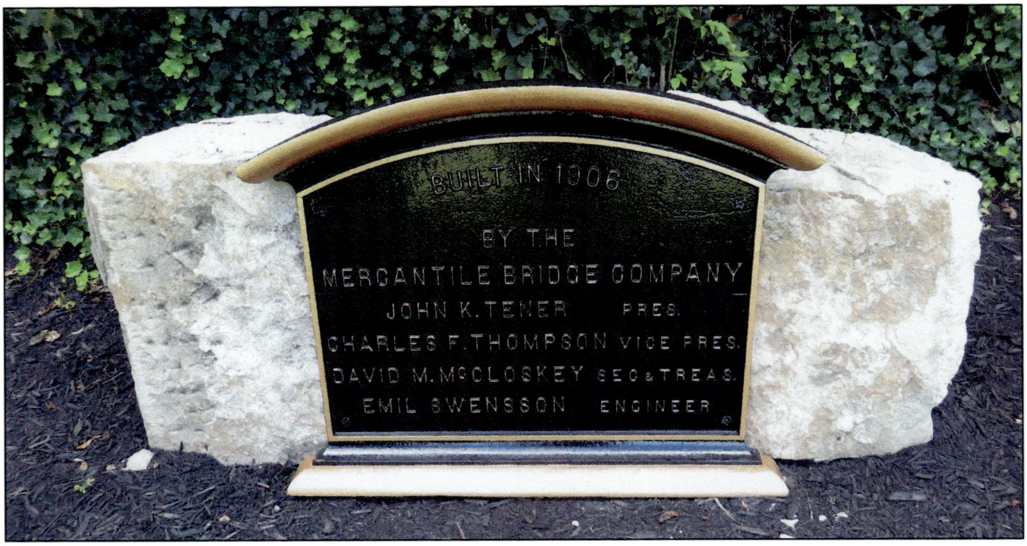

Although it is located in nearby Charleroi, this plaque was taken from the old Charleroi-Monessen Bridge. The plaque was recently restored and placed in a small park near the bridge on the Charleroi side of the river. Monessen also received the same plaque, which was located on Monessen's side of the bridge. (Courtesy of Karla Spangler.)

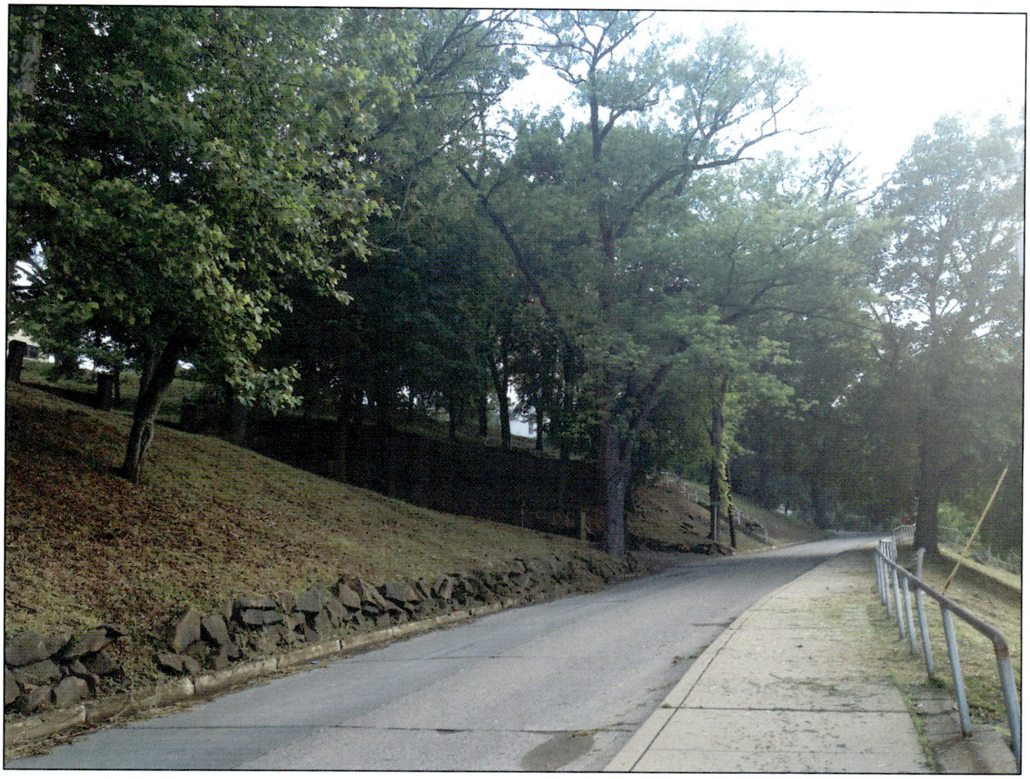

Hillside Park, also known as Sixth Street Park, is Monessen's oldest park. Hillside Park was constructed when homes were built on McKee Avenue and Parkway. The families that lived on these streets were wealthy and wanted a nice park they could enjoy. The park was beautifully landscaped with tree-lined paths, and it was an oasis from the smoke-filled skies of the city. (Courtesy of Karla Spangler.)

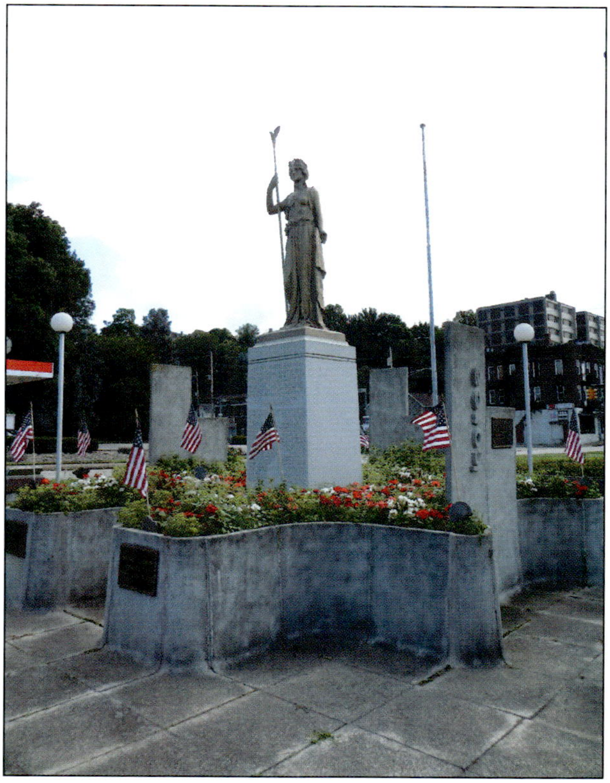

One of the city's war memorials is located on Veteran's Way between Schoonmaker and Donner Avenues in the Eastgate section. The statue, which is dedicated to those who served in World War I, was originally located in Hillside Park. It was relocated to its current location at Eastgate in the 1970s. (Courtesy of Karla Spangler.)

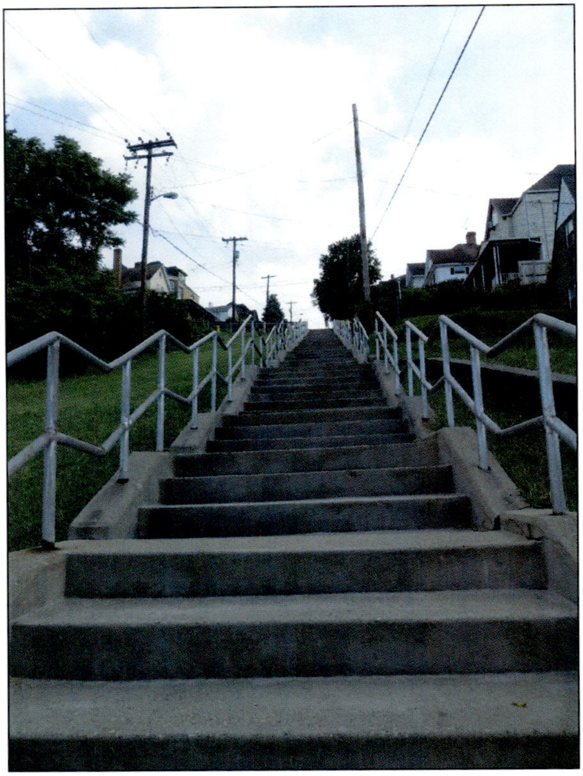

Since the city of Monessen was built on hilly terrain, there are many public stairways within the city. The longest stairway in Monessen is located at Fourth Street and Schoonmaker Avenue. Homes were built along the steep grade of Fourth Street in the early 20th century, but they were not accessible because the grade was too steep for carriages and would be steep for early automobiles as well. (Author's collection.)

This Art Deco metal statue is located on the corner of Third Street and Donner Avenue, near the Monessen Public Library. It was installed after the current library was constructed and moved from Fifth Street. The sculpture was restored in 2011, when the library was undergoing renovations of its own. (Author's collection.)

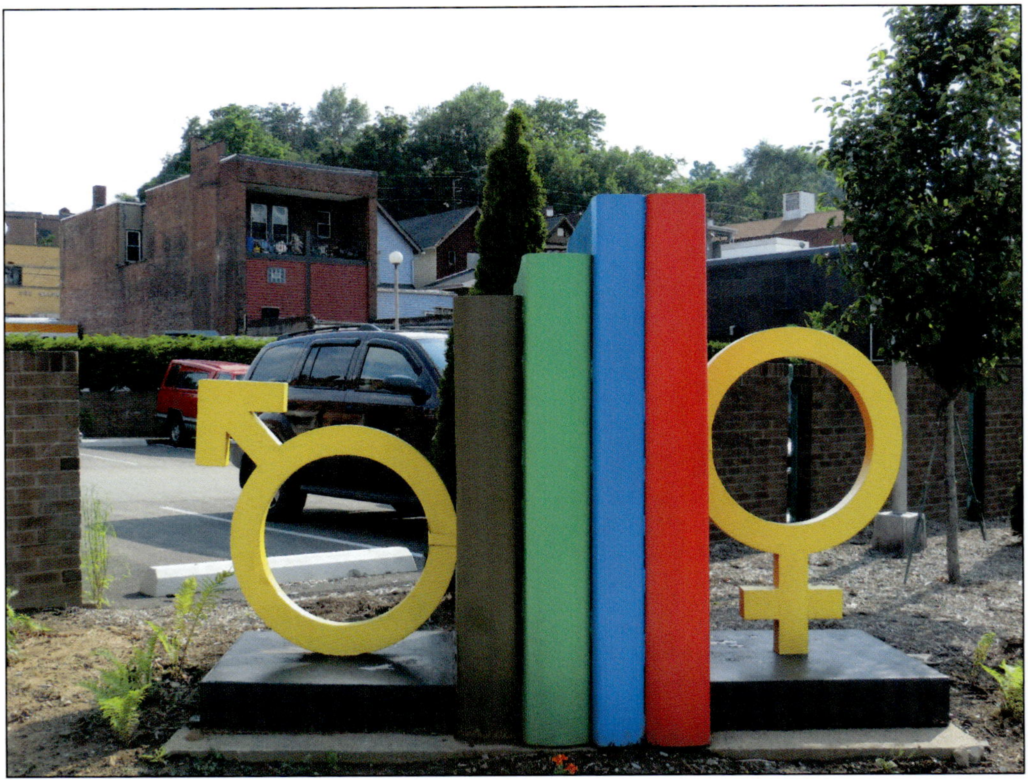

The Monessen Elementary Center is one of two buildings that are within the Monessen Public School system. The building is located on Rostraver Street and originally served as the vocational-technical school, until it was converted into an elementary school. Children who are in kindergarten through fifth grade attend school here. (Courtesy of Karla Spangler.)

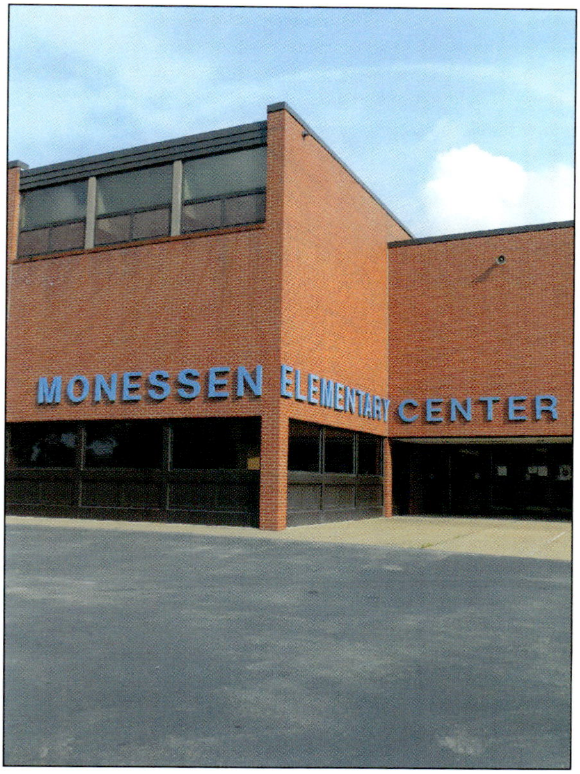

The Monessen Memorial Stadium is located on Rostraver Street, next to the elementary center. The stadium, a WPA project, is used throughout the year by the Monessen School District for various practices and games. The Monessen Greyhound football team also practices and plays here each season. It is one of the largest and oldest stadiums in the area. (Courtesy of Karla Spangler.)

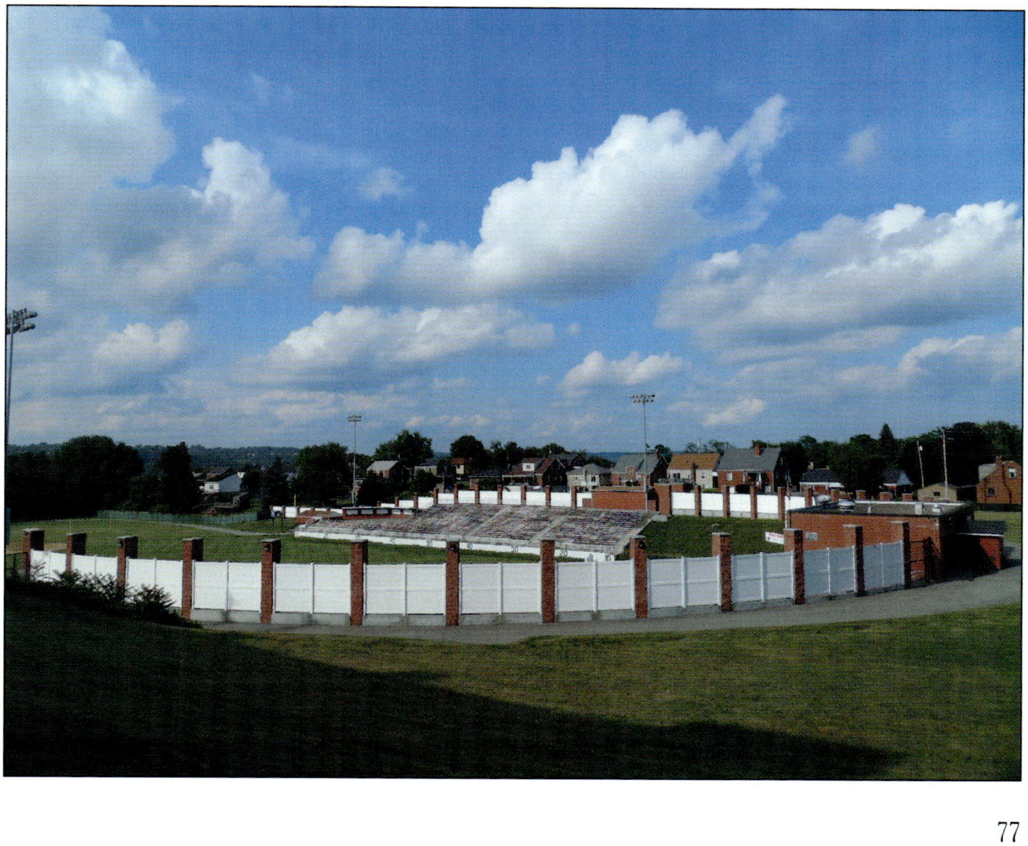

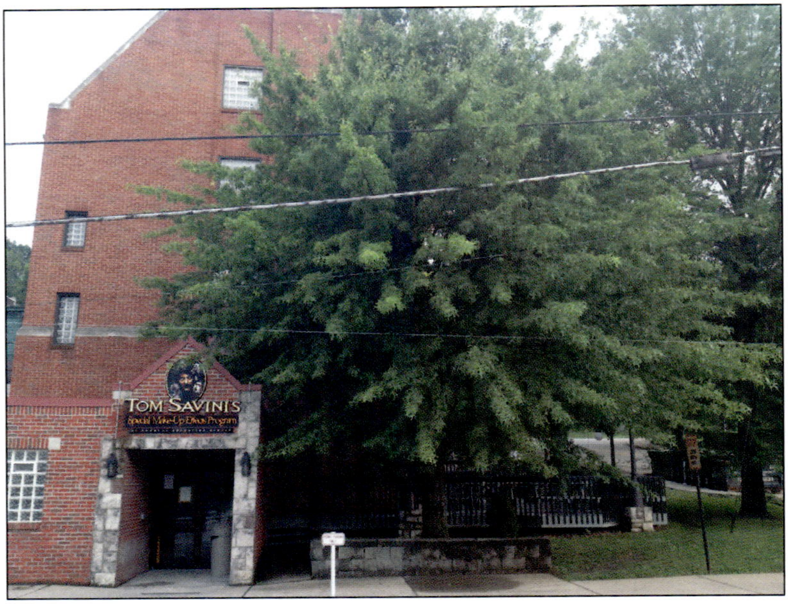

Tom Savini's Special Make-Up Effects Program is located on Donner Avenue and Eighth Street. The program is part of the Douglas Education Center. The building originally housed a nunnery for the nuns that taught at St. Leonard's parochial school, which is nearby. St. Leonard's Church sits next door. (Courtesy of Karla Spangler.)

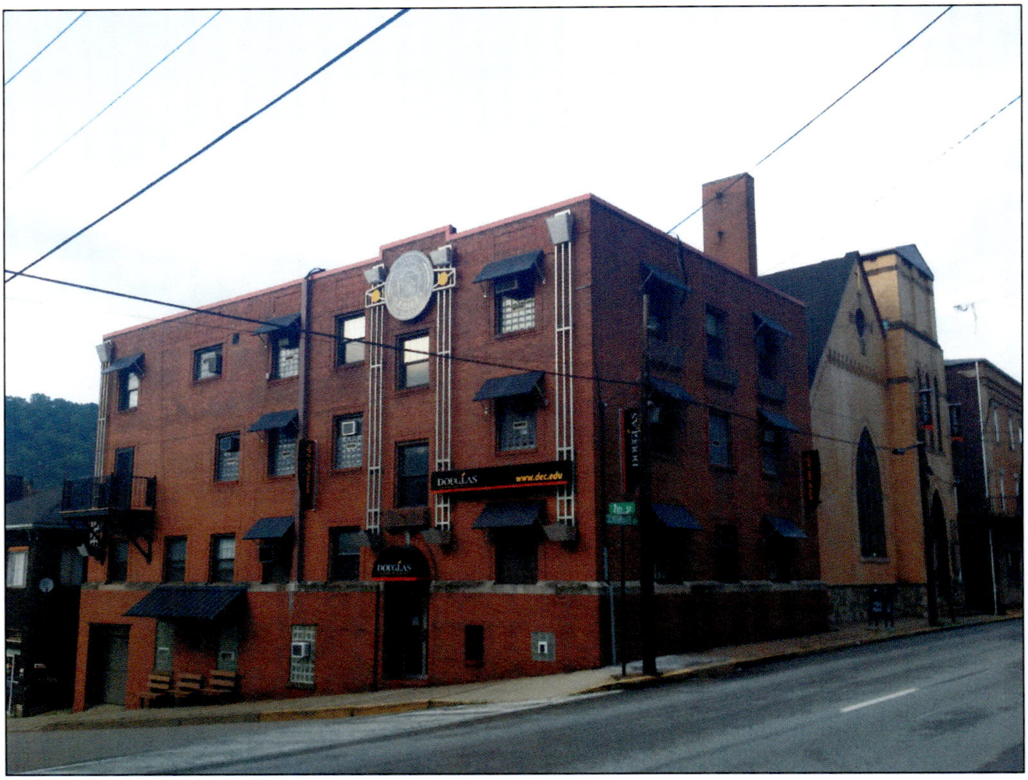

The Douglas Education Center building was once the school's only structure. The school expanded and added various programs such as film, special effects, cosmetology, and many others. The Seventh Street building used to house the Gimmell Hospital before the Douglas School acquired it. Douglas Business School, as it was originally called, was established in Monessen in 1904. (Courtesy of Karla Spangler.)

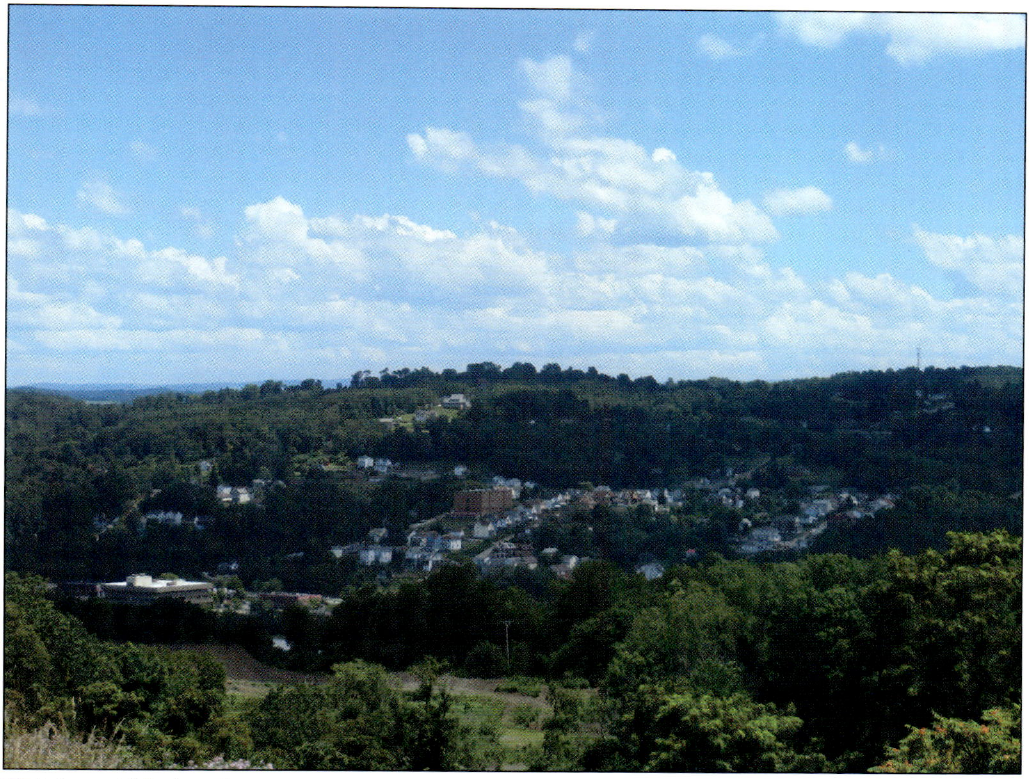

This beautiful view from across the Monongahela River in Carroll Township shows Monessen nestled in the Pennsylvania hills. The Eastgate section of the city can be seen as well as parts of the Park Plan and upper Midtown. (Author's collection.)

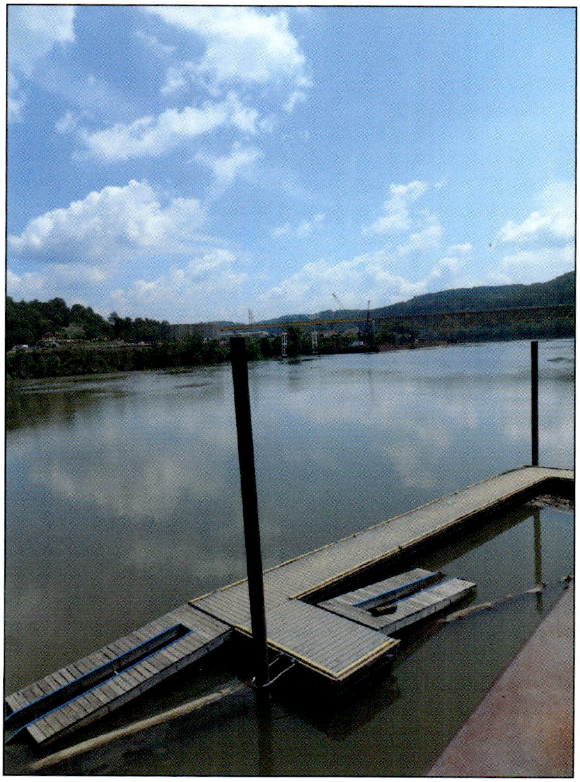

Pictured here is the Herman Mihalich Boat Launch along the Monongahela River, off Monongahela Street. Local anglers and boaters enjoy the serenity of the once-busy river. The launch was named after Mihalich, who was one of Pennsylvania's state representatives. In 1997, he passed away while in office. Mihalich was a Monessenite who loved his community. (Courtesy of Karla Spangler.)

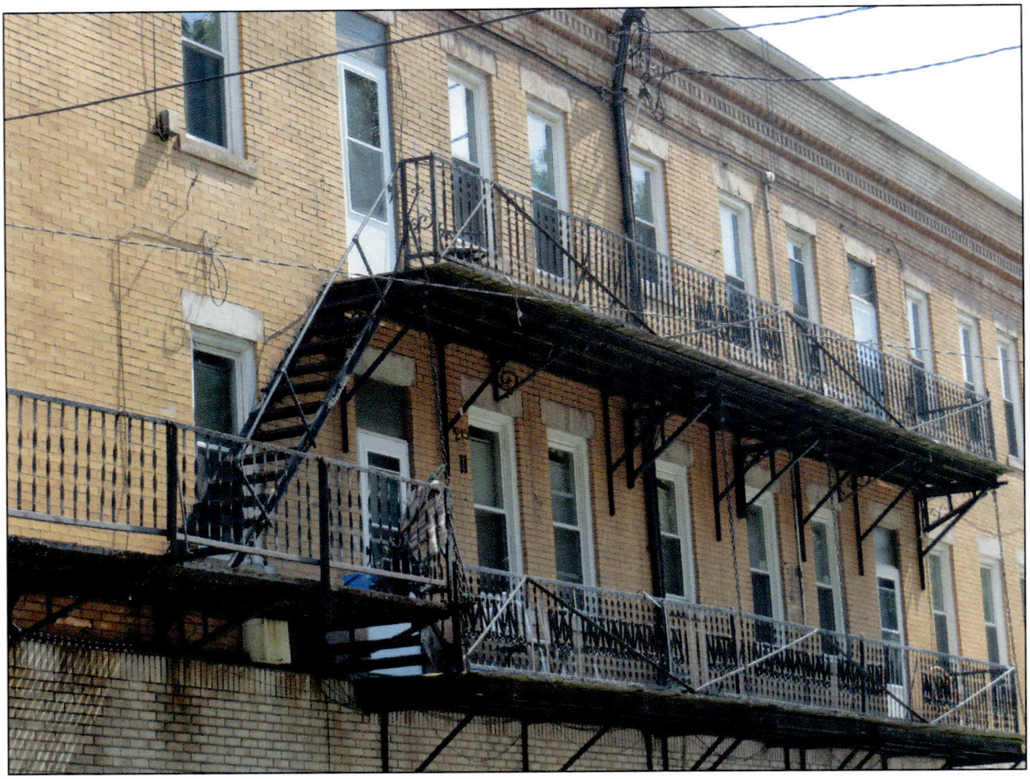

This is what typical apartment buildings looked like throughout the 20th century in Monessen. This is one of the few apartment buildings remaining. It is located on Sixth Street at Schoonmaker Avenue and used to house First Federal Savings Bank before the bank moved down the street. (Courtesy of Karla Spangler.)

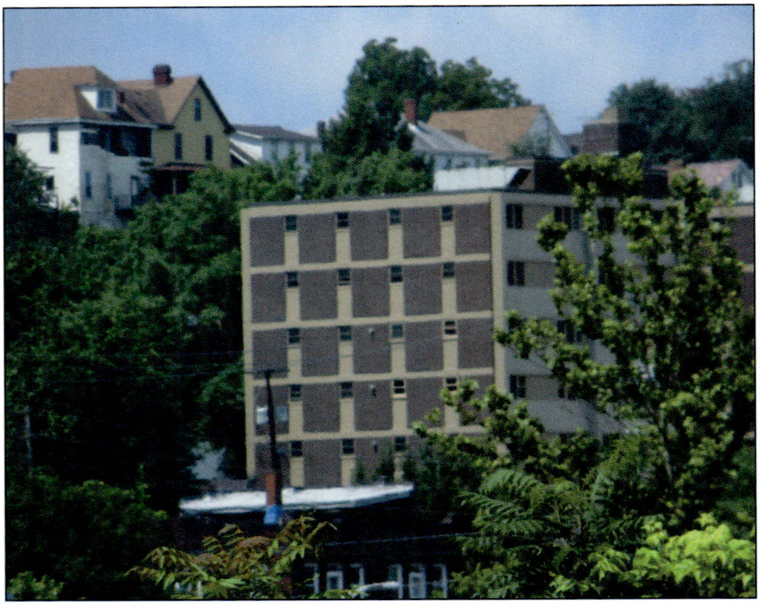

During the 1960s and early 1970s, there was a building boom in Monessen due to its economic successes. Three high-rise buildings were constructed in the city to be used as public housing. The Eastgate Manor was built where the old Iowa school structure stood, at Oneida Street and Schoonmaker Avenue. (Courtesy of Karla Spangler.)

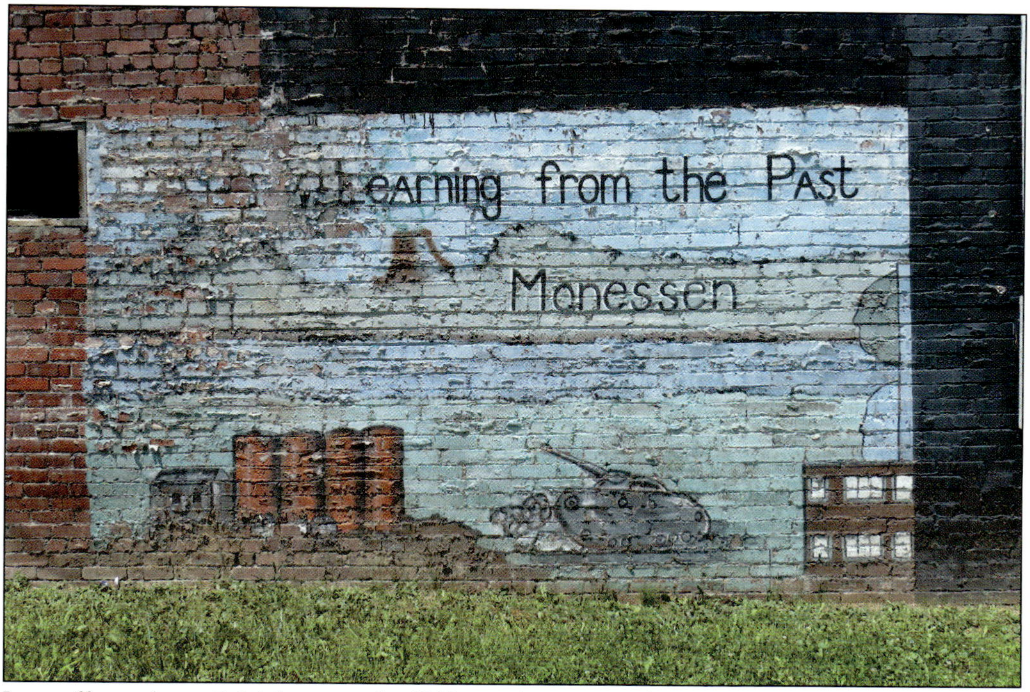

In an effort to beautify Midtown in the 1990s, students painted a mural on the side of a commercial property. The mural faces a lot where the Monessen Grand Hotel once stood; it is now used as a small urban park. The worn-out mural reads, "Learning from the Past, Monessen." (Courtesy of Karla Spangler.)

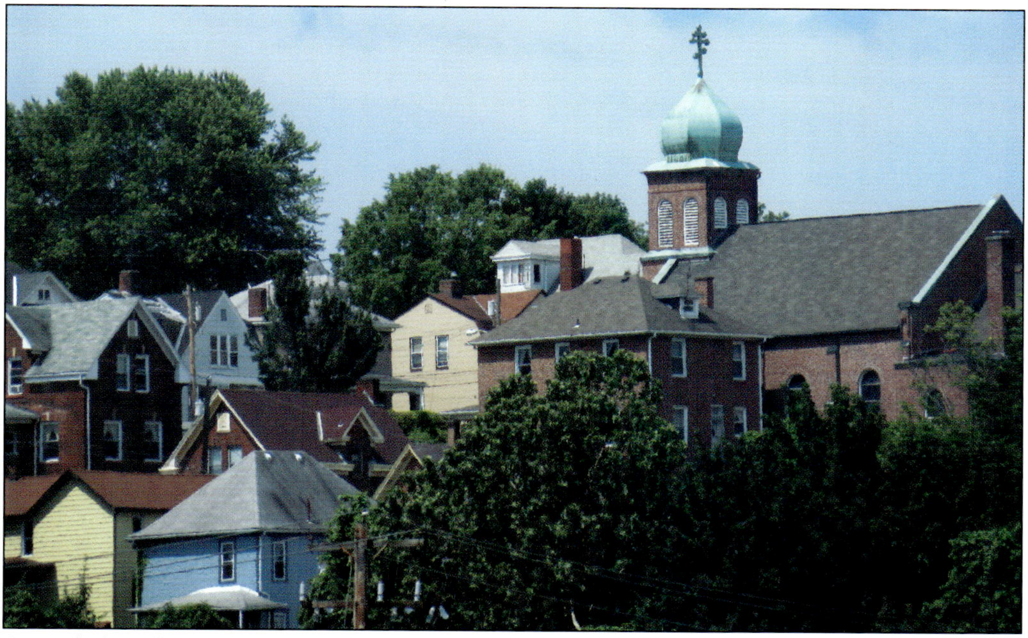

St. Nicholas Ukrainian Orthodox Church is one of Monessen's oldest and most quaint churches. It is located on Reed Avenue in upper Midtown. At the time of its construction, the brick structure was built near a more affluent neighborhood of the city, despite the fact that it was an immigrant church. (Courtesy of Karla Spangler.)

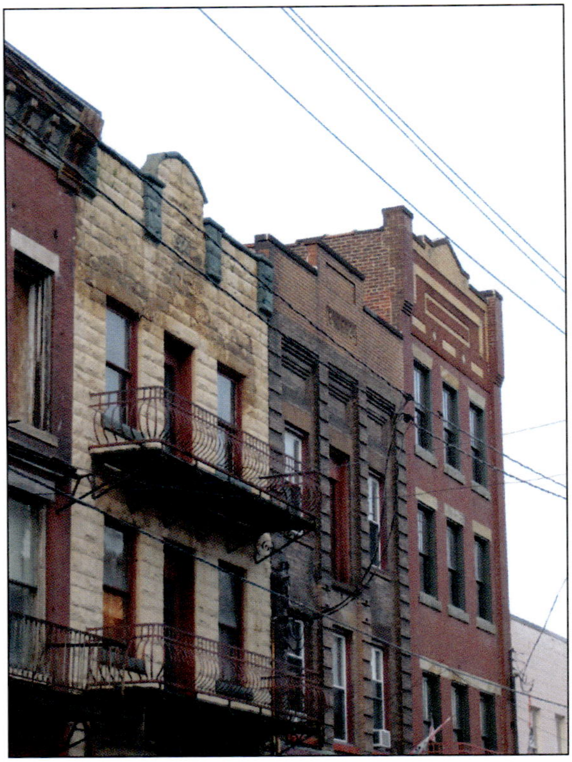

Pictured here is the last intact row of commercial structures in the downtown area of old Monessen. The structures were built in the early 1900s in the style typical for that era. Many of the buildings are 15 feet wide by 100 feet deep, much smaller than today's standards. (Courtesy of Karla Spangler.)

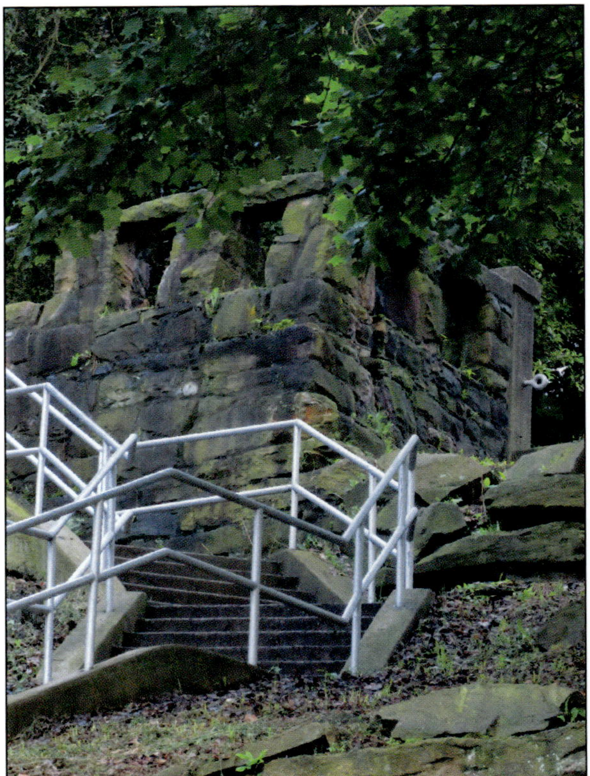

The Sixth Street steps are part of Hillside Park, which is located near McKee Avenue, Parkway, and Schoonmaker Avenue. The stone railing at the top of the steps was a WPA project. Hillside Park provided a nice piece of nature for those that lived in the smoke-filled downtown area. (Courtesy of Karla Spangler.)

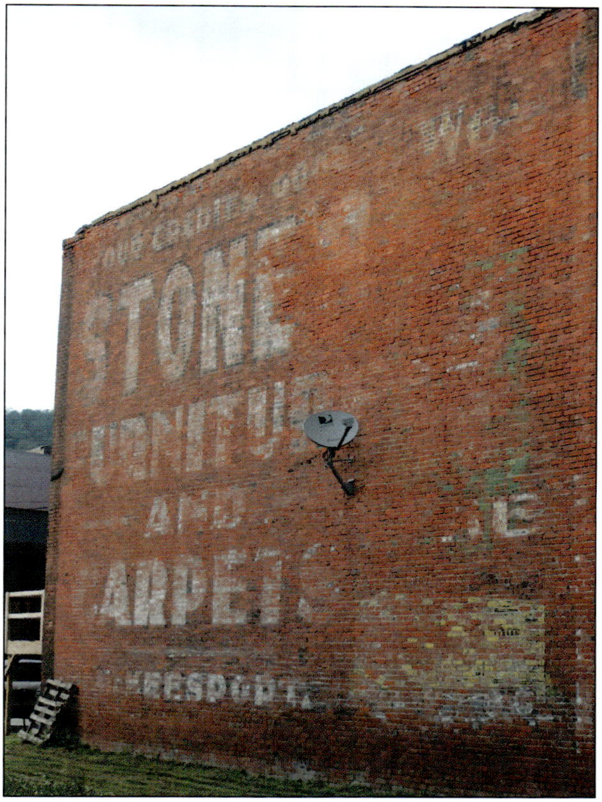

Another advertisement can be seen on Donner Avenue in the middle of downtown. The Krasik Building, which is now demolished, once hid this painted mural. It is rarely seen by anyone now because the flow of traffic has been changed since it was painted in the early 1900s. It advertises a store that was located in McKeesport, Pennsylvania. (Courtesy of Karla Spangler.)

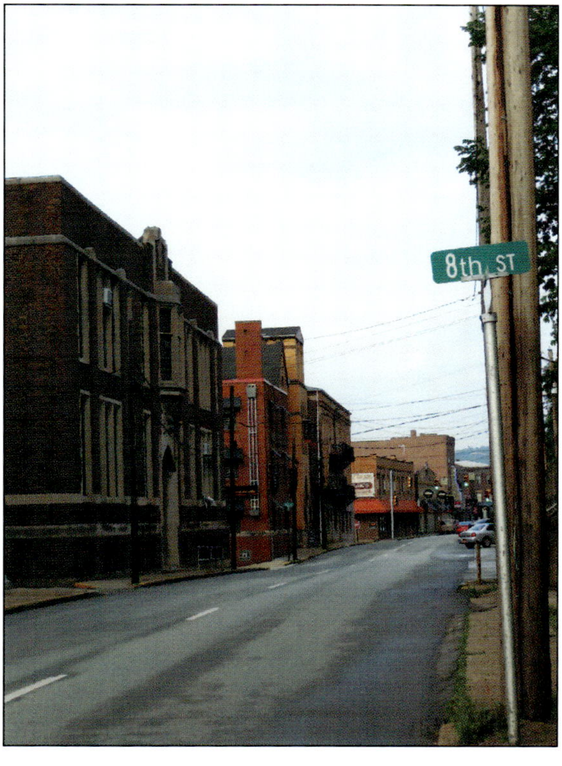

This is a view of Schoonmaker Avenue from Eighth Street, looking east. The first building on the left is the Schooner Youth Center, which is operated by Orchard Christian Church. Many of the other buildings are part of the Douglas Education Center. The marquee for their film school can be seen in the distance. (Courtesy of Karla Spangler.)

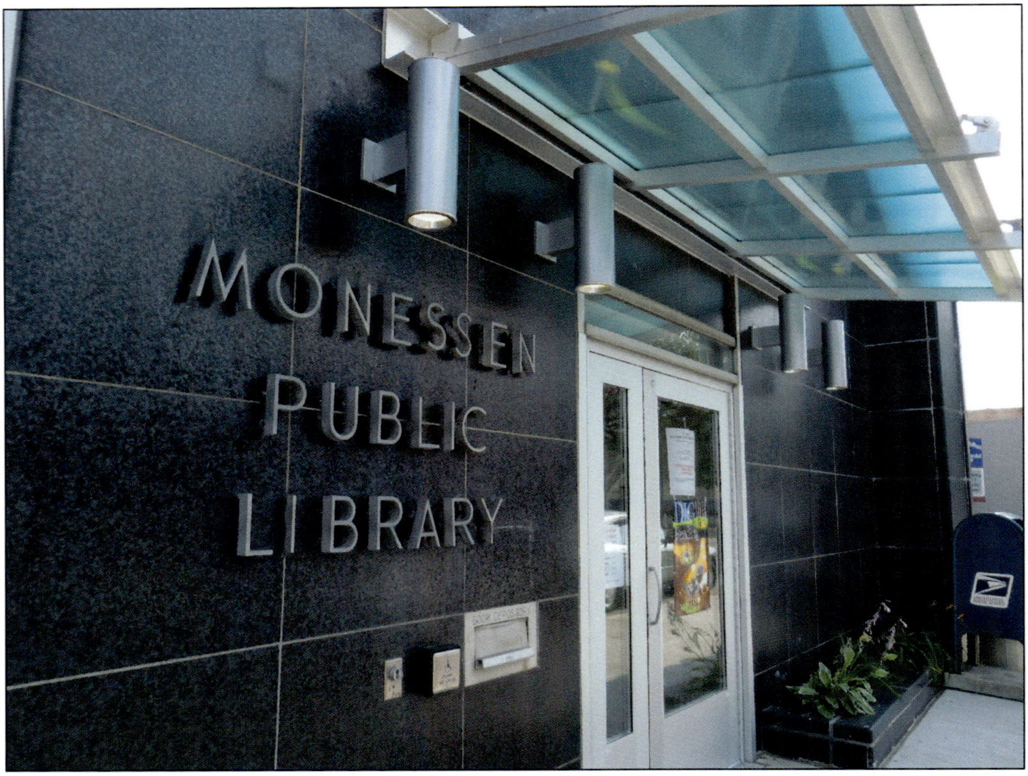

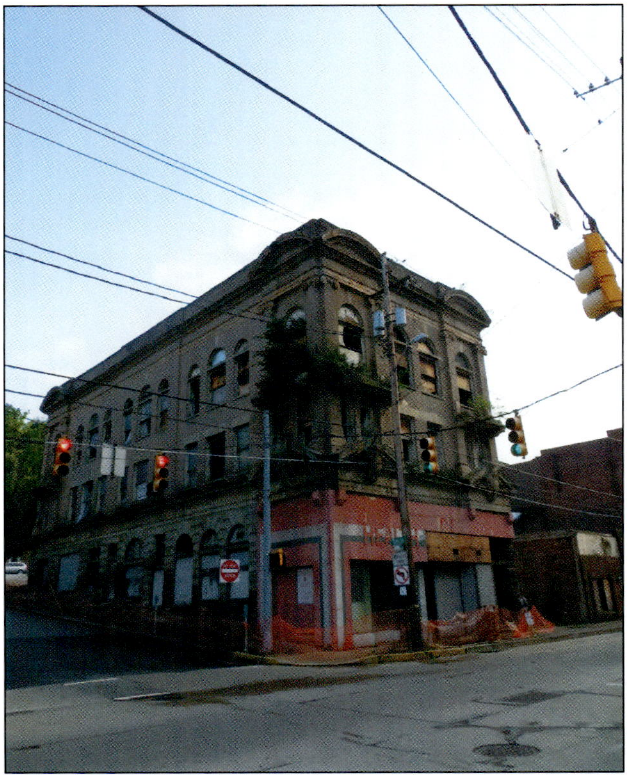

This photograph shows the newly renovated entrance of the Monessen Public Library and Cultural Center. It has been in its Donner Avenue and Third Street location since the 1960s. When the library was moved from Fifth Street to Third Street and Donner Avenue, students formed a chain and carried its book collection to the new building. (Courtesy of Karla Spangler.)

One of the largest and most ornate structures in Monessen is the former Monessen Savings and Trust Company building at Fifth Street and Donner Avenue. It has been abandoned for several decades, but interest has grown in the property. It is hoped that efforts will be made to salvage this building and use it as an anchor for the downtown area. (Courtesy of Karla Spangler.)

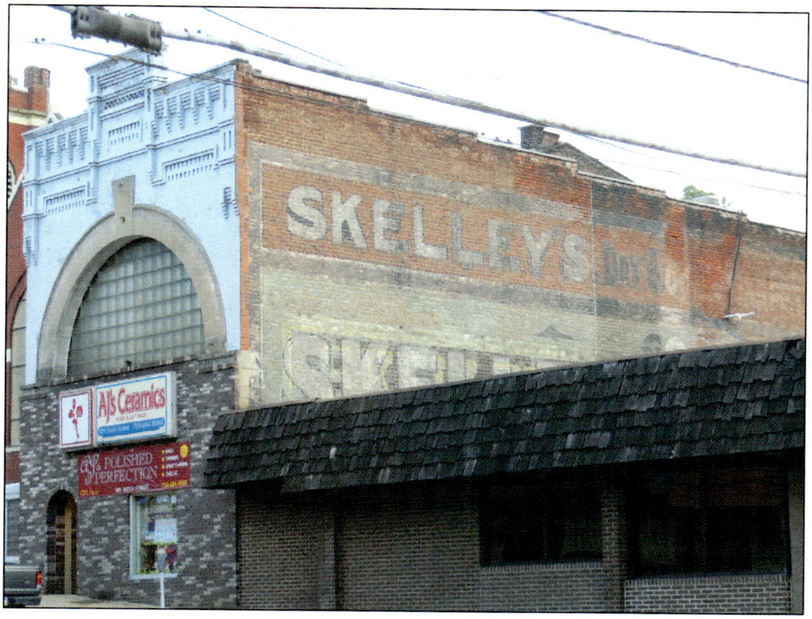

Currently, one of the city's oldest buildings stands on Sixth Street. The side of the building shows an advertisement that was painted there in the early 1900s. The building is advertising Skelley's Dry Goods Store, a popular business that operated in the city for many years. (Courtesy of Karla Spangler.)

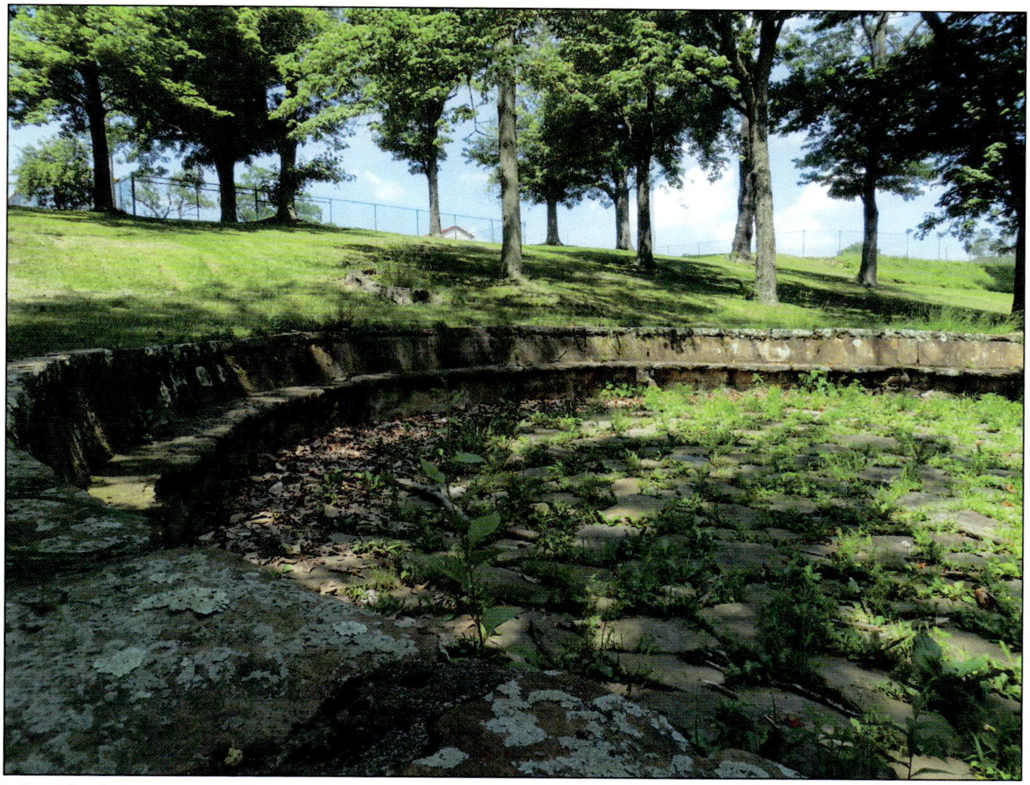

Many barbeque pits and picnic areas like this one exist in Monessen City Park. The stone areas were built under the WPA program during the Great Depression. Civic groups are looking into the idea of restoring these areas, so that people can better enjoy them. (Courtesy of Karla Spangler.)

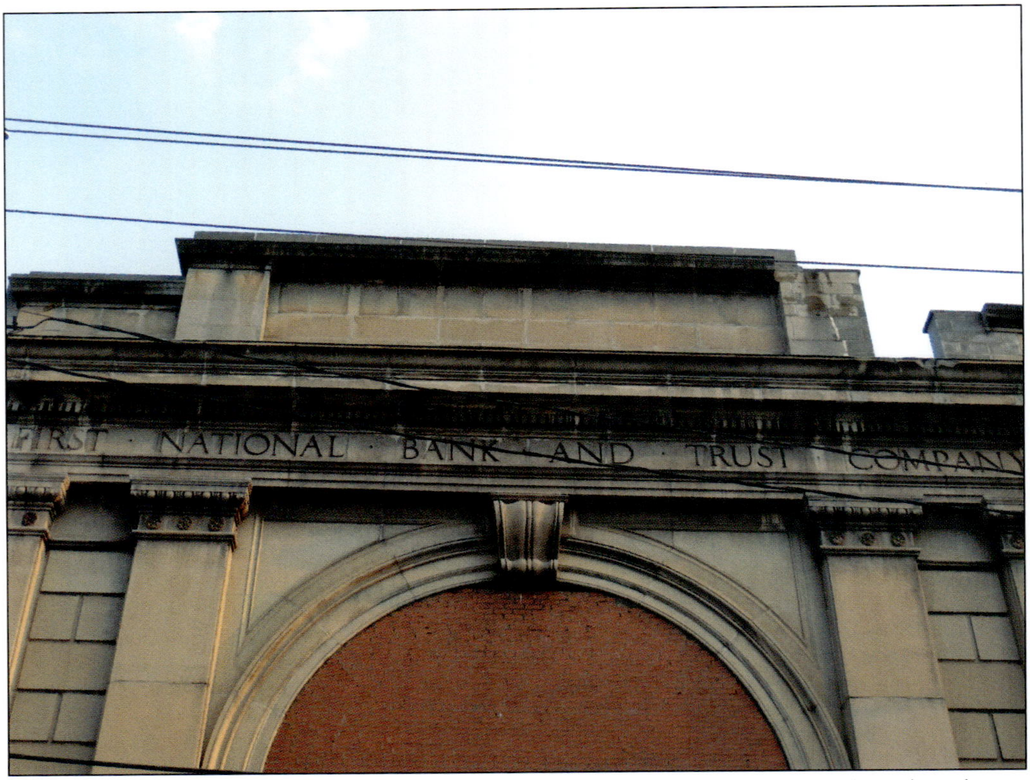

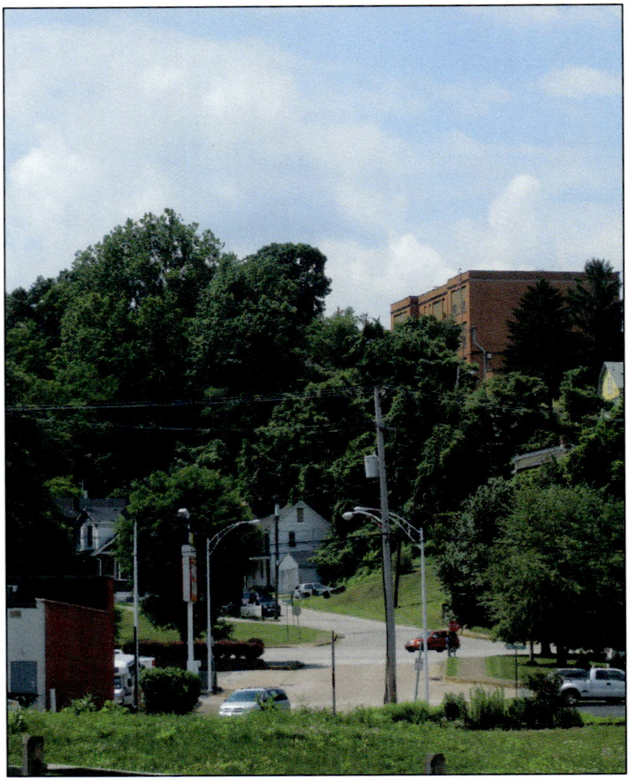

The First National Bank and Trust Company operated on the opposite corner as the Monessen Savings and Trust Company. Both banks struggled to survive and did not make it after the Great Depression. The First National Bank served as a department store for several decades before it became a gymnastics studio. Most of the exterior architecture of the building is still intact. Rumor has it that a tunnel under Fifth Street connected the two banks. (Courtesy of Karla Spangler.)

This photograph provides a view of the city from the river. The old Benjamin Franklin primary school building can be seen on the hill, and it is one of two remaining schools of that era that still exist in the city. The building now serves as the Ben Franklin Apartments. (Courtesy of Karla Spangler.)

The Landmark Place building was constructed at Eighth Street and Donner Avenue in the 1920s. The structure originally served as the steelworkers' union building. It has many amenities such as bowling and showers. Landmark Place was used as a dance hall for many years. The building is not used anymore, but it is a beautiful example of the architecture that existed in the city during its heyday. (Courtesy of Karla Spangler.)

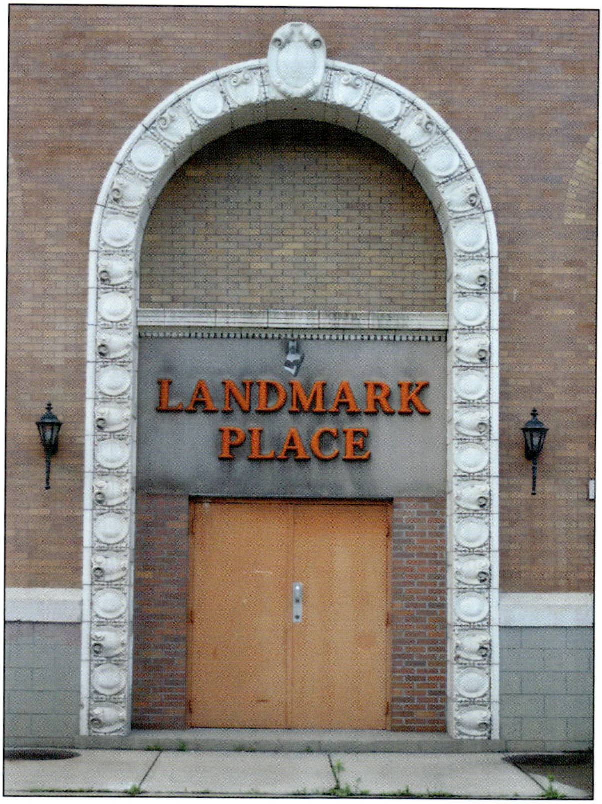

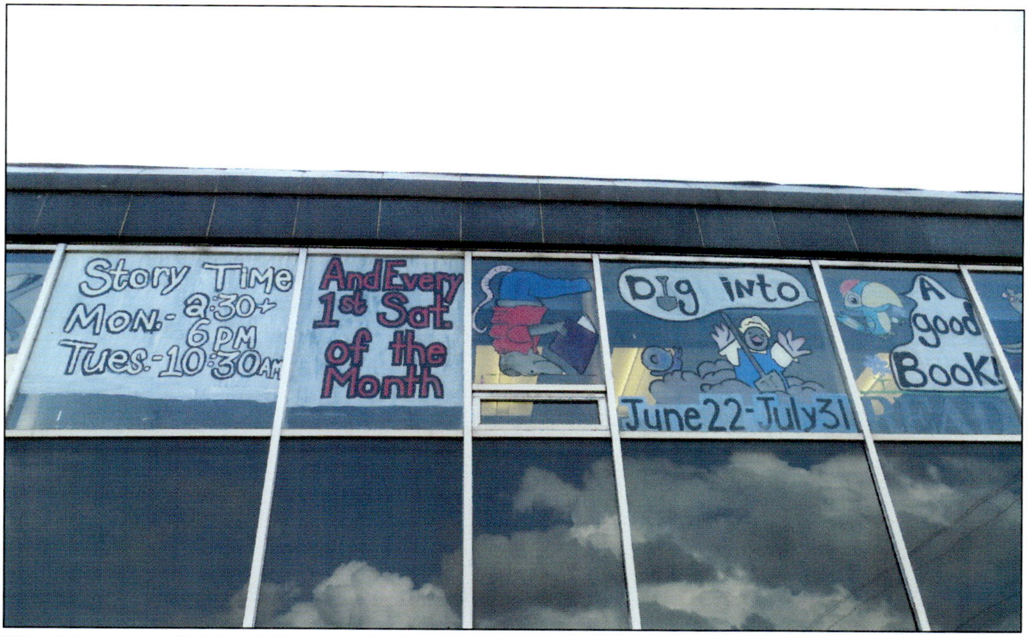

The Monessen Public Library, which also serves as a cultural center, provides activities for children as well as adults. The library staff always decorates the windows in a fun way to advertise upcoming events. The library has realized its vital role in helping the city revive itself. (Courtesy of Karla Spangler.)

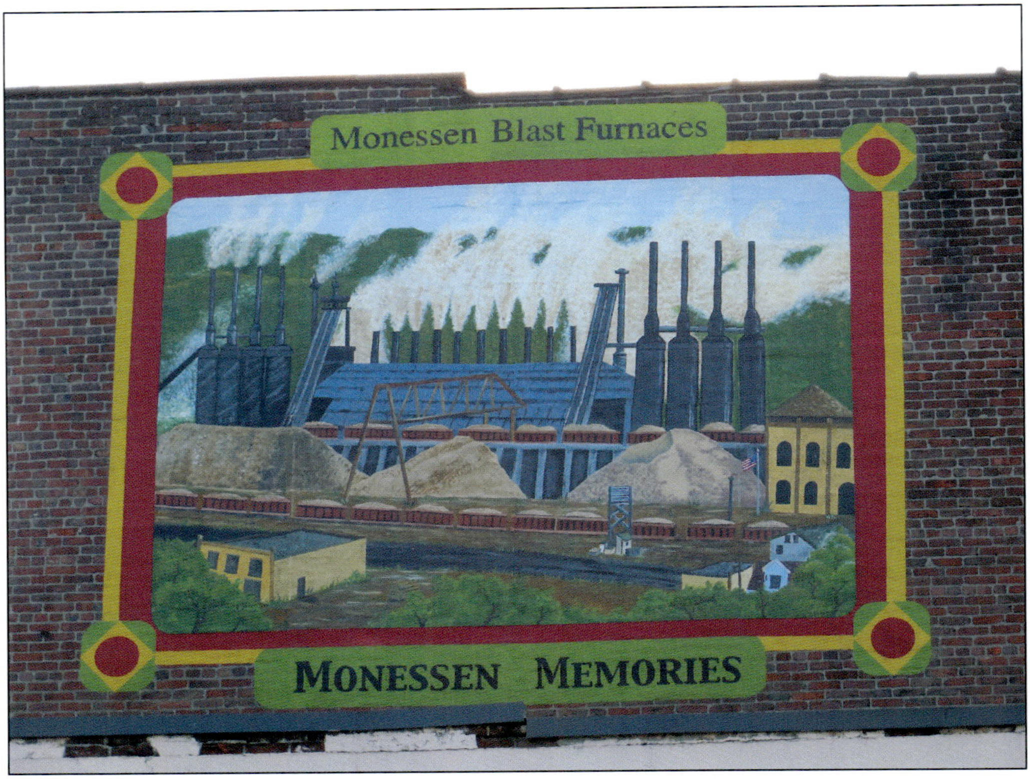

In 2012, the Greater Monessen Historical Society decided to get motorists and pedestrians to look up at the often-beautiful architecture of the old buildings in the city. It was decided that a mural would be painted at the top of the society's building on a wall facing oncoming traffic. It was common practice throughout the 20th century to paint large advertisements on the sides of buildings. (Courtesy of Karla Spangler.)

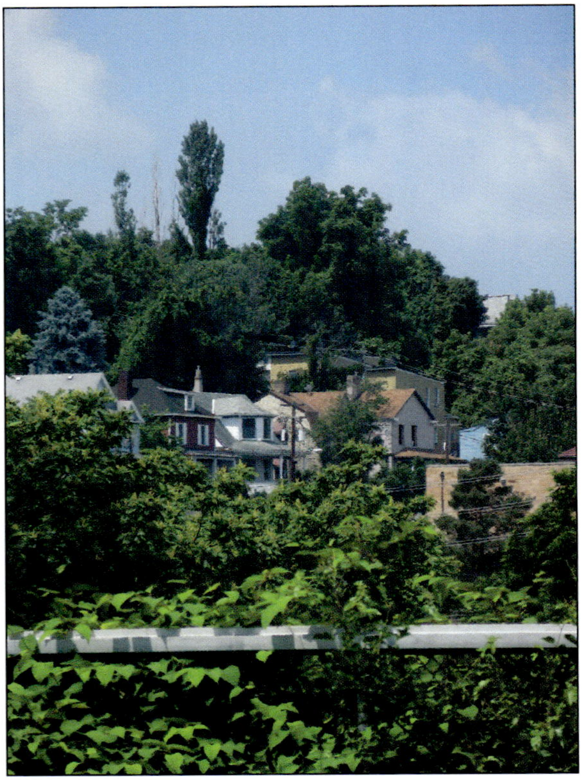

This section of McKee Avenue is located between First and Second Streets. Once called Millionaire's Row, McKee was one of the most affluent neighborhoods in the city. Now, it has become one of the hardest-hit neighborhoods in regards to vacancy. The once-beautiful homes and mansions are slowly falling into disrepair. (Courtesy of Karla Spangler.)

Pictured here is an old painted advertisement on the side of a commercial building between Fifth and Sixth Streets on Donner Avenue. The sign, which advertises Brooks Department Store, was hidden for decades until the building next to it was demolished. Brooks was a popular department store in early Monessen. (Courtesy of Karla Spangler.)

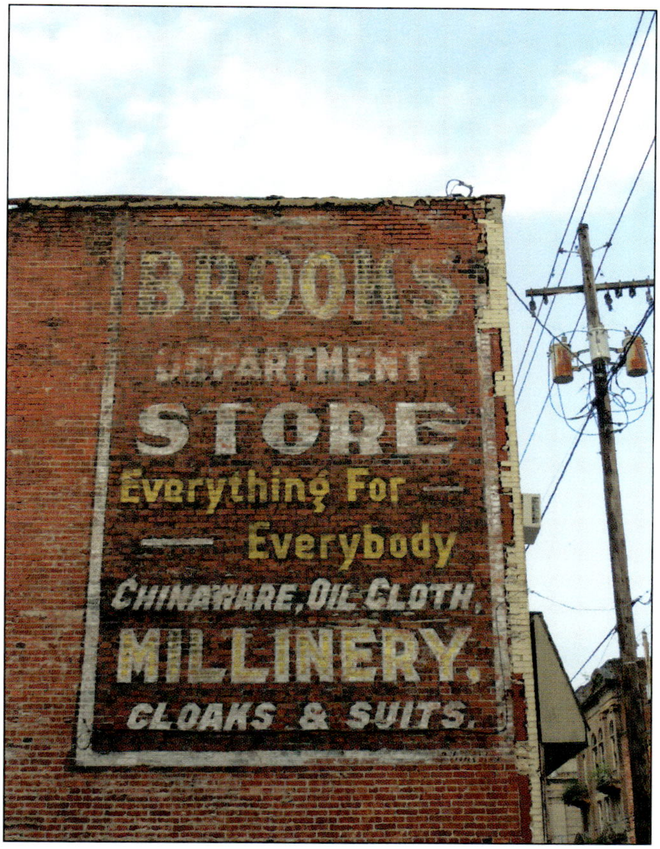

This sign welcomes visitors to the Monessen Memorial Stadium on Rostraver Street. The facility is one of the largest and nicest high school football stadiums in the area. The stadium was built as a WPA project during the Great Depression. Materials used to build the stadium were obtained from Page's Wire Mill.

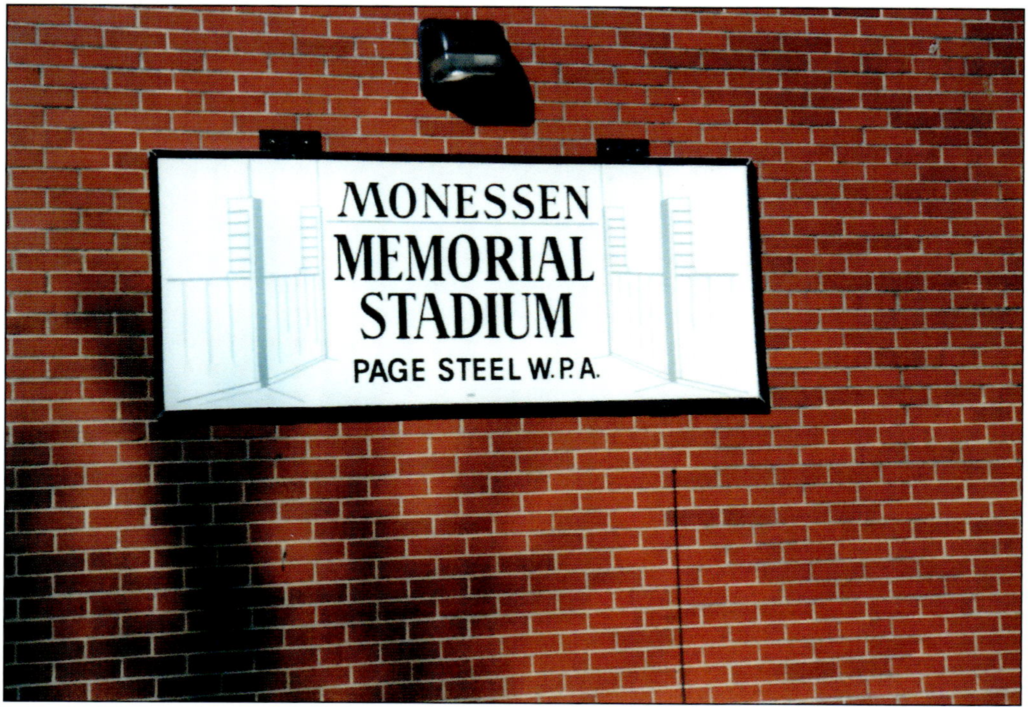

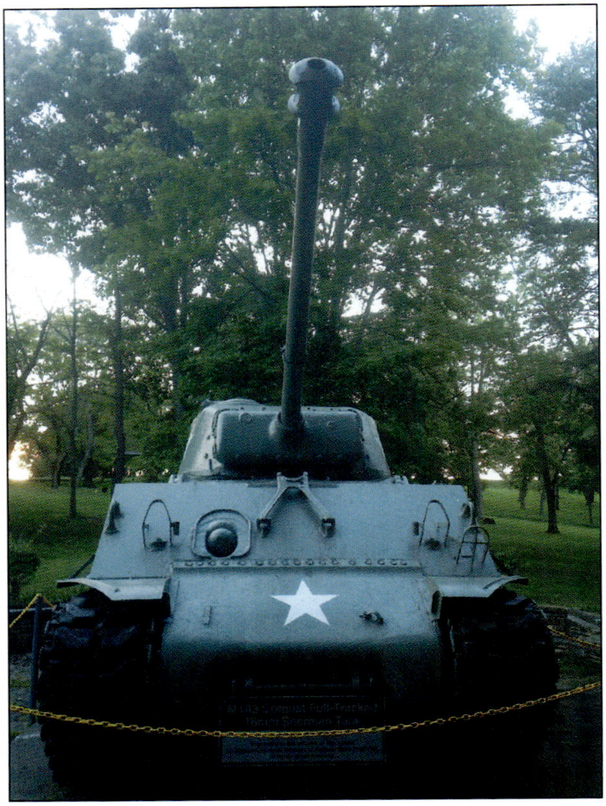

An old Sherman tank stands guard in Monessen City Park as a reminder to all of the past. The Veterans of Foreign Wars, Post 1190, presented the tank to the City of Monessen in honor of all veterans. In 2013, the tank was painted by local Eagle Scout Troop 1543. (Author's collection.)

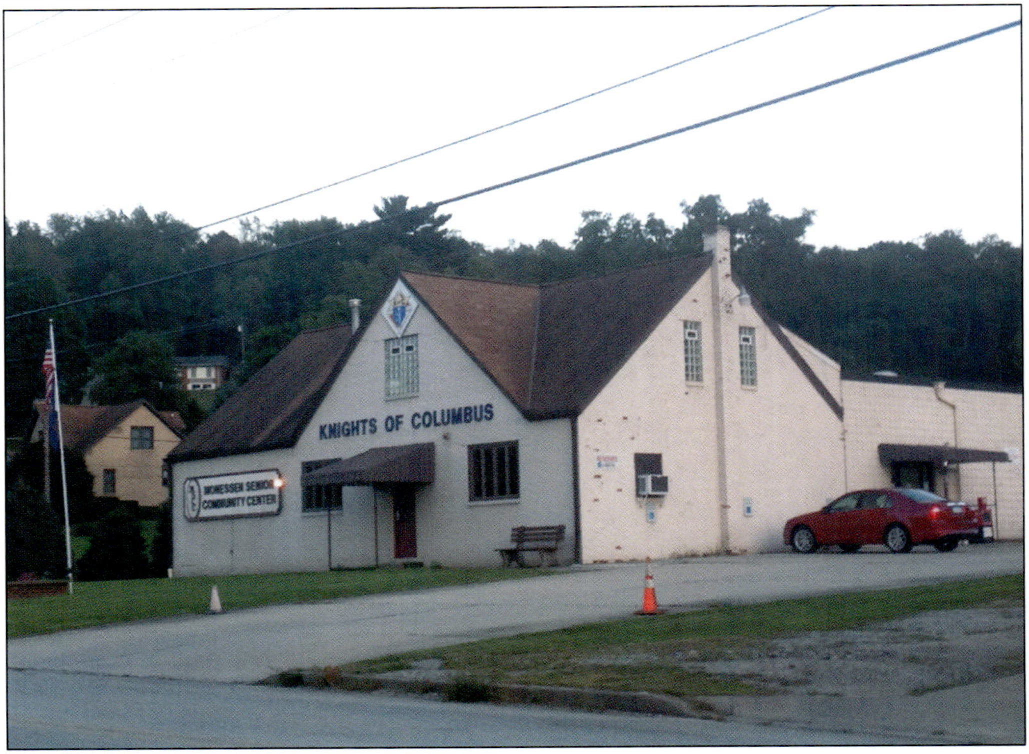

The Monessen Knights of Columbus and Senior Citizens Center is located on Grand Boulevard. It is across the street from Monessen City Park in its Park Plan neighborhood. The organization provides various programs for senior citizens. (Author's collection.)

The newly constructed John K. Tener Bridge provides a scenic atmosphere for a walk. The bridge was completed in 2013 and replaces the former Charleroi-Monessen Bridge. There is a pedestrian walk on the bridge, which includes benches and plaques about the history of the original span and John K. Tener. (Author's collection.)

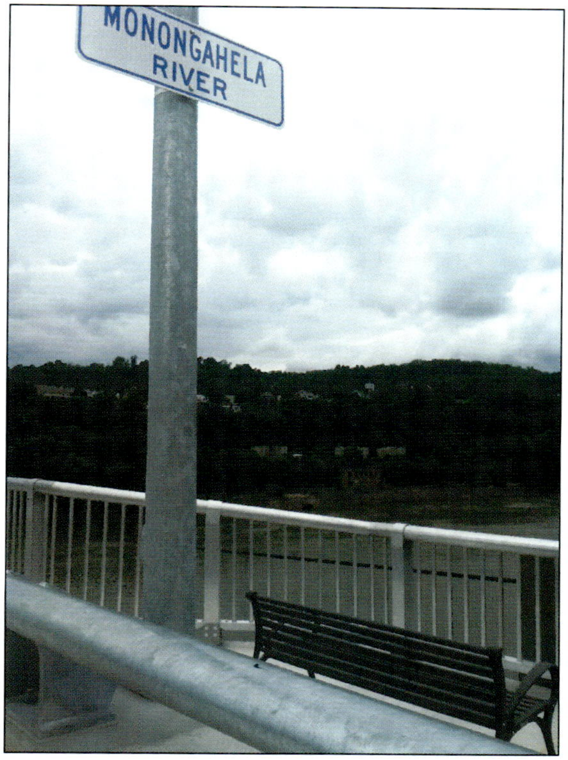

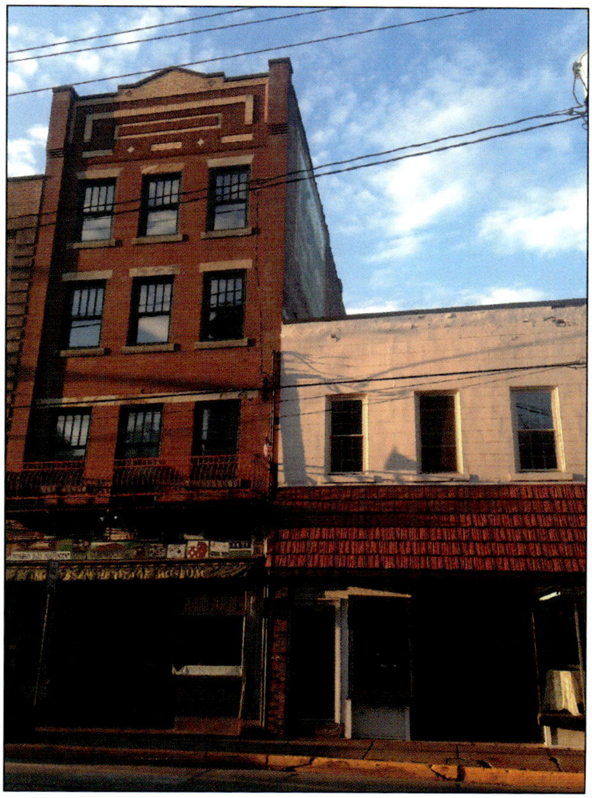

The Greater Monessen Historical Society took up residence in the 500-block of Donner Avenue in downtown. There they hold various events such as fundraisers and seminars. They also have rotating exhibits on the first floor and a library and archives on the second floor. The society recently acquired the building to the right and are working to renovate it and install a permanent Monessen-related exhibit. (Author's collection.)

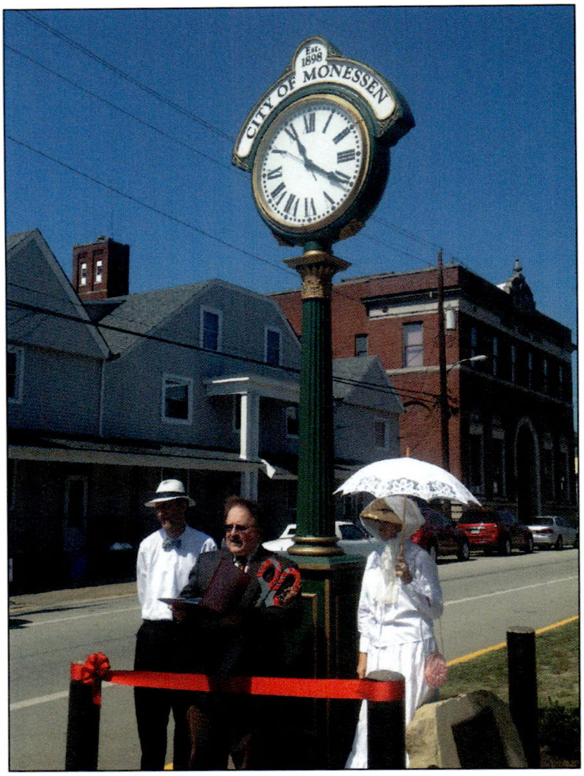

Members of the Greater Monessen Historical Society pose for a photograph in front of the newly installed Brown Street clock. The new street clock is located on Donner Avenue in front of the new public safety building. The clock was purchased by the city and private donors. Brown Street clocks were produced in Monessen in the early 20th century and shipped all over the country. (Author's collection.)

An a cappella group from California University of Pennsylvania (Cal U) performs at the newly refurbished Monessen Public Library and Cultural Center. Cal U is a local university located about 11 miles south of Monessen. Monessen is trying to connect to Cal U and reestablish itself as an education and cultural hub. (Author's collection.)

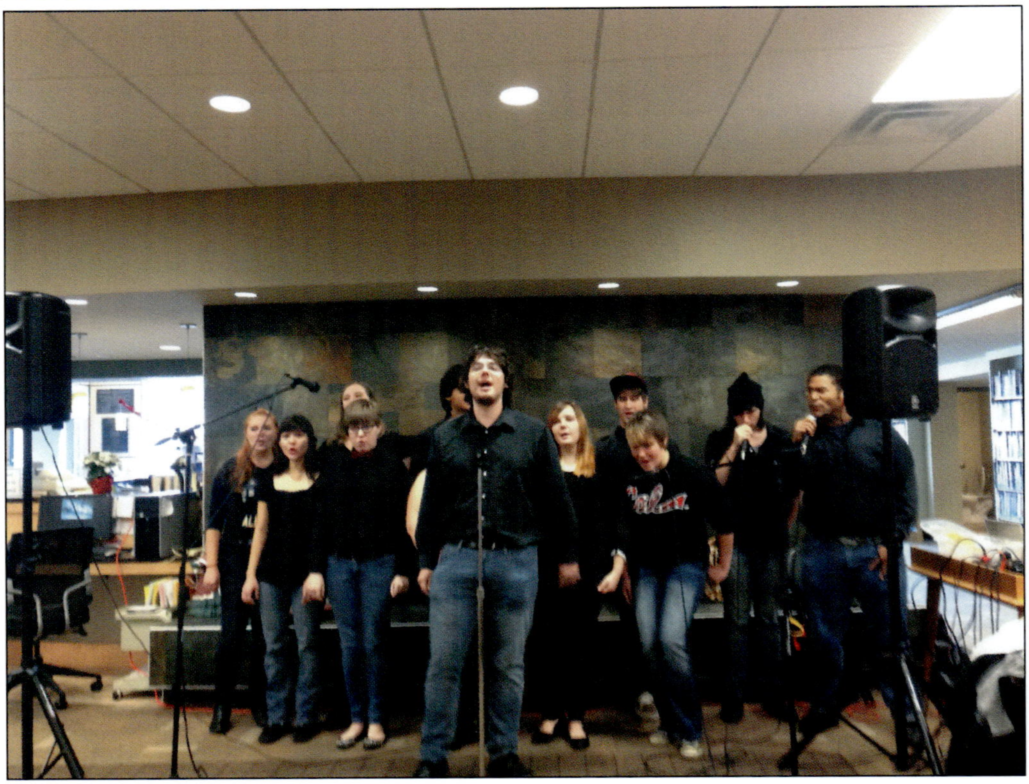

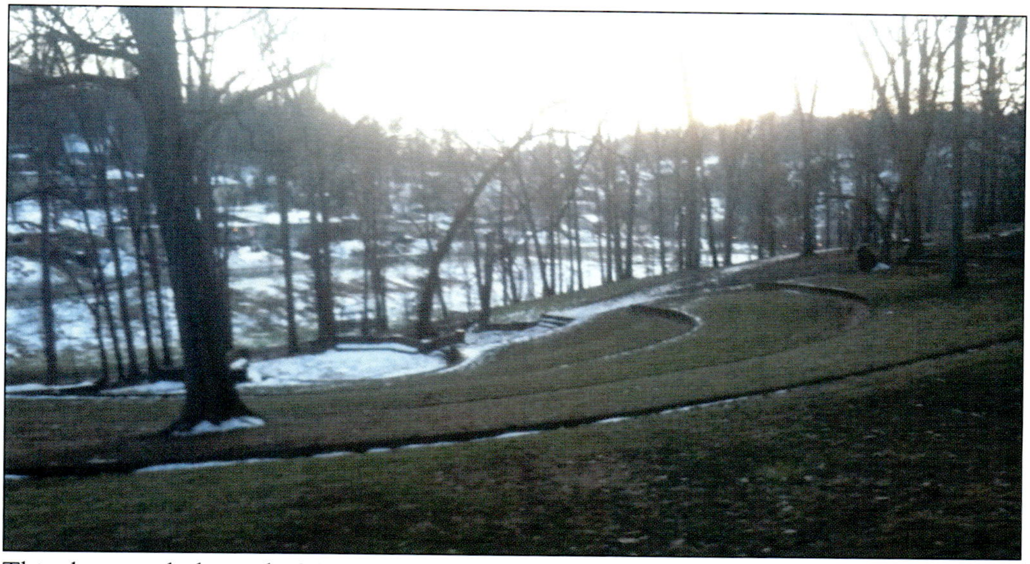

This photograph shows the Monessen City Park amphitheater as it was originally designed. The amphitheater was built in 1931 and used throughout the 20th century as a bandstand in Monessen City Park. It became overgrown and fell into disuse from several years of neglect. It was renovated in 2014. (Author's collection.)

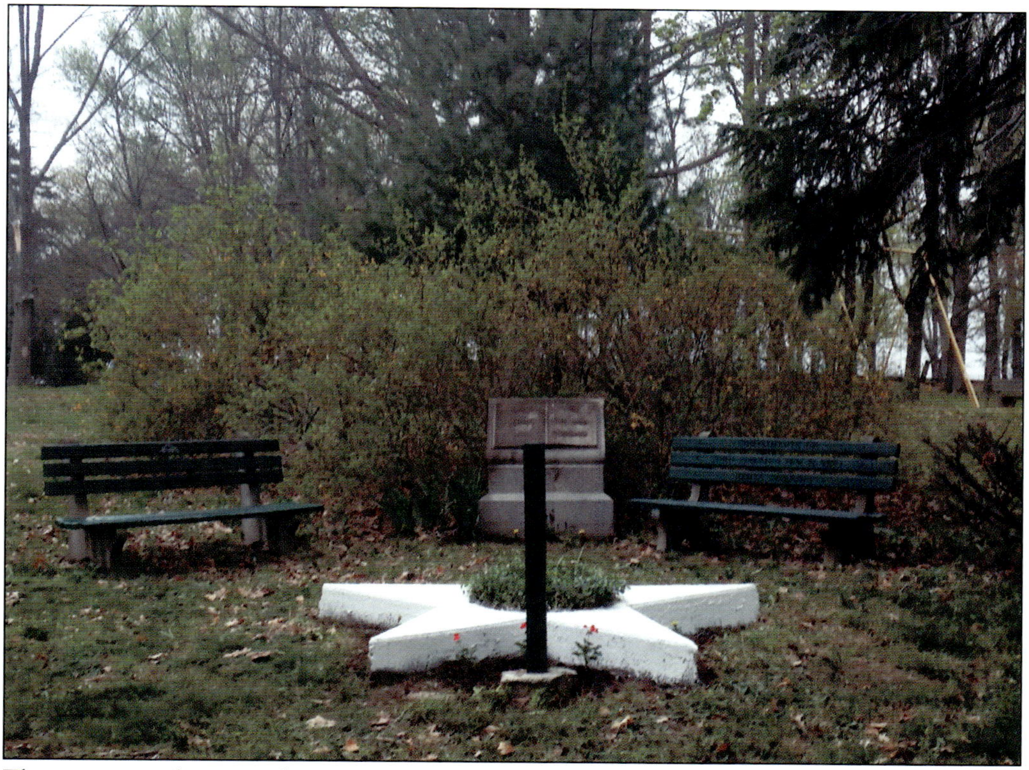

There are several memorials at Monessen City Park. This photograph shows one of the memorials after students cleared weeds and debris, planted flowers, and painted the benches. Monessen City Park is the largest of several parks in the city. Recently, efforts have been made to clean the parks so that they can be used as an attraction to the city. (Author's collection.)

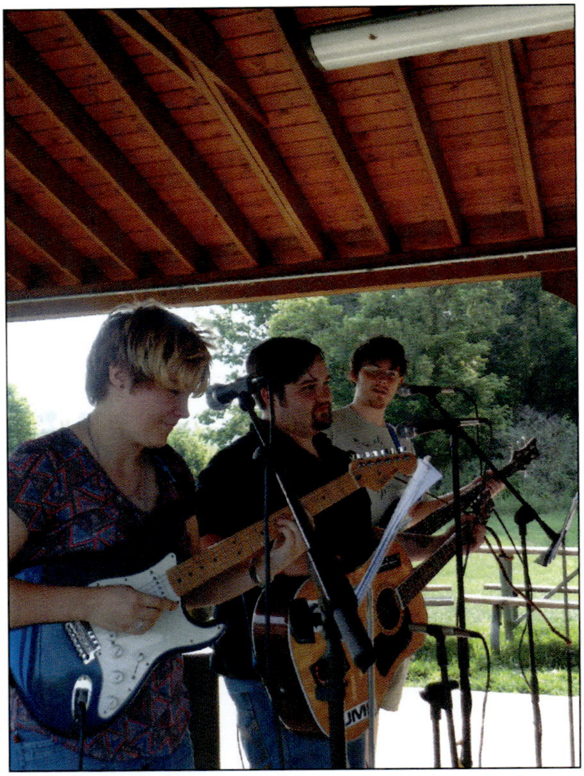

Students are performing folk music at the Herman Mihalich Boat Launch. Many of the city's parks and recreational facilities have pavilions and areas where people can perform music and participate in other cultural activities. The pavilion sits near the Monongahela River and offers a beautiful view for those sitting nearby. (Author's collection.)

In the area behind the pavilion at the boat launch, the former Mon Valley Health Center, now the municipal complex, can be seen. The area surrounding the boat launch was part of Page's Wire Mill before it was demolished in the early 2000s. The land was turned into a small park and boat launch to promote recreation along the Monongahela River. (Author's collection.)

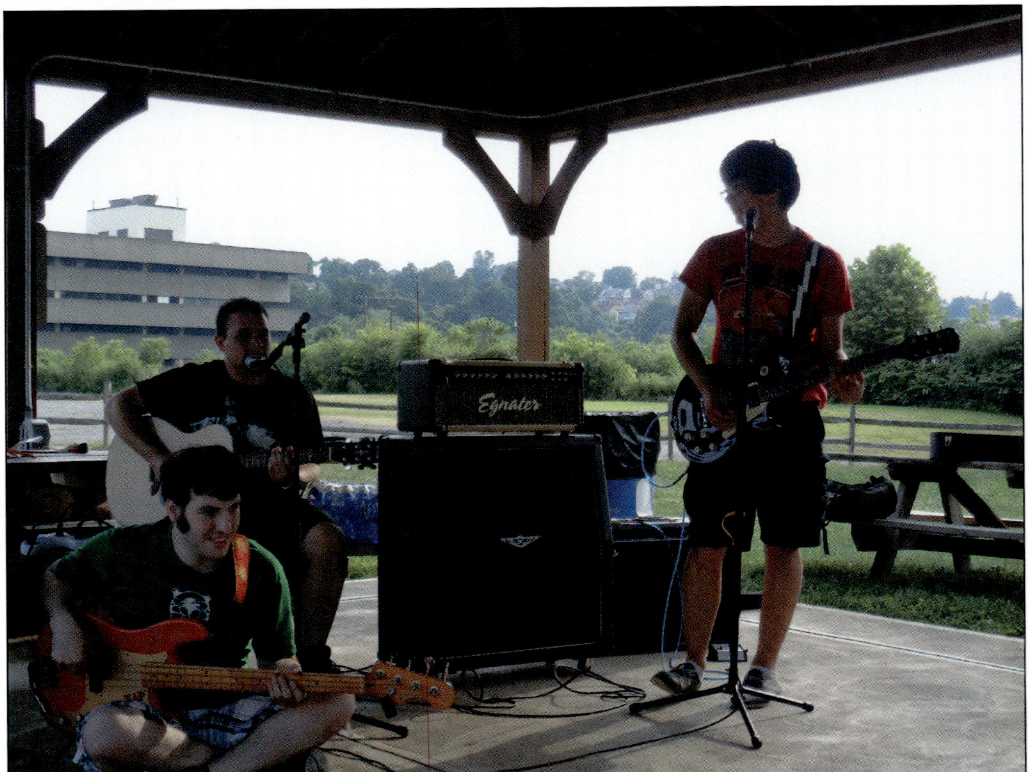

About the Greater Monessen Historical Society

The Greater Monessen Historical Society shall promote and foster knowledge, understanding, and appreciation of history in general and of the city of Monessen and its environs in particular. The objective of this society shall be to study, collect, and preserve for the city historical records and antiquities relating to the history of Monessen and environs and its people; to preserve items of current events that may have historical interest in the future; to interest and unite the city in a finer public spirit, through a fuller understanding of the traditions and history, both past and in the making, of our city and its neighboring communities.